MULTICULTURAL EDUCATION SERIES

JAMES A. BANKS, *Series Editor*

Human Rights and Schooling: An Ethical Framework for
Teaching for Social Justice
AUDREY OSLER

We Can't Teach What We Don't Know:
White Teachers, Multiracial Schools, Third Edition
GARY R. HOWARD

Teaching and Learning on the Verge:
Democratic Education in Action
SHANTI ELLIOTT

Engaging the "Race Question":
Accountability and Equity in U.S. Higher Education
ALICIA C. DOWD AND ESTELA MARA BENSIMON

Diversity and Education: A Critical Multicultural Approach
MICHAEL VAVRUS

First Freire: Early Writings in Social Justice Education
CARLOS ALBERTO TORRES

Mathematics for Equity:
A Framework for Successful Practice
NA'ILAH SUAD NASIR, CARLOS CABANA, BARBARA SHREVE,
ESTELLE WOODBURY, AND NICOLE LOUIE, EDS.

Race, Empire, and English Language Teaching:
Creating Responsible and Ethical Anti-Racist Practice
SUHANTHIE MOTHA

Black Male(d): Peril and Promise in the Education of
African American Males
TYRONE C. HOWARD

LGBTQ Youth and Education: Policies and Practices
CRIS MAYO

Race Frameworks:
A Multidimensional Theory of Racism and Education
ZEUS LEONARDO

Reaching and Teaching Students in Poverty:
Strategies for Erasing the Opportunity Gap
PAUL C. GORSKI

Class Rules:
Exposing Inequality in American High Schools
PETER W. COOKSON JR.

Teachers Without Borders? The Hidden Consequences of
International Teachers in U.S. Schools
ALYSSA HADLEY DUNN

Streetsmart Schoolsmart:
Urban Poverty and the Education of Adolescent Boys
GILBERTO Q. CONCHAS AND JAMES DIEGO VIGIL

Americans by Heart: Undocumented Latino Students and
the Promise of Higher Education
WILLIAM PÉREZ

Is Everyone Really Equal? An Introduction to Key
Concepts in Social Justice Education
ÖZLEM SENSOY AND ROBIN DIANGELO

Achieving Equity for Latino Students: Expanding the
Pathway to Higher Education Through Public Policy
FRANCES CONTRERAS

Literacy Achievement and Diversity:
Keys to Success for Students, Teachers, and Schools
KATHRYN H. AU

Understanding English Language Variation
in U.S. Schools
ANNE H. CHARITY HUDLEY AND CHRISTINE MALLINSON

Latino Children Learning English: Steps in the Journey
GUADALUPE VALDÉS, SARAH CAPITELLI, AND LAURA ALVAREZ

Asians in the Ivory Tower: Dilemmas of Racial Inequality
in American Higher Education
ROBERT T. TERANISHI

Our Worlds in Our Words: Exploring Race, Class, Gender,
and Sexual Orientation in Multicultural Classrooms
MARY DILG

Culturally Responsive Teaching:
Theory, Research, and Practice, Second Edition
GENEVA GAY

Why Race and Culture Matter in Schools:
Closing the Achievement Gap in America's Classrooms
TYRONE C. HOWARD

Diversity and Equity in Science Education:
Research, Policy, and Practice
OKHEE LEE AND CORY A. BUXTON

Forbidden Language:
English Learners and Restrictive Language Policies
PATRICIA GÁNDARA AND MEGAN HOPKINS, EDS.

The Light in Their Eyes:
Creating Multicultural Learning Communities,
10th Anniversary Edition
SONIA NIETO

The Flat World and Education: How America's
Commitment to Equity Will Determine Our Future
LINDA DARLING-HAMMOND

(continued)

MULTICULTURAL EDUCATION SERIES, *continued*

Teaching What Really Happened:
How to Avoid the Tyranny of Textbooks and
Get Students Excited About Doing History
JAMES W. LOEWEN

Diversity and the New Teacher:
Learning from Experience in Urban Schools
CATHERINE CORNBLETH

Frogs into Princes: Writings on School Reform
LARRY CUBAN

Educating Citizens in a Multicultural Society,
Second Edition
JAMES A. BANKS

Culture, Literacy, and Learning:
Taking Bloom in the Midst of the Whirlwind
CAROL D. LEE

Facing Accountability in Education:
Democracy and Equity at Risk
CHRISTINE E. SLEETER, ED.

Talkin Black Talk:
Language, Education, and Social Change
H. SAMY ALIM AND JOHN BAUGH, EDS.

Improving Access to Mathematics:
Diversity and Equity in the Classroom
NA'ILAH SUAD NASIR AND PAUL COBB, EDS.

"To Remain an Indian": Lessons in Democracy from a
Century of Native American Education
K. TSIANINA LOMAWAIMA AND TERESA L. MCCARTY

Education Research in the Public Interest:
Social Justice, Action, and Policy
GLORIA LADSON-BILLINGS AND WILLIAM F. TATE, EDS.

Multicultural Strategies for Education and Social Change:
Carriers of the Torch in the United States and South Africa
ARNETHA F. BALL

Un-Standardizing Curriculum: Multicultural Teaching in
the Standards-Based Classroom
CHRISTINE E. SLEETER

Beyond the Big House:
African American Educators on Teacher Education
GLORIA LADSON-BILLINGS

Teaching and Learning in Two Languages:
Bilingualism and Schooling in the United States
EUGENE E. GARCÍA

Improving Multicultural Education:
Lessons from the Intergroup Education Movement
CHERRY A. MCGEE BANKS

Education Programs for Improving Intergroup Relations:
Theory, Research, and Practice
WALTER G. STEPHAN AND W. PAUL VOGT, EDS.

Walking the Road:
Race, Diversity, and Social Justice in Teacher Education
MARILYN COCHRAN-SMITH

City Schools and the American Dream:
Reclaiming the Promise of Public Education
PEDRO A. NOGUERA

Thriving in the Multicultural Classroom:
Principles and Practices for Effective Teaching
MARY DILG

Educating Teachers for Diversity:
Seeing with a Cultural Eye
JACQUELINE JORDAN IRVINE

Teaching Democracy:
Unity and Diversity in Public Life
WALTER C. PARKER

The Making—and Remaking—
of a Multiculturalist
CARLOS E. CORTÉS

Transforming the Multicultural Education
of Teachers: Theory, Research, and Practice
MICHAEL VAVRUS

Learning to Teach for Social Justice
LINDA DARLING-HAMMOND, JENNIFER FRENCH, AND
SILVIA PALOMA GARCIA-LOPEZ, EDS.

Culture, Difference, and Power
CHRISTINE E. SLEETER

Learning and Not Learning English:
Latino Students in American Schools
GUADALUPE VALDÉS

The Children Are Watching:
How the Media Teach About Diversity
CARLOS E. CORTÉS

Multicultural Education, Transformative Knowledge,
and Action:
Historical and Contemporary Perspectives
JAMES A. BANKS, ED.

Human Rights and Schooling

An Ethical Framework for Teaching for Social Justice

AUDREY OSLER

TEACHERS COLLEGE PRESS

TEACHERS COLLEGE | COLUMBIA UNIVERSITY

NEW YORK AND LONDON

Published by Teachers College Press, 1234 Amsterdam Avenue, New York, NY 10027

Copyright © 2016 by Teachers College, Columbia University

Cover photo by laflor (iStock by Getty Images).

Library of Congress Cataloging-in-Publication Data

Names: Osler, Audrey, author.
Title: Human rights and schooling : an ethical framework for teaching for
    social justice / Audrey Osler.
Description: New York, NY : Teachers College Press, 2016. | Series:
    Multicultural education series | Includes bibliographical references and
    index.
Identifiers: LCCN 2016004244 (print) | LCCN 2016013397 (ebook) | ISBN
    9780807756768 (pbk. : alk. paper) | ISBN 9780807756775 (case : alk. paper)
    | ISBN 9780807773925 (ebook)
Subjects: LCSH: Human rights—Study and teaching. | Social justice—Study and
    teaching. | Democracy and education.
Classification: LCC JC571 .O844 2016 (print) | LCC JC571 (ebook) | DDC
    323.071—dc23
LC record available at http://lccn.loc.gov/2016004244

ISBN 978-0-8077-5676-8 (paper)
ISBN 978-0-8077-5677-5 (hardcover)
ISBN 978-0-8077-7392-5 (ebook)

Printed on acid-free paper
Manufactured in the United States of America

23 22 21 20 19 18 17 16   8 7 6 5 4 3 2 1

For Logan and Julie, Yarin and Mina

Contents

Series Foreword   *James A. Banks*   ix

Acknowledgments   xiii

1. Human Rights Education, Politics, and Power   1

2. The Right to Human Rights Education   14

3. Intersectionality, Human Rights, and Identities   32

4. Narrative in Teaching for Justice and Human Rights   46

5. Human Rights, Education, and the Nation   61

6. Human Rights, Peace, and Conflict   81

7. Child Rights: The Heart of the Project   104

8. Reimagining a Cosmopolitan Future   119

Notes   130

Appendix A: The Universal Declaration of Human Rights   134

Appendix B: Unofficial Summary of the U.N. Convention
    on the Rights of the Child   140

Appendix C: Does Your School Environment
    Give Everyone a Chance to Enjoy Their Rights ?   147

List of Abbreviations   150

References   151

Index   169

About the Author   178

Series Foreword

The tumultuous situation in Europe caused by the Syrian refugee crisis (Barnard, 2016; Cohen, 2016), the worldwide terrorism led by ISIS (Hisham, 2016), and events in nations around the world that manifest racism, xenophobia, and structural inequality (Banks, 2009) have stimulated contentious and searing debates and analyses about social justice, citizenship, and human rights. The growth of international migration as well as migration within nations has also intensified and deepened debates about issues and developments related to human rights (Castles, 2014). In 2013, there were approximately 232 million international migrants in the world (United Nations Department of Economic and Social Affairs, Population Division, 2013). Many of these migrants have ambiguous citizenship status and are victims of structural exclusion, racial microaggressions, cultural erasure, deculturalization (Spring, 2010)—and sometimes violence.

This informative and engaging book is timely, needed, and visionary because of these developments and events. One of the most important, original, and creative contributions of this book is the broad and inclusive way in which Osler conceptualizes and theorizes human rights. Human rights violations, as she points out, are often regarded by school practitioners and other educators in the United States as well as in other nations in the Global North as issues that exist primarily in nations in the Global South— especially when despotic leaders victimize their own citizens or media workers and citizens from nations in the Global North. In other words, educators in the Global North often view "human rights" violations as an issue for "them" and not for us.

With her compelling analysis and powerful examples, Osler conceptualizes human rights as an issue within all communities, institutions, societies, and nations. She maintains that human rights issues exist for students and teachers in families, local communities, the classroom, and the school. Consequently, one of the salient points made in this discerning book is that human rights is not about the other in distant lands but it is about all of us and the everyday lives of students and teachers. Osler also provides teachers and students with a powerful legal and moral framework that can be used to guide the analysis of human rights issues in classroom discussions and deliberations. This insightful, heartfelt, and compassionate book provides students and teachers with a new conception of human rights that focuses on their everyday experiences, struggles, and possibilities. It emphasizes how the experiences of people in the Global North are connected to—rather than disparate from—the lives of people in Global South nations in Africa, Asia, Latin America, and the Middle East.

In addition to providing a visionary and transformative conception of human rights, Osler describes what human rights look like "on the ground" and in the lives of teachers and students. The ways in which she concretizes human rights is an antidote to the nebulous ways in which the concept is often used, especially within political discourse. Osler uses practical and engaging anecdotes to illustrate how human rights are actualized and violated. She describes protests by high school students against national examinations in South Korea to illustrate how students in a highly developed and Westernized nation can take action to push for human rights. In a graduate class she taught at a university located in Utah—a state in the United States with a high Mormon population—Osler invited the teachers in this graduate seminar to examine the principles of human rights and "apply them to their own schools and communities." In an ingenious lesson that focused on same-sex marriage and religion, Osler facilitated a rich and productive discussion of "both the right to same sex marriage and the right to religious freedom within the framework of the Universal Declaration of Human Rights." The examples of the protest by high school students in South Korea and Osler's university seminar illustrate how the author makes human rights practical and feasible for teachers and students. This book includes myriad examples of how teachers can make human rights education engaging, practical, and effective. A figure in Chapter 2, for example, presents a guide that students can use to examine human rights issues in their community, including school, place of worship (e.g., church, mosque, synagogue, or temple), hospital, cinema, civic office, and other institutions in the community.

This book is being published in the Multicultural Education Series at Teachers College Press, Columbia University. The major purpose of the Multicultural Education Series is to provide preservice educators, practicing educators, graduate students, scholars, and policymakers with an interrelated and comprehensive set of books that summarize and analyze important research, theory, and practice related to the education of ethnic, racial, cultural, linguistic, and religious groups in the United States and other nations and the education of mainstream students about diversity.

The dimensions of multicultural education developed by Banks (2004) and described in the *Handbook of Research on Multicultural Education* and in the *Encyclopedia of Diversity in Education* (Banks, 2012), provide the conceptual framework for the development of the publications in the Series. The dimensions are content integration, the knowledge construction process, prejudice reduction, equity pedagogy, and an empowering institutional culture and social structure. The books in the Multicultural Education Series provide research, theoretical, and practical knowledge about the behaviors and learning characteristics of students of color, language minority students, low-income students, and other minoritized population groups, such as LGBTQ youth (Mayo, 2014). Osler's book is a significant and timely one to add to the Multicultural Education Series because the most cutting-edge issues related to multicultural education, diversity, and human rights today have international dimensions and require global solutions.

This book is also timely and noteworthy because globalization has significantly weakened national borders and made conceptions of citizenship that are highly nationalistic and patriotic obsolete because national borders are increasingly porous. Appadurai (1996) uses "diasporic public spheres" to describe the ways in which people who live in different nations connect, interact, and work to expand social justice and human rights. Consequently, citizenship education within this age of globalization and mass migration must reach beyond national borders and incorporate ways in which students can develop identities and commitments to improve human rights for individuals in nations around the world. Scholars such as Nussbaum (2002), Appiah (2006), as well as Osler (Osler & Starkey, 2003)—in this book as well in other publications—call such individuals "cosmopolitan citizens." Cosmopolitan citizens are efficacious individuals who take action not only to improve human rights for people within their local communities and nations, but also for people in other parts of the world. They are consequently transformative citizens (Banks, 2008) because they are willing to take action that advances human rights even though they might violate existing laws and customs. Osler views empowering students to become change agents and to take transformative civic action to advance equality and justice as important goals of human rights education.

Osler is a pioneering scholar who has for several decades been a forceful and influential voice for human rights education. In 2004, she founded the Centre for Citizenship and Human Rights Education (CCHRE) at the University of Leeds in the United Kingdom and has influenced human rights education around the world with prolific lectures and publications. This book demonstrates, once again, that Osler is one of the world's most eloquent, authoritative, and compassionate voices that speaks for human rights education. I am pleased to welcome her book to the Multicultural Education Series and hope that it will attain the wide readership and influence that it deserves.

James A. Banks

REFERENCES

Appadurai, A. (1996). *Modernity at large: Cultural dimensions of globalization.* Minneapolis, MN: University of Minnesota Press.

Appiah, K. A. (2006). *Cosmopolitanism: Ethics in a world of strangers.* New York, NY: Norton.

Banks, J. A. (2004). Multicultural education: Historical development, dimensions, and practice. In J. A. Banks & C. A. M. Banks (Eds.), *Handbook of research on multicultural education* (2nd ed., pp. 3–29). San Francisco, CA: Jossey-Bass.

Banks, J. A. (2008). Diversity, group identity, and citizenship education in a global age. *Educational Researcher, 37*(3), 129–139.

Banks, J. A. (2009). *The Routledge international companion to multicultural education.* New York, NY: Routledge.

Banks, J. A. (2012). Multicultural education: Dimensions of. In J. A. Banks (Ed.), *Encyclopedia of diversity in education* (vol. 3, pp. 1538–1547). Thousand Oaks, CA: Sage Publications.

Barnard, A. (2016, February 8). Syrians desperate to escape what U. N. calls "extermination" by government. *The New York Times.* Retrieved from http://www.nytimes.com/2016/02/09/world/middleeast/syria-united-nations-report.html

Castles, S. (2014). International migration at a crossroads. *Citizenship Studies, 18*(2), 190–207.

Cohen, R. (2016, February 4). Europe's huddled masses. *The New York Times.* Retrieved from http://www.nytimes.com/2016/02/05/opinion/europes-huddled-masses.html

Hisham, M. (2016, January 14). Living under the sword of ISIS in Syria. *The New York Times.* Retrieved from http://www.nytimes.com/2016/01/15/opinion/living-under-the-sword-of-isis-in-syria.html

Mayo, C. (2014). *LGBTQ youth and education: Policies and practices.* New York, NY: Teachers College Press.

Nussbaum, M. (2002). Patriotism and cosmopolitanism. In J. Cohen (Ed.), *For love of country* (pp. 2–17). Boston, MA: Beacon Press.

Osler, A., & Starkey, H. (2003). Learning for cosmopolitan citizenship: Theoretical debates and young people's experiences. *Educational Review, 25*(3), 243–254.

Spring, J. (2010). *Deculturalization and the struggle for equality: A brief history of the education of dominated cultures in the United States* (7th ed.). New York, NY: McGraw-Hill.

United Nations Department of Economic and Social Affairs, Population Division (2013, October 3–4). Retrieved from http://www.oecd.org/els/mig/dioc.htm

Acknowledgments

I would like to thank most warmly my former students and colleagues Chalank Yahya and Juanjuan Zhu for their generous permission to use our collaborative work in this book:

"Challenges and Complexity in Human Rights Education: Teachers' Understandings of Democratic Participation and Gender Equity in Post-conflict Kurdistan–Iraq" by A. Osler and C. Yahya, 2013, *Education Inquiry*, *4*(1), pp. 189–210 (available at www.education-inquiry.net/index.php/edui/article/view/22068).

"Narratives in Teaching and Research for Justice and Human Rights," by A. Osler and J. Zhu, 2011, *Education, Citizenship, and Social Justice*, *6*(3), pp. 223–235 (available at esj.sagepub.com/content/6/3/223).

Chapter 4 draws in part on work with Zhu, and Chapter 6 on work with Yahya.

A number of other chapters also build on my own previously published work:

"Bringing Human Rights Back Home: Learning from 'Superman' and Addressing Political Issues at School," by A. Osler, 2013, *The Social Studies*, *104*(2), pp. 67–76 (available at dx.doi.org/10.1080/00377996.2012.687408).

"Human Rights, Scholarship, and Action for Change," by A. Osler, 2014, in *Intersectionality and Urban Education: Identities, Policies, Spaces, and Power* (pp. 249–265), by C. Grant and E. Zwier (Eds.), Charlotte, NC: Information Age.

"Human Rights Education, Postcolonial Scholarship, and Action for Social Justice," by A. Osler, 2015, *Theory & Research in Social Education*, *43*(2), pp. 244–274 (available at dx.doi.org/10.1080/00933104.2015.1034393).

Any book project relies on a network of friends and supporters, as much as on the determination of the author. First, I want to thank James Banks for proposing this book and for his imagination in conceiving a number of stimulating projects in which I have had the good fortune to be involved. I also appreciate all who have challenged and sustained me while writing, including students and colleagues at University College of Southeast Norway, particularly Hein Lindquist, Lena Lybæk, Ådne Valen-Senstad, and Bjørn Flatås. Working in Norway has opened my eyes to new ways of seeing. I am also grateful to Steven Camicia, Virginia Cawagas, and Yan Wing Leung for inviting me to join them as a visiting professor at Utah State University; the U.N. University for Peace, Costa Rica; and Hong Kong Institute of Education and for the new insights which you and your various students and colleagues offered me. Short visits to Beijing Normal University and Shangdong Normal University in China also caused me to reflect in new ways on my work. I very much appreciate the support of Wanda Cassidy and access to Simon Fraser University and University of Leicester libraries. I am particularly grateful for those times when I was able to escape to peaceful and inspiring surroundings to write and reflect. And so I thank Ellen Moore and Scott Harrison for the use of their amazing tree house in Nederland, Colorado—it felt as though it had been built with escaping scholars in mind—as well as for their insights and conversation. And special thanks also to the fabulous Helen R. Whiteley Center at Friday Harbor Laboratories, University of Washington, for hosting me. I feel I am never so productive or creative as when I am there. Finally, I wish to thank Hugh Starkey for continuing to act as my first reader and Brian Ellerbeck at Teachers College Press for running with this project and showing tremendous patience.

CHAPTER 1

Human Rights Education, Politics, and Power

Human Rights and Schooling: An Ethical Framework for Teaching for Social Justice aims to examine ways in which education, and specifically schools and education authorities, might develop so as to enable and support the original goals of the human rights project, namely freedom, justice, and peace in the world—in local communities, workplaces, homes, and schools. As Eleanor Roosevelt, who chaired the committee that drafted the Universal Declaration of Human Rights, expressed it:

> Where, after all, do universal human rights begin? In small places, close to home—so close and so small that they cannot be seen on any maps of the world. Yet they are the world of the individual person; the neighborhood he lives in; the school or college he attends; the factory, farm, or office where he works. Such are the places where every man, woman, and child seeks equal justice, equal opportunity, equal dignity without discrimination. Unless these rights have meaning there, they have little meaning anywhere. Without concerted citizen action to uphold them close to home, we shall look in vain for progress in the larger world. (Roosevelt, 1958)

Within this vision, the realization of justice and peace in the world depends, first, on realizing justice and peace in families, in neighborhoods, in local communities, and in national communities. This human rights vision is not primarily about international politics, but about everyday living. It is about challenging microaggressions, overcoming everyday racism, and everyday sexism. And schools have a key role in enabling these processes to be realized.

The second, interrelated purpose of *Human Rights and Schooling* is to consider how teachers might draw on human rights to achieve the widely agreed goal of realizing greater justice and equitable schooling for their students, or in Eleanor Roosevelt's words, of supporting and enabling school systems where every student can claim their entitlement to "equal justice, equal opportunity, and equal dignity without discrimination." Following from this, the third purpose is to explore how human rights might be harnessed to empower students to become agents of change for human rights, in other words, how students might be enabled to become cosmopolitan citizens, ready to take action to support the struggles of others, in the local community, the national community, and in other parts of the globe. These kinds of solidarities are central to the success of the human rights vision.

The overall focus of *Human Rights and Schooling* is to explore various facets of human rights education as well as the potential of human rights as principles for living together in multicultural nation-states and communities and as a framework for realizing equitable and just learning communities. Since all education takes place within specific social, cultural, and political contexts, one key concern here will be to explore the meanings of *universal* human rights within *diverse* contexts.

Since 1948 and the proclamation of the Universal Declaration of Human Rights, human rights rhetoric has triumphed. That is to say, human rights are commonly invoked by governments to justify their actions and, in many contexts, by disadvantaged or oppressed groups to seek support for their cause. They are likewise invoked by international organizations to put pressure on governments to act or desist from a particular course of action. Yet human rights are commonly associated first and foremost with the political positioning of governments, and sometimes with point scoring between nation-states, rather than recognized as principles for everyday life. This rhetoric has become the common currency of governments eager to further their specific political agendas.

Such political rhetoric has brought human rights into disrepute in many quarters. Hopgood (2013) suggests we have reached the "endtimes of Human Rights" because of widespread skepticism arising from the use and abuse of human rights language, both by governments and by some powerful nongovernmental organizations (NGOs). As discussed below, he distinguishes between human rights, which are embraced by local communities around the globe in their struggles for greater justice, and Human Rights (uppercase), which are the discourses embedded in U.N. machinery and instruments.

Human Rights and Schooling: An Ethical Framework for Teaching for Social Justice is, as the title suggests, about human rights on the ground, and about their relevance to the everyday professional lives of teachers and their students, to the curriculum, and to the policies and practices associated with the day-to-day processes of schooling. I argue that human rights provide teachers with a powerful moral and legal framework for enabling greater social justice and more equitable outcomes in a variety of social and cultural contexts across the globe, particularly in multicultural schools and communities. In this endeavor, I draw on key international human rights instruments, particularly the United Nations' 1948 Universal Declaration of Human Rights (UDHR) and 1989 Convention on the Rights of the Child (CRC), as key documents that teachers can deploy in this enterprise.

If Hopgood is right, then the goals of human rights, as articulated in the preamble of the UDHR, namely human dignity and the equal rights of all and, ultimately, "freedom, justice and peace in the world" (U.N., 1948, pre-amble) are now more dependent on locally embedded human rights cultures than they ever were. Schools and teachers have a key role to play in creating a culture of human rights and for encouraging students to develop a sense of empathy and solidarity with their fellow humanity.

HUMAN RIGHTS CLOSE TO HOME

Inequalities and injustices exist in all societies; no country is immune. Human rights discourse is frequently deployed in local communities struggling against injustice, poverty, and violence. For example, the Kensington Welfare Rights Union and Poor People's Economic Human Rights Campaign in the United States brought together people living in poverty and homeless people to raise the issue of poverty "as a violation of human rights, basing their claim on the Universal Declaration of Human Rights" particularly, Article 23 (the right to work for just pay and the right to organize); Article 25 (the right to health, housing and social security); and Article 26 (the right to education). Effectively, these rights, as set out in the UDHR, became the rallying cry of their struggle in the Kensington District of Philadelphia. The campaign-ers discovered that human rights provided them with "a set of international rights principles, laws, methods, and strategies" that were conceptual and practical tools for action (Cox & Thomas, 2004, p. 53).

Their campaign began in the late 1990s when Cheri Honkala and five other women, whose children had nowhere to play in the neighborhood, took over an abandoned welfare center and set up a community center, since they lacked these basic facilities. They were arrested and held for 6 days in jail. Found not guilty on all counts, they made a strong case for their take-over and harnessed a degree of public support for their cause. These women eventually joined with others to found the Kensington Welfare Rights Union, established on the belief that they did not have to accept a downward spiral of poverty. Beginning with action to secure the human rights of their children, in many respects theirs has been a struggle for the recognition of women's rights as human rights.

They challenged the negative impacts of welfare reform, which not only left them in a weakened and insecure economic position but also undermined their sense of self through the construction of discourses that individualize poverty. Such discourses provoke a sense of shame in poor people, which un-dermines and corrodes human dignity, preventing human flourishing (Bap-tist & Bricker-Jenkins, 2002; Lister, 2013). The language of human rights acts as a powerful counterweight to the dehumanizing and sometimes de-monizing language used to describe the poor and homeless, moving the issue away from the rhetoric of personal responsibility to one of dignity and rights, within which the wider community shows solidarity with the poor.

These antipoverty campaigners and others, such as those working for women's rights, disability rights, gay rights, racial justice, and environmental justice, recognize the power of human rights frameworks for their cause. They can harness the power of human rights to form alliances to address common concerns, thereby challenging the huge and often widening gap between human rights discourse and the harsh realities of everyday life. Cox and Thomas (2004) argue that they also challenge conceptions of patriotism in the United States that tie it to unilateralism. Instead, they assert the need to make concrete links between local struggles and struggles for global justice and to reclaim ideals that contributed to the creation of the United Nations and the UDHR. Such ideals recall the powerful words of the poet Langston Hughes: "Let America be America again." The struggle for human rights and social justice, in the United States and elsewhere, is often a long and arduous undertaking, requiring energy and commitment, but also a vision of a better future:

> The struggle to build a movement for human rights in the United States is not for the faint of heart. It seeks a transformation in U.S. society. . . . It faces substantial obstacles, not least of which is the increasing unilateralism of the U.S. government and its long history of exceptionalism with respect to the domestic application of human rights . . . . Let it be said by future generations that in the 21st century, the United States finally gave its full attention to the words that The Reverend Dr. Martin Luther King, Jr. uttered nearly 40 years ago: "I think it is necessary to realize that we have moved from the era of civil rights to the era of human rights." (Cox & Thomas, 2004, p. 18)

U.N. CALL FOR HUMAN RIGHTS EDUCATION

In 2011 the United Nations made a very explicit call for human rights education globally, with the adoption of the United Nations Declaration on Human Rights Education and Training (DHRET; U.N., 2011). Although this is a nonbinding treaty, like the UDHR it has moral force and is a key step in enabling human rights education globally. It provides a working definition of *human rights education* (HRE), against which member-states, NGOs, and other educational shareholders, including teachers, parents, and students, can assess progress and demand change. Importantly, it defines HRE as encompassing education *about, through,* and *for* human rights. Education *about* rights includes providing knowledge and understanding of human rights norms and principles, the values that underpin them, and the mechanisms for their protection. Education *through* human rights includes learning and teaching in a way that respects the rights of both educators and learners.

Finally, education *for* human rights is about empowering learners to enjoy and exercise their rights and to respect and uphold the rights of others (U.N., 2011, art. 2.2).

Teachers will be aware of the right to education, but the right to human rights education is generally less well known. The right to HRE was first articulated in the UDHR in 1948. Its preamble states: "Member States have pledged themselves to achieve, in co-operation with the United Nations, the promotion of universal respect for and observance of human rights and fundamental freedoms" noting that "*a common understanding of these rights and freedoms is of the greatest importance for the full realization of this pledge* [emphasis added]" (U.N., 1948). This "common understanding" was to be realized through education, with Article 26 stating that "Education shall be directed . . . to the strengthening of respect for human rights and fundamental freedoms."

O'Cuanachain (2010) suggests that one of the earliest articulations of human rights education *as a right* in the education research literature can be dated to Osler and Starkey (1996). (See also Starkey, 1991.) Chapter 2 of this book explores the right to HRE and education as an enabling right for other human rights. The United Nations's 2011 call for HRE is stressed here because it serves as a powerful political lever in the struggle for human rights. One key element of "concerted citizen action" (Roosevelt, 1958) to uphold human rights is education. It is education that also makes possible effective citizen action in the field of human rights. Of course, HRE is not by any means confined to schooling, but school is a near universal institution and therefore a potentially powerful site of human rights education.

Yet before turning to education, this chapter confronts the broader international politics of human rights, not least because international politics and the discourses associated with them have a considerable impact on individuals' understandings about the relevance of human rights to our daily lives and therefore the relevance of HRE. These understandings vary across and between nation-states and are influenced by such factors as prevailing regional and national discourses about nationhood, citizenship, and belonging and whether the communities and individuals in question belong to mainstream or marginalized groups. In other words, they are influenced by power relationships between nations and between individuals and communities in those nations.

HUMAN RIGHTS AND INTERNATIONAL POLITICS

In western Europe, where human rights discourses are promoted by many national governments and by international bodies such as the Council of Europe (founded in 1949 to promote human rights in the region in the wake of World War II and with 47 member states today), human rights discourses

are relatively strong, and nation-states are generally willing to commit themselves to international human rights treaties. As a result, human rights
education—in principle, if not in practice—is generally seen as relevant and
uncontroversial (with some recent exceptions, discussed below), regardless of
whether the party in power is from the left or the right.

In the United States, by contrast, although human rights education is
actively promoted by organizations such as Amnesty International USA, it is
less well known, and often unheard of within the academy. When I arrived as
a visiting professor at Utah State University in autumn 2010 to teach a course
on human rights education to doctoral candidates, an administrator in the international office asked me what I was planning to teach. When I mentioned
human rights, she carefully explained that this was probably not relevant to
most Americans, and went on to suggest that this course would probably be
better targeted in other parts of the world, where people faced serious human
rights violations. Her response reflects a common misperception (not limited
to the United States) that human rights education is largely a study of rights
denials. But it also reflects a dominant national political culture in which
certain human rights (such as freedom of expression; freedom of thought,
conscience, and religion; nondiscrimination; the right to own property) are
defined as civil rights, properly guaranteed by the Constitution and domestic
law and not linked to international human rights standards.

Nevertheless, there are indications that HRE is under threat in some
European states. In 2006 the Spanish parliament approved the Education
Act 2/2006, which introduced a new course, "Education for Citizenship
and Human Rights," in line with Recommendation CM/Rec (2010)7 of the
Committee of Ministers on the Charter on Education for Democratic Citizenship and Human Rights Education of the Council of Europe (Council
of Europe, 2010). Teaching was to address the subject in primary, secondary, and baccalaureate programs, and include a cross-curricular element at
each stage. The law incorporated social and civic competences into the basic
competences to be acquired by all students by the end of compulsory education, to enable them to participate as citizens. Immediately, there was an
assault on the course by sections of the hierarchy of the Catholic Church, the
Popular Party, and right-wing media, who encouraged campaigns by parents
demanding its removal, and efforts to claim conscientious objection to the
program and, consequently, exemption from attendance. The Spanish Supreme Court subsequently ruled that the program was legal and legitimate,
but following the 2011 elections in which the Popular Party came into power, the proposals for the program have been supressed through the passing of
an education reform law, despite the legitimacy, constitutionality, and legality
of the program and a European-wide campaign to protect students' right to
HRE (Fundación Cives, 2013; Muñoz Ramirez, 2014).

There is a common perception in many western nations that the most
abhorrent violations of human rights take place in other regions of the world.

This binary between "heavenly" western nations and "hellish" countries of the Global South is challenged by a number of human rights scholars (Mutua, 2001; Okafor & Agbakwa, 2001). This binary can be illustrated by the context in which the United States ratified the 1966 International Covenant on Civil and Political Rights (ICCPR; U.N., 1966a) in 1992. Although the United States was heavily involved in the drafting of this treaty, its argument was that it had no real need to ratify the treaty, as domestic law adequately protected citizens. The inference here seems to be that other "hellish" human rights countries have greater need to be bound by the covenant and international mechanisms for its enforcement. However, there was a degree of contradiction and discomfiture on the part of the United States in taking this position since at the time of ratification it made numerous reservations to the ICCPR so as to *avoid* bringing domestic law in line with international standards (Baxi, 1996). These include reservations relating to the limitations on free speech (Article 20), leaving vulnerable minorities less well protected against hate speech than in other nations, and the State's right to impose capital punishment, including such punishment for crimes committed by persons below 18 years of age (Article 6). Nine European states (Belgium, Denmark, France, Finland, Germany, Norway, Portugal, Spain, and Sweden) filed objections to the various reservations of the United States (Okafor & Agbakwa, 2001).

The United States is not a State Party to the International Covenant on Economic, Social and Cultural Rights (CESCR; U.N., 1966b). Economic and social rights, such as the right to work and the right to social security, have cost implications and are consequently less well protected.[1] So, for example, the 1979 Convention on the Elimination of Discrimination Against Women (CEDAW), the 1965 International Convention on the Elimination of All Forms of Racial Discrimination (CERD), and the 1989 Convention on the Rights of the Child (CRC) have not been ratified by the United States. Unlike the Universal Declaration of Human Rights (UDHR), these treaties carry more than moral weight. State parties that ratify them hold themselves accountable to international bodies, something the United States is generally reluctant to do. The reluctance of the United States to ratify these treaties effectively weakens the international human rights framework, and in the eyes of other U.N. members and NGOs, undermines its moral authority and credibility to speak on human rights matters.

In the 21st century there appears to be a growing skepticism both about the way human rights rhetoric is selectively deployed by powerful nations and about the ways in which humanitarian and military aid is frequently conditionally tied to fulfillment of selected human rights norms (Hopgood, 2013). There is also growing skepticism about human rights institutions and about the global structure of laws, courts, norms, and organizations that claim to speak in the name of humanity as a whole. A number of international NGOs, which may or may not have a mass membership, also use human rights language to further their power and influence, engaging in fund raising—often through slick campaigns using social media—writing reports, and lobbying governments, all in the name of a universal, secular moral authority, namely, that of human rights (Hopgood, 2013).

Some may detect a direct parallel between 21st-century appeals in the name of human rights, whereby all societies are expected to adopt global norms, and the 19th-century mission of the Christian churches, dominated by middle-class European values, to civilize working-class, urban populations at home and colonized peoples abroad. Certainly, human rights often appeal to a comfortable middle-class constituency, who can donate to a cause without necessarily engaging in any meaningful way with those they see themselves as supporting. These necessarily short-term campaigns and activities are often a world away from grassroots struggles for social justice by oppressed people, which often last many decades.

Meanwhile, the United Nations, through its Security Council and other bodies, often appears slow or helpless to intervene in unfolding humanitarian crises, as witnessed by the war in Syria (ongoing at the time of writing) and the disastrously slow response by the World Health Organization (WHO) to the 2014 Ebola epidemic in West Africa, where impoverished postconflict societies with weak health systems were left vulnerable for many months. The latter episode has led to urgent calls for the reform of the WHO, not only to provide security against epidemic threats, but also to meet everyday health needs, thus realizing the right to health (Gostin & Friedman, 2015). The failure of U.N. bodies to guarantee the human rights of vulnerable communities leads to widespread skepticism not just about U.N. bodies but about human rights mechanisms more broadly.

In this context, reform of international institutions (generally a slow and laborious process requiring a high degree of international cooperation) is critical, but so too is the empowering of local communities to take action. Both the commitment to international solidarity and the empowering of local communities to struggle for justice require human rights awareness in populations across nation-states. Human rights education has a key role to play in enabling and equipping people to struggle for rights at all scales—local, national, and international. Schools are a key site for such education, yet the conditions in schools may sometimes appear unfavorable. It is to this issue that I now turn.

TESTING, STANDARDS, AND HUMAN RIGHTS EDUCATION

In 2007 I visited South Korea, where the Ministry of Education, in cooperation with the Korean Commission for Human Rights, was engaged in an initiative to introduce HRE into schools, and was holding a series of conferences for school principals, education personnel, members of youth organizations, and other stakeholders in three cities: Seoul, Busan, and Gwangju. On our arrival at the Gwangju conference, we were not surprised to see a group of young people outside, protesting with placards. We had been told that there might be protests outside the conference concerning the U.S. and British military invasion of Iraq. The city is known for its commitment to justice and democratic participation. The collective memory of the Gwangju May 18 Democratic Uprising remains powerful, when in a demonstration against martial law in 1980 over 150 people lost their lives and many thousands were wounded, quashed by military forces.

In fact, the protesters, high school students, and members of the Movement for Teenagers Human Rights, were protesting about the high-stakes testing regime in Korean schools. Their placards, prepared in both Korean and English, proclaimed:

> Korean teenagers are living in exam hell
> U must know the truth that Korean education is teenagers-killing education.

We asked the students to explain their protest. Their argument was that a curriculum reform that introduced human rights content meant very little while high school students were under such intense examination pressure that they experienced a denial of basic rights in and beyond school.

Examination pressures force Korean school students to work excessive hours with little sleep, both at regular school and then in the evening at cram school, driving a number to take their own lives.[2] High youth suicide rates reflect wider problems among youth, problems that are generated as an outcome of this excessive examinations-driven school system. They suggest serious difficulties in realizing rights in and beyond school, with large numbers of young people failing to achieve a basic sense of well-being.

The Korean high school students protesting outside the HRE conference had not learned *about* rights as part of the school curriculum, since this was a new initiative. This knowledge had been gained beyond school. They felt strongly that rights *through* education were denied to them and their peers because of the intense examination-orientated nature of schooling. Despite these shortcomings in their education, they were aware that rights are something that need to be struggled for. These protesters were invited into the conference and given the opportunity to speak from the platform and voice their concerns to conference delegates. The Korean high school students' protest highlights the importance of addressing both education *about* rights and education *through* rights as part of a balanced curriculum. In fact, the HRE initiative in Korean schools has subsequently been severely impeded by the high-stakes testing processes that continue.

Keet (2006, 2012), drawing first and foremost on his experience of human rights and HRE in South Africa and framing his analysis in the context of such initiatives as the U.N. Decade for Human Rights Education 1995–2004 and the subsequent World Programme for Human Rights Education (2005–ongoing), highlights the dangers of what he calls a "declarationist" approach to human rights education, whereby all human rights truths are assumed to come solely from international instruments. His observations have particular resonance in examination-driven learning contexts since they have direct implications for pedagogy. He writes: "HRE has developed as a *declarationist, conservative, positivistic, uncritical, compliance-driven framework*" (2006, p. 218, italics in the original), which assumes all truths come from international instruments. He argues for a human rights pedagogy that draws centrally on learners' own life experiences and critically examines international texts, recognizing the historical and political context in which they were drafted, rather than approaching international instruments unquestioningly as if they are quasi-sacred texts that must be accepted as a matter of faith. Importantly, teaching and learning about human rights needs to be situated in the specific sociopolitical context of the learners, allowing them to examine rights as possible tools for enabling social justice. When learners examine human rights texts, they need to interrogate the texts' possible meanings and value for their lives and those of others.

The struggle of the Korean Movement for Teenagers Human Rights and the wider Korean experience of schooling support this case. The student protesters were well placed to draw on a specific, collective local and national history of struggle for democracy and human rights. Their own struggle related directly to their lived experiences of school and to shocking levels of teen suicides. Together their knowledge and experience, and that of the wider Gwangju community, had made them effective advocates for justice, able to critique constructively a national HRE initiative that was being introduced on their behalf, and to communicate effectively their concerns. Arguably, HRE should be introduced in cooperation with such students.

In her book *Un-standardizing Curriculum*, Christine Sleeter (2005) considers whether teachers can work with standards and multicultural education at the same time. Her concern is that in many U.S. schools and school districts, the attention being given to Common Core Standards and tests has diverted the focus away from teaching culturally and linguistically diverse students. She seeks to address a common claim by teachers that they lack time for multicultural education since they need to prepare their students for these tests. Multicultural education, like human rights education, is concerned with equitable schooling and seeks to address students' diverse identities, interests, languages, and communities to enable greater equity, and so her arguments have some resonance for HRE. The challenge is to enable students to claim their entitlement to equal justice and equal dignity and to empower both students and teachers to become agents of change, exploring rights as a means of realizing these goals. Key to this process is teachers' ability to reconcile such goals with enabling their students to succeed in the standardized tests that form part of their reality. It is particularly important if we are to avoid the pitfall that the Korean high school students anticipated, namely, that an attempt by school authorities to introduce HRE as education *about* human rights, without reviewing the ways in which students' human rights need to be secured in the school setting, was unlikely to be effective.

First, Sleeter emphasizes that students will do better academically if teachers stop teaching to the test and focus on the specific needs of the students within a culturally diverse society. She calls on teachers to use curriculum standards as a "backbone" for developing a multicultural, academically rigorous curriculum that is meaningful to students. Using the concept of "backward design" (Wiggins & McTighe, 2005), she invites teachers to plan content that is focused enough to teach, broad enough to maneuver, and potentially meaningful to students. Sleeter works with the concept of "transformative intellectual knowledge" (Banks, 2014) to encourage her graduate students to research a question relating to their teaching plans from the perspective of a marginalized group, so as to avoid the stereotyping that so easily happens if we teach about the "other" without reflection. If feasible, Sleeter also guides teachers to learn some of the "cultural wealth" (Yosso, 2005) or "funds of knowledge" (Gonzalez, Moll, & Amanti, 2005) in the communities from which their students are drawn. In this way, teachers can uncover community resources and organizations that might support their work. By encouraging teachers to aim high on behalf of their students, examine their own beliefs and judgments about the students and communities with whom they work, and give classroom-based assessments and feedback, she hopes to overcome low teacher expectations of marginalized students. All these steps can be applied to human rights learning, helping teachers to work with standards to benefit students, rather than teach to the test.

This chapter has highlighted that while school is a key site for human rights education, not all HRE takes place in school. Museums are another key site for HRE, acting as a resource for teachers and communities. Curators and museum educators also need to examine their practices in relation to HRE. Golding (2014), in her discussion of how museums might contribute, draws on the traditional Indian story of the five blind men who discover an elephant, each describing different features—tail, trunk, flank, leg, or ear—by sense of touch. She uses the tale to challenge museum study that privileges Western perspectives. It is a metaphor for multiperspectivity, so critical to sound HRE. She argues for museums to raise their voices against human rights abuses around the world, to uphold universal principles, and stand firm against injustice. Tai (2010) discusses the case of the Osaka Human Rights Museum, which was created by those engaged in the liberation of the (formerly outcast) Buraku people of Japan, demonstrating how education at the museum is a product of an interesting interaction of global and local perspectives on human rights, and examining how curators there have adopted and appropriated the universal concept of human rights to changing strategies of

human rights activism as enacted in the context of the city of Osaka. They
have gradually extended the museum's original scope to enable visitors to
make links between different struggles for rights, including those of resident
Koreans in Japan, women, people with disabilities, and sexual minorities. The
goal is to break down the dichotomy between visitors and those who experience discrimination in Japanese society and to invite all visitors to reflect on
and recognize their own discriminatory attitudes.

An important additional site of HRE is in colleges and universities. In
many regions of the world, students are increasingly encouraged, and sometimes expected, to engage in civic learning. A report from the National Task
Force on Civic Learning and Democratic Engagement (2012) stressed the
importance of preparing students with knowledge and *for action*. Although
there is no explicit mention of human rights, there are openings for HRE, in
enabling higher education institutions to meet such goals, an issue that is further explored in Chapter 8, where I consider how a human rights framework
might strengthen such programs.

CREATING A LOCAL CULTURE OF HUMAN RIGHTS

On March 17, 2003, the U.N. High Commissioner for Human Rights, Ser-
gio Vieira de Mello, addressing the 59th Session of the U.N. Commission on
Human Rights in Geneva, said:

> The culture of human rights must be a popular culture if it is to have
> the strength to withstand the blows that will inevitably come.
> Human-rights culture must be a popular culture if it is to be able to
> innovate and to be truly owned at the national and sub-national levels.
> (Vieira de Mello, 2003)

When Vieira de Mello highlighted the need for a popular culture of human rights, he was recognizing implicitly the gap between the grand rhetoric
of human rights deployed at the global level and everyday struggles for justice. He recognized the power of human rights in local contexts and within
local cultures. In particular, he recognized the potential of embedded human
rights and anticipated the realization of a popular culture of human rights
through education:

> "Education" is the word we use to describe this process, and it deserves
> more attention. We must work harder at communicating the human
> rights story through all available means, not least electronic media.
> Security will be enhanced as we fill in the lacunae of ignorance, empow-
> er the dispossessed and enable them to recognize and claim their rights.
> (Vieira de Mello, 2003)

His words are particularly poignant, since 5 months later, on August 19, 2003, a suicide truck bombing of the U.N. building in Baghdad killed 22 humanitarian workers, including Vieira de Mello. His vision of the future of education for human rights and its potential to empower the dispossessed means that whether or not we share Hopgood's (2013) thesis that we are now in the endtimes of Human Rights, HRE needs greater attention in the coming years. This education needs to be critical and to be carefully theorized, to avoid the conservative and compliance-driven agendas that continue to travel from western nations to other parts of the world, assuming a mistaken model of themselves as a human rights paradise, while identifying other places as hellish sites of human rights violations. This simplistic view is not only mistaken but ineffective in enabling rights. All HRE needs to be linked more closely to everyday struggles and everyday injustices, whether we are addressing the education of the powerful or the dispossessed.

Of course there remains a role for education in international human rights law. But the education of the wider public, and particularly of the next generation, cannot be a watered-down version of this and it cannot solely focus on a U.N. culture of rights. Learners may be encouraged and inspired by the utopia imagined by those who drafted the UDHR (Osler & Starkey, 2010), but they also need to imagine their own utopias and develop skills to struggle for and to realize their own just communities. The processes of human rights education must necessarily empower learners to become more effective in the ongoing struggle for rights. It must enable them to critique existing power structures, and equip them with the skills for transformation and change. Only then will education *for* human rights be effective.

CHAPTER 2

The Right to Human Rights Education

Davis Guggenheim's 2010 documentary film *Waiting for "Superman"* (Chilcott & Guggenheim, 2010) highlights how for many children, particularly those from low-income minority groups, the American public school system operates as a lottery, potentially undermining their right to education. Bianca is a kindergartner in Harlem, NY. Her mother Nakia worries about sending her to a local public school. Nakia pays US$500 a month for Bianca's tuition at a Catholic school, but struggling to find steady work, she falls behind with the school bills. Like the four other children profiled in *Waiting for "Superman,"* living in disadvantaged neighborhoods in New York, Washington, D.C., and Los Angeles, and even in the comfortable surroundings of Silicon Valley, Bianca is entered into a lottery to win a place in her family's school of choice, a free charter school. In every case, the odds are stacked heavily against the child (Weber, 2010).

Both the movie and the charter school movement have been contentious topics. Introduced with the ostensible purpose of offering school choice and with the potential for educational innovation, while minimizing government bureaucracy, Minnesota was the first state to authorize charter schools in 1991. California and Colorado quickly followed suit, and by 2011 there were 5,453 such schools across the country (Weiler & Vogel, 2015). The claim that charter schools can help realize a more equitable and just public school system in the United States has been challenged by a number of researchers (Frankenberg & Lee, 2003; Minow, 1999).

Swalwell and Apple (2011) make the case that *Waiting for "Superman"* is an appropriation by the powerful of the language of those whose rights are denied. They see the film as an attempt to reinterpret the social world of those it portrays, namely, those who are denied access to various social and educational goods. They suggest that the film neglects many vital questions, particularly ones of power, race, and class, contradicts many of its own assertions, and serves to cut off rather than open up discussion.

Concerns have been expressed about the high level of racial segregation in such schools and the potential for discrimination within a system that is "premised on self-segregation and sorting" and ultimately favors the affluent and well-informed (Minow, 1999, p. 282). Frankenberg and Lee (2003) found in their nationwide study of 1,855 charter schools that 95%

were located in 16 states and were more segregated than the noncharter public schools in those locations. According to Martin (2004), the charter school movement is responsible for "enhancing opportunities for well-to-do and well-informed families while reducing opportunities for the poor and the less informed, especially minority families residing in low-income, urban districts" (p. 331). In an empirical study of charter schools in Colorado, Weiler and Vogel (2015) found several school practices that threaten equity: charging fees for full-time kindergarten enrolllment, books, athletics and other extracurricular activities, and school uniforms; testing of students as part of the registration process; requirements that parents serve a specified number of volunteer hours at the school; and suggested donations by parents.

These are important considerations in examining equitable access to education, but not reasons to avoid using *Waiting for "Superman"* as a pedagogical tool to examine the right to education and rights in education. The film highlights everyday rights and injustices in education with which most students will identify and provides rich material both for high school students and students participating in professional education courses to critically analyze and deconstruct the film. It is important to note that the film does not use the language of international human rights. Students might consider how applying a human rights discourse and framework in the film would influence how viewers might understand the cases of the five children represented.

This chapter illustrates how human rights principles might inform everyday processes of schooling and learning to live together. It considers rights *to*, *in*, and *through* education, exploring ways in which Banks et al.'s (2005) assertion that human rights should underpin citizenship education might be applied by social studies teachers. Chapter 1 introduced the U.N. Declaration on Human Rights Education and Training (U.N., 2011), which refers to human rights education (HRE) as encompassing education *about* rights, *through* rights, and *for* rights. This equates with the knowledge, experiential processes (skills), and outcomes of HRE (attitudes and action orientations). In this chapter I take a step back to look first at the right *to* education, which includes the right to HRE and the knowledge, skills, and attitudes this might include. Rights *in* education addresses legal and policy frameworks as well as the attitudes of students and the consequent climate of the learning community. Rights *through* education is about the outcomes of the educational process; it includes the creation of a rights-respecting community and the ways in which education is an enabling right providing access to other rights (McCowan, 2012).

This chapter illustrates how a human rights framework permits a critical examination of politically or socially sensitive issues close to home, but also opens up opportunities for a global dimension; thus rights and social justice can be centered in the classroom but analyzed in various settings with the result that commonalities and differences can be better understood. Using the film *Waiting for "Superman"* as a starting point, it suggests ways in which teachers can work with students to reflect on the processes and politics of education to examine and enable ways for schooling to become "*available, accessible, acceptable* and *adaptable*" to all (Tomaševski, 2001, p. 13, emphasis added), in line with internationally agreed-upon standards. These four concepts are discussed below.

WAITING FOR "SUPERMAN" AND THE "LEARNING TO LIVE TOGETHER" GRADUATE SEMINAR

Waiting for "Superman" assumes, quite rightly, that there are a number of elements contributing to a quality education and a quality school system, including high standards in math and reading, equitable access for minority students, appropriate support to enable success for students with special needs, opportunities to progress to college, and, above all, effective teachers. The film aims to serve as a wake-up call, inspiring parents and guardians, teachers, and concerned citizens to work together to improve schools. After all, education is a basic human right, and this implies more than just a school place for every child. The 1990 Jomtien Declaration acknowledged growing recognition across the globe that the right to education implies efforts by governments to ensure that conditions exist for every child to be able to access high-quality teaching and learning (World Conference on Education for All, 1990).

Of course in 102 minutes no film can fully explore what constitutes a quality education, nor can it necessarily examine all aspects of education as a human right. During fall 2010, public school teachers and administrators in my graduate seminar at Utah State University (USU) grappled with the concept and underlying principles of human rights as applied to schools, school systems, communities, and, most importantly, students. While none of us would claim to have answers to all the challenges facing America's schools, the seminar nevertheless provided opportunities to examine in depth the shared professional responsibilities of teachers, especially social studies teachers. Specifically, we considered the role of human rights in schooling for democratic participation, examining the right *to* education, rights *in* education, and rights *through* education.

This chapter draws on my experiences as a visiting professor at USU. I led a 10-session credit-bearing seminar, offered as an elective to graduate students. They came from a range of academic backgrounds, with some specializing in social studies, one specializing in language education, and others teaching mathematics and science. Most were combining their studies with full- or part-time work in public schools. Two were teaching classes at university level and supervising teacher education students. All but one were either U.S. citizens or longstanding U.S. residents. The exception was an international student from China.

The graduate seminar was entitled Learning to Live Together and included the following descriptor: "We will consider human rights as principles for living together and focus on human rights education as a possible means to working toward the cosmopolitan ideals of justice and peace." The students were told: "The tutor is from the United Kingdom. It is expected that there will be a genuine cultural exchange between participants and tutor as well as mutual learning. . . . As part of the preparation for the various classes, you will reflect on your own positioning in relation to various human rights and justice issues." Eight students registered. During the seminar we read a number of academic papers addressing both children's human rights in education and human rights education as a curriculum subject in different national contexts. Students also read *Teachers and Human Rights Education* (Osler & Starkey, 2010) to provide a common starting point for discussion and debate.

During the period of the seminar, the film *Waiting for "Superman"* was on general release, but it did not come to Logan, UT. I, and some of the class, saw it when we attended a conference in Denver, CO. The topic of the film, the availability and accessibility of quality schooling was, however, one that was vigorously debated in class. Other human rights standards identified by Tomaševski (2001) and relating to the acceptability and adaptability of schooling were explored using other resources, discussed below in Chapter 7, in relation to child rights. A number of seminar members also used these other resources with their own classes, both in teacher education and in middle and high schools.

In class, many of the day-to-day human rights topics that arose were ones of considerable local and/or international sensitivity. Generally, these topics were introduced by students, who drew from the news, from their own classrooms, and from debates taking place on campus. We sought to make links between these topical concerns and education. It is beyond the scope of this chapter to address all these human rights issues, but they included religious freedom, LGBT rights, immigration controls, multiculturalism, violence against women and girls, and, during banned books week,[1] censorship in schools and children's libraries.

Although many of these subjects are socially and politically sensitive, generating strong emotional reactions, in class we endeavored to observe three ground rules: We respect each other's dignity and identities; we remain open to learning from each other's personal and professional experiences; and our assertions should be evidence-based.

THE RIGHT TO EDUCATION

Waiting for "Superman" is an excellent stimulus for opening a discussion about education as a human right. The opening scenes reveal how the movie got its name: Social activist Geoffrey Canada, who grew up in the South Bronx, explains:

> One of the saddest days of my life was when my mother told me "Superman" did not exist. Cause even in the depths of the ghetto you just thought he was coming. . . . She thought I was crying because it's like Santa Claus is not real. I was crying because no one was coming with enough power to save us.

Today, Canada is only too conscious that communities cannot afford to wait for "Superman" or any other hero to drop in and rescue schools in neighborhoods torn apart by poverty, crime, and other social problems. He's a passionate advocate for education reform, having established Harlem Children's Zone (HCZ) in 1990. Importantly, he raises the question of power, and while this is not a theme that is explicitly developed in the film, we, as teachers, might usefully reflect on the uneven distribution of power and our own professional practice. As Sensoy and DiAngelo (2012) remind us, "society is stratified (i.e., divided and unequal) in significant and far reaching ways along social group lines that include race, class, gender and ability" (p. xviii), which means that all teachers are, by their actions or inactions, implicated in processes that either support or undermine struggles for justice:

> Each of us does have a choice about whether we are going to work to interrupt these systems or support their existence by ignoring them. There is no neutral ground; to choose not to act against injustice is to chose to allow it. (p. xxii)

For many children, there need to be broader changes in their lives, if they are to effectively claim the right to education. The HCZ project adopts a holistic approach to rebuilding a community so that children can stay on track through college and into the job market. The project's goal is

> to create a "tipping point" in the neighborhood so that children are surrounded by an enriching environment of college-oriented peers and supportive adults, a counterweight to "the street" and a toxic popular culture that glorifies misogyny and anti-social behavior. (HCZ, n.d.)

The neighborhood needs to develop so that high-achieving young adults want to remain, rather than move away. Over 20 years HCZ has expanded to become a comprehensive system of programs covering nearly 100 blocks of Central Harlem. Programs address parental support and include in-school, after-school, social-service, health, and community-building initiatives. The premise is that for children to succeed, their families also need to do well and feel empowered. What is interesting here is the ability of people to work together for change. By doing so they exercise agency, whereas individually they remain powerless.

HCZ works to operationalize the right to education. Former U.N. Special Rapporteur on the Right to Education Katarina Tomaševski noted that simply providing schools is insufficient. She encapsulated the right to education as the "4 As" (Figure 2.1): Schools must fulfill criteria guaranteeing their *availability* to all and must also be *accessible, acceptable,* and *adaptable* to all children (Tomaševski, 2001).

Tomaševski recognized that the nation-state, as primary duty bearer, must take steps to guarantee the 4 As, but that other stakeholders, including the child, the parents/guardians, and teachers, have key roles to play. Teachers can use Figure 2.1 as a checklist with middle and high school students to investigate and assess education provision in their own and other communities. Teacher education students might review Figure 2.1 and build on it, drawing on their knowledge of the research literature to discuss whether they consider any element to be missing from Tomaševski's analysis. One starting point is the portrayal of education as a lottery system in *Waiting for "Superman,"* suggesting that in the United States, quality schooling is neither available nor accessible to all. Learners can investigate the following: What are the particular concerns of the parents and children featured in the film? What evidence is put forward to support or challenge their claims? Are students able to uncover any counterevidence? Where resources are limited, is a lottery a fair means of allocating school places? Does it discriminate against any particular groups of learners? What alternative solutions might address school availability and accessibility to all? How is public schooling funded? What laws are in place to protect children's right to education? Are they effective? Students can also make international comparisons, using Figure 2.1 to examine challenges that children elsewhere encounter in claiming the universal right to education.

The film has little to say about the *acceptability* (curriculum and teaching) and *adaptability* (addressing community and minority needs) of U.S. schools, as defined by Tomaševski (2001). By focusing on the uneven provision of quality schools, the film addresses indirect discrimination, but it does not consider in any depth either curriculum content or how children experience schooling. These are issues that are discussed in more depth in Chapter 7.

THE RIGHT TO HUMAN RIGHTS EDUCATION

As noted in Chapter 1, the right to human rights education was first articulated in the Universal Declaration of Human Rights (UDHR; U.N., 1948). HRE, or education about rights, was foreseen as a central part of the human rights project. Those who drafted the UDHR envisaged a copy being present

Figure 2.1. The 4 As of the Right to Education

Availability

- Education is universal, free, and compulsory
- Infrastructure ensures adequate student books and materials
- Buildings meet safety and sanitation standards
- Recruitment, proper training, and appropriate retention to ensure enough qualified teachers

Accessibility

- All children have equal access to school services regardless of gender, race, religion, ethnicity, socioeconomic, and other statuses
- Efforts are made to ensure the inclusion of marginalized groups, for example, refugee children, homeless, and those with disabilities
- No forms of segregation or denial of access to any student
- Laws are in place against child labor or exploitation
- Schools must be within a reasonable distance, or transportation provided
- Education should be affordable to all

Acceptability

- No discrimination in quality education, schooling is relevant and culturally appropriate for all
- Students are not expected to conform to specific religious or ideological views
- Teaching methods and materials reflect a wide range of ideas and beliefs
- Health and safety are emphasized and comply with minimum standards applicable in adult workplaces
- Discipline procedures respect child dignity

Adaptability

- Educational programs are flexible and can be adjusted to community needs
- Students' observance of religious or cultural holidays is respected
- Adequate attention is given to students with disabilities; buildings and facilities adapted to their needs

Source. Information in figure adapted from *Human rights obligations: Making education available, accessible, acceptable, and adaptable,* by K. Tomaševski, 2001, Lund, Sweden: Raoul Wallenberg Institute. (Available at www.right-to-education.org/sites/right-to-education.org/files/resource-attachments/Tomasevski_Primer%203.pdf)

in every classroom (Osler & Starkey, 1996), and the United Nations acknowledged the school as central in guaranteeing, protecting, and promoting human rights, recognizing the relationship between rights knowledge and rights implementation. As Osler (2012b) notes: "With the proclamation of the UDHR, education and human rights became inextricably linked" (p. 2257). McCowan (2012) suggests that human rights within education

> are justified neither solely through the intrinsic importance of upholding rights, nor solely through their instrumental benefits. Instead, the frontier between the two starts to dissolve as we move into a space in which the learning of human rights and the expression of human rights are fused. (p. 79)

Nevertheless, the UDHR is nonbinding, acting as a moral, rather than legal force. So it is with subsequent binding instruments that the right to HRE has become firmly established. The International Covenant on Economic, Social and Cultural Rights (CESCR; U.N., 1966b) and the Convention on the Rights of the Child (CRC; U.N., 1989) are two binding instruments that confirm the right to education in human rights, although the latter is better known to schools internationally, partly because of its focus on children's human rights and consequent direct professional relevance to teachers, and also because it has been almost universally ratified. The CESCR's Article 13 states that parties to the Covenant

> agree that education shall be directed to the full development of the human personality and the sense of its dignity, and shall *strengthen the respect for human rights and fundamental freedoms* [emphasis added]. They further agree that education shall enable all persons to participate effectively in a free society, promote understanding, tolerance and friendship among all nations and all racial, ethnic or religious groups, and further the activities of the United Nations for the maintenance of peace. (U.N., 1966b)

In this formulation, specific links are made between education for human rights, human dignity, and tolerance of difference across nations, racial groups, ethnicities, and religions. One aim of education is to promote human rights and, following from this, to encourage respect and tolerance in the context of diversity. Thus intergroup respect and tolerance is seen as a prerequisite for human rights; educational initiatives that enable such respect are fundamental to the wider human rights education project. The aims of education are further developed in the CRC. Article 29 spells out the aims of education, which include those articulated in the CESCR and are modified and extended to address:

> The development of respect for the child's parents, his or her own cultural identity, language and values, for the national values of the country in which the child

is living, the country from which he or she may originate, and for civilizations different from his or her own; The preparation of the child for responsible life in a free society, in the spirit of understanding, peace, tolerance, equality of sexes, and friendship among all peoples, ethnic, national and religious groups and persons of indigenous origin; . . . The development of respect for the natural environment. (U.N., 1989, art. 29)

Here there is a new emphasis on peace and on gender equity and an obligation on school systems not only to create respect for national values but also for the child's own culture and for that of other traditions and civilizations. This does not imply a culturally relativist approach where anything goes, since other child rights guaranteed in the CRC cannot be undermined in the name of cultural identity. The CRC, like all human rights instruments, needs to be understood as a whole. Parental choices or cultural preferences, in education or elsewhere, cannot supersede other rights guaranteed by the CRC. No individual article in the Convention trumps all others.

As both Grover (2007) and Osler (2010b) have highlighted, the CRC therefore affirms that a form of intercultural or multicultural education is every child's right, where children come to understand and respect their own culture and those of others. Children cannot be educated in a "spirit of understanding, peace, tolerance, equality of sexes, and friendship among all peoples, ethnic, national and religious groups and persons of indigenous origin" unless they are educated together (not separated—as happens in a number of places in the world—in different schools according to language, ethnicity, or other characteristics) and have curricular access to a range of cultures and experiences beyond the ones readily available to them in their immediate family and community. The reference in the CRC to "persons of indigenous origin" highlights how the human rights project has developed since the 1960s in response to the struggles of indigenous peoples across the globe. The Declaration on the Rights of Indigenous Peoples (U.N., 2007) was finally adopted by the United Nations General Assembly in 2007, following more than 2 decades of negotiations between governments and indigenous peoples' organizations.[2] Significantly, the declaration addresses both individual and collective rights; education rights and other rights directly related to education, including cultural rights and identity; and language rights. The additional aim of "respect for the natural environment" within the CRC appears to acknowledge that human life is part of a wider ecosystem and that human flourishing depends on an interrelationship between all lifeforms.

In Europe, human rights education was firmly on the agenda of the Council of Europe from the mid-1980s. Recommendation No. R (85) 7 on *Teaching and Learning About Human Rights in Schools* (Council of Europe, 1985), was not only an important step in standard setting but also included valuable practical guidance in the form of an appendix (Starkey, 1991). Not only is human rights education a right, but education itself is an enabling right (McCowan, 2013), securing access to other rights, including health and well-being, an adequate standard of living, and various elements of participation, including political participation.

The end of the Cold War and the growing acknowledgment that all rights (civil, political, economic, social, and cultural) are, in fact, interrelated and interdependent gave impetus to various international initiatives to put human rights education onto the agendas of governments. These initiatives include the U.N. Decade for Human Rights Education 1995–2004 and the subsequent World Programme for Human Rights Education (2005–ongoing); UNESCO's (1995) higher prioritization of HRE following the *Declaration and Integrated Framework of Action on Education for Peace, Human Rights and Democracy*, which is given new impetus in UNESCO's (2014) current work programme (2014–2017) through work on "global citizenship education." This, of course, builds on earlier standard setting such as UNESCO's (1974) *Recommendation Concerning Education for International Understanding, Co-operation and Peace and Education Relating to Human Rights and Fundamental Freedoms.*

The Council of Europe's (2010) *Recommendation CM/Rec (2010) 7 . . . Charter on Education for Democratic Citizenship and Human Rights Education* also marks an important step in re-emphasizing the role of human rights within the broader Council of Europe initiatives in this field. Importantly, the Council of Europe has put in place a series of measures for the support of member-states and for the enablement of this initiative, with the first Europe-wide conference to assess progress taking place in 2012 (Osler 2013b, 2014b) and the next scheduled for 2015.

The adoption of the U.N. Declaration on Human Rights Education and Training (U.N., 2011), although a nonbinding treaty, gives considerable impetus to the work of human rights educators. As we have seen, it defines HRE as encompassing education *about, through,* and *for* human rights: In other words it is primarily concerned with educational processes that enable human rights. In this chapter I have also focused on how rights can be enabled through education, considering the right to education (which includes the right to HRE), rights in education (learners' entitlements), and rights through education (how education supports the human rights project). In other words, I am considering the broader relationship between the human rights project and education.

The U.N. Declaration on Human Rights Education and Training reminds us that HRE extends beyond education *about* rights. Education *through* human rights addresses rights in school, including the way schools are organized, as well as the processes of learning and teaching. All need to be managed in a way that respects the rights of both students and teachers. Education *for* human rights is about empowering learners to enjoy and exercise their rights and to respect and uphold the rights of others (U.N., 2011, art. 2.2). Clearly, education *for* rights enables the realization of rights *through* education, but it is not the whole story.

Returning to the U.N. definition, the three elements are obviously related. Education *about* rights implies that HRE has a basis in human rights law. It is useful to extend it by looking to the U.N. Convention on the Rights of the Child. For children, including young children, education *about* rights would include knowing that children have human rights and that these are formulated in the Convention on the Rights of the Child. But this knowledge is also accompanied by the application of these rights and young people's experiences of schooling. This is, in the United Nations' (2011) definition, referred to as education *through* rights, which also implies that teachers and administrators give thought to young people's perspectives (Osler, 2010a), to classroom methodologies, and to educational structures that might support or undermine those same rights (Lundy, 2007; Osler, 2010a, 2010b). In other words, the CRC places duties on adult actors, including teachers, who are responsible for children's schooling. I understand education *for* rights as implying a transformatory education and one where educational outcomes are in conformity with human rights standards. Education for rights and for transformation is discussed further in Chapter 8.

EDUCATION ABOUT RIGHTS (KNOWLEDGE)

It is critical that high school students have the opportunity to study global human rights issues, and that their teachers feel confident to address human rights, because in our globalized age their actions and choices may have direct and indirect impacts on the lives of strangers in distant places. Similarly, decisions made by the governments we elect may directly affect the human rights of people in other parts of the world.

Rather than focusing exclusively on human rights abuses, it is important that school students explore positive aspects of human rights and their implications for everyday life. Learning about human rights and the ways in which international norms have been used and are being used in struggles for justice can be an empowering experience for learners, encouraging them to recognize the potential strength of these instruments in effecting change in their own lives.

For example, the people of South Africa were able to secure support and solidarity across the international community in their struggle against apartheid by raising awareness of their struggle within the framework of universal rights and a universal standard of human dignity. They appealed to our common humanity. Likewise, toward the end of his life, civil rights leader Malcolm X suggested activists would only succeed if they presented their case to the whole world. When rights are framed in terms of global solidarity rather than domestic citizenship rights, "anyone, anywhere on this earth can become your ally" (X, 1964/1992, p. 175). Diverse groups across the globe, including the Dalit (untouchables) in India and LGBT activists, continue to appeal to universal human rights standards in their struggles for rights, recognition, and equality of dignity.

I wanted the Utah teachers to look afresh at the principles of international human rights and apply them to their own schools and communities. I urged them to engage with school students in considering children's and young people's rights in and through education. The challenge we faced, and one facing all teachers, arises from the question: How do we address human rights right here, right now? Eleanor Roosevelt and those who codrafted the Universal Declaration of Human Rights envisioned it would be available in every classroom. When Roosevelt (1958) posed the question "Where do universal rights begin?" and responded "In small places, close to home," she was referring to the individual's day-to-day responsibility to defend human rights and the power of human rights as a framework for everyday living in community. At the same time, she was implicitly acknowledging a contradiction in demanding human rights standards in distant places without engaging in struggles to achieve these same standards at community and national levels. Within this vision, not only is the right to education secured, but also the right to human rights education is guaranteed as a fundamental aspect of schooling. These rights are enshrined in the UDHR and in subsequent human rights instruments. For learners to claim their rights and defend the rights of others, they need opportunities to study and understand human rights.

Figure 2.2., Human Rights in the Community, is a useful tool for examining the Universal Declaration of Human Rights (U.N., 1948) not simply as a historical document but as one that has the power to remain relevant in our everyday lives and in the communities in which we live. The exercise works equally well with learners in school and with student teachers. It can be adapted for younger students by adding photos or drawings of the places listed, such as school, shops, a park, places of worship, a train station, or bus stops. Some learners may find it easier to use a plain language version of the UDHR. (http://www.ohchr.org/Documents/Publications/ABCannexesen.pdf)

Students are asked to link these everyday places with rights. The exercise can be done in three stages: first, identifying rights associated with each place using existing knowledge, and then examining the articles of the UDHR to link actual rights to each place. In a third stage, students can see which rights are not linked to any listed place and identify other locations to which any remaining rights can be linked. When the exercise is complete, not only do students see the relevance of the UDHR to everyday life but they have read, studied, and become familiar with the document. The exercise raises awareness of human rights close to home, although the purpose is not to suggest that this is where human rights concerns should end.

Social justice and human rights awareness require a degree of critical self-reflection by individuals and wider society and recognition that there are local and global implications to the ways in which those in the Global North

Figure 2.2. Human Rights in the Community

This tool is designed to give you an opportunity to familiarize with the Universal Declaration of Human Rights and to demonstrate the extent to which human rights are embedded in the life and structures of our society.

You will need: this sheet and a copy of the Universal Declaration of Human Rights

Think about each of the following places in the local community where you live.

Next to each place, write against each of them human rights that may be associated with that place.

You can do this in two stages, first using just your own knowledge and then checking the articles of the Universal Declaration of Human Rights. Or you can do the whole task by consulting the Universal Declaration.

- Schools
- Civic offices/town hall
- Community center/public hall
- Railway station/bus station/bus stop
- Library
- Church/mosque/synagogue/temple/other place of worship
- Park
- Sports center
- Police station
- Prison
- Law courts
- Banks/shops
- Factories/industries
- Private homes
- Hospitals
- Bar/public house/cafe/restaurant/dance club
- Cinema/theaters
- Newsagent/newspaper offices/radio stations/TV services
- Other places (please specify)

When you have done this, check how many of the 30 articles you have now included.

Identify those articles that you have not yet included. Can you now link them to a place in the community?

Which of the places can you identify as having a particular role in promoting human rights? Note down a brief explanation for each. Are there places in your community where you consider human rights might be abused in some way? Note these with a brief explanation.

conduct themselves, for example, as tourists or consumers. As discussed in Chapter 1, in the United States, as in many other western countries, human rights are most commonly associated with foreign policy or the plight of strangers in distant places. For my students in Logan, UT, the term human rights initially conjured up cases from distant places. Invited early on in the course to identify a human rights news story, they came with cases such as that of Sakineh Mohammad Ashtiani, the Iranian woman sentenced to death in 2010 by stoning for alleged adultery; children engaged in manual labor in impoverished Kenyan communities; and children engaged as sex workers in the seamy side of Bangkok's tourist industry.

Not all students began by focusing on human rights abuses in the Global South. One student brought a news item relating to former basketball star John Amaechi, who was denied access to a night club in Manchester, England, in September 2010, allegedly because he was Black (BBC News, 2010). She presented the case as one of racial discrimination and encouraged her classmates to discuss the issue of racial justice in the United Kingdom, before then revealing that the bar in question was a gay bar. This opened up a discussion of LGBT rights as human rights, which was a particularly hot topic on campus at that time.

It prompted another student subsequently to bring to class the case of a specific Mormon church vandalized in California in 2008, after the LDS (Church of Jesus Christ of Latter Day Saints) leadership supported California's Proposition 8, which defined marriage as the union between one man and one woman, overturning an earlier ruling that permitted same-sex marriage in the state.[3] The class then examined both the right to same-sex marriage and the right to religious freedom within the framework of the Universal Declaration of Human Rights, looking at the case through the lens of the various articles, and applying the principles of equal dignity and equal rights, freedom of belief, and freedom from fear.

I posited that the enactment of these principles (to which students had previously said they subscribed) allowed students (and teacher) to have a conversation across difference and to listen to other perspectives and concerns. This setting of the discussion within the framework of the UDHR, with which all were by then familiar, allowed students to deliberate the issues and to listen deeply (perhaps in some cases for the first time) to a range of perspectives and concerns. All agreed that freedom of belief did include freedom to worship without fear, but did not include imposing your views on others. Students did not agree on whether same-sex marriage should be supported by government, but they were able to engage in a sensitive and moving discussion, addressing parents' recognition or denial of their own children's sexual identities and the tensions and stresses in the life of an individual who might identify as both gay and Mormon.

Questions that arose included the degree to which religious leaders tend to speak on behalf of believers, particularly when male leaders pronounce on questions relating to women's lives and women's rights, and how religious teaching may be modified over time. Subsequently, some students researched how same-sex marriage is addressed in other jurisdictions, discovering that the issue was not contentious in other Western societies. Like the high school students discussing controversial issues within a structured framework as part of their civic education (Avery, Levy, & Simmons, 2013), these graduate students did not set out to win an argument but to address a genuine issue of public concern, and some later reported that they had modified their views and understood the complexity of the issues as an outcome of this work.

Understanding the importance of social, cultural, and historical context in interpreting human rights was another important outcome in this particular learning community. Importantly, this case allowed students not only to look at the issues from a fresh perspective, but also to critically examine the UDHR rather than accept it as the secular equivalent of a sacred text, where critical questioning or examination is not permitted. On this occasion, by focusing on the text rather than on emotional responses to a hot topic, class members were able to deliberate a genuine example of a perceived tension between freedom of religion and the right to equal dignity and equal treatment before the law. They were also able to reflect on the degree to which human rights themselves offer a framework for learning to live together in a society that is simultaneously secular and multifaith.

EDUCATION THROUGH RIGHTS
(EXPERIENCES, SKILLS, AND ATTITUDES)

Children who are learning about human rights in school need also to know that their rights are upheld in the classroom and in the educational processes to which they are subject. They need opportunities to examine and practice human rights in their own worlds as well as in the larger world of which they are a part. Learners will quickly identify the contradictions in learning about rights at school if their own rights in school are disregarded.

Learners can be given the opportunity to reflect on their own schooling and to study Tomaševski's concepts of school acceptability and adaptability. Using Figure 2.1 as a checklist, students can design a model school that meets the needs of all. They can then survey their peers to find out the degree to which they feel that their schools used appropriate and culturally inclusive methods and materials to meet the needs of different groups of students.

James A. Banks and an international panel of researchers gave some thought to teachers' responsibilities in making young people aware of their human rights. They concluded: "The teaching of human rights should underpin citizenship education courses and programs in multicultural nation-states" (Banks et al., 2005, pp. 5, 12). Banks and his colleagues were concerned with developing some broad principles for educating citizens in a global age. Not only did they wish to promote reflection on ways of preparing students to become effective citizens in a global context, but they set out principles that might be applied in different regions of the globe.

The U.S. Constitution, or any other national constitution, cannot be a globally shared reference point, but the UDHR can. Citizenship education has traditionally focused on the nation and continues to do so in most nation-states (Reid, Gill, & Sears, 2009). Education systems reinforce a sense of national identity and national citizenship, which is, at best, inadequate preparation for living in an interdependent world. At worst, they may actually foster indifference to the rights of other people in distant places and even hostility, war, and violence (Harber, 2004).

The principle offered by Banks et al. (2005)—that human rights underpin citizenship education—makes a radical departure from the standard approach by encouraging young people to think of themselves as global or cosmopolitan citizens (see Chapter 8), who do not have an exclusive affinity to their fellow nationals but to all humanity, regardless of where they live. The human rights project is based on recognition of the equal dignity of all people and on recognition of the global community as interconnected and interdependent.

Banks and his colleagues' (2005) concept of citizenship education does not inevitably detract from the local or national community but adds another dimension to citizenship: commitment to our fellow humanity. The principle recognizes our responsibilities to others *across difference*, at local, national, and global scales. Extending our gaze across difference means being prepared to defend the rights of those with whom we may not agree and even being prepared to defend the rights of those who themselves do not respect human rights.

Citizenship education founded on human rights implies intercultural learning. From the perspectives of Grover (2007) and Osler (2010b), the right to intercultural education is also articulated in the Convention on the Rights of the Child (U.N., 1989) and is an essential element of learning to live together in a diverse global community and in schools and local communities characterized by diversity. Human rights apply to us all, but they offer special protection to those who are marginalized or excluded. For this reason they are particularly valuable tools for the protection of minorities, as Malcolm X (1964/1992) recognized.

Banks and his colleagues (2005) reviewed the literature on education for democratic citizenship and argued that

> The ethical framework proposed by universal human rights standards is particularly important in multicultural schools . . . [since it] provides members of the school community with a basis for dialogue and can help ensure that all voices are recognized and all points of view are considered. (p. 12)

The Banks principle is pertinent to a discussion of the *Waiting for "Superman"* film because it allows us not only to analyze education provision against national norms but also to assess young people's educational entitlements against international minimum standards. The film becomes a useful classroom resource for high school or teacher education students if used in this way. Before viewing the film, students can develop their own questions concerning equity in education, researching problems and challenges, and drawing up their own principles for realizing social justice in and through schooling. They can investigate how education is funded and whether the outcomes of current funding systems are just. In particular, they can review whether charter schools have proved an effective or comprehensive solution to educational challenges in the United States. They can research problems faced by learners in other comparable nations and the ways in which these have been addressed or resolved.

Education in human rights opens up the possibilities of education *for* rights, which implies a transformative goal in human rights education. Teaching for transformation relates to a fundamental purpose of human rights and of education in democracies, namely, that of social justice. It implies addressing oppression at the microlevel of interpersonal relationships, including student–student and student–teacher relationships. It cannot be separated from education about rights (curriculum content), nor can it be divided from enabling learners to enact their rights at school. This question of education *for* rights is further discussed in Chapter 7, with specific reference to child rights and in relation to the bigger question of enabling rights through education.

SUMMARY

In this chapter I have addressed the right to education and specifically the right to human rights education, drawing on international instruments, particularly the UDHR, and on my experiences of teaching a graduate class. The teaching was structured so that learners could make links between their own everyday personal and professional experiences and the theory and practice of human rights. To paraphrase Eleanor Roosevelt, without concerted teacher–citizen action to uphold rights in school, we shall look in vain for progress in the larger community. The enacting of rights *in* education is central to Eleanor Roosevelt's project of bringing rights back home and also critical in ensuring that teaching *about* rights is effective.

I have suggested that social studies and citizenship or civics education teachers can draw on human rights instruments and human rights principles to navigate difficult, sensitive, and complex classroom debates. Internationally agreed-upon principles also support teachers who want to open up debate but are anxious about whose values should hold sway in contexts of social, cultural, and political diversity. Not only do these principles help establish procedural rules for classroom discussion, but they can also engage students in examining questions of justice, peace, and human dignity in their own lives and in the lives of others.

Eleanor Roosevelt identified her involvement in the drafting of the UDHR as her greatest achievement. The UDHR marked an important step forward for human dignity and social justice because it codified human rights, not as entitlements deriving from citizenship of a nation-state, but as universal entitlements. This is the essence of human rights: They are not the gifts of governments but belong to all, wherever we live. If the teaching of human rights underpins citizenship education courses in the way that Banks and his colleagues proposed, such courses are likely to be more relevant to all, both citizens and noncitizens alike. All students, regardless of their formal citizenship status, can critically examine international human rights standards and compare them with rights secured through citizenship. The methods proposed here provide some entry points to a study of the right to education, education about rights, and rights in education.

Here I focused on student learning. I argued that the teacher's role is not to endorse or challenge a specific ideology but to enable students to assess what is needed so that all students are able to access an education in keeping with their rights and their specific circumstances. I have also argued that education for social justice is central to the professional responsibility of the teacher. The next chapter focuses more closely on the teacher and on questions of intersectionality and teacher positionality in addressing human rights and schooling. It is concerned with how we might theorize HRE so as to enable social justice through education.

CHAPTER 3

Intersectionality, Human Rights, and Identities

In this chapter I explore the possibilities offered by combining the concepts of intersectionality and human rights to provide a framework to analyze and enable social justice in and through education, focusing on concepts, language, and legal frameworks. I argue that by bringing intersectionality theory to human rights, we have the possibility of engaging in a deeper way with learners' multiple identities and enabling social justice through education.

In our global age we need theories and tools that will support educational research and development and that can be applied in different sociocultural contexts and at different scales: local, cultural, national, regional, and global. Among those committed to multicultural education, intersectionality theory has attracted much debate and controversy (Grant & Zwier, 2011). Here I seek to relate it to human rights and human rights education. Human rights stress human dignity and the complex and varied identities held by both teachers and learners. Intersectionality theory recognizes multiple and flexible identities. The concept of intersectionality, which signifies the complex interweaving of strands of social life (Crenshaw, 1989), enables us to better interpret the complex ways learners experience justice/injustice and equality/inequality. Within the human rights framework the concept of intersectionality is implicit. Here, I will seek to make this implicitness explicit.

Before examining together the concepts of intersectionality, identities, and human rights and ways in which they may enhance our analysis of injustice or inform struggles for justice, I recount my own epistemological journey toward human rights. I do this not only to situate my thinking within the context of my own experiences and to be explicit about my own positionality, but because I am arguing that all of us need to be reflexive and self-critical in the wider project of human rights and social justice education. My own story outlines my steps toward bridging the concepts of human rights and intersectionality in education research and practice.

AN EPISTEMOLOGICAL JOURNEY TOWARD HUMAN RIGHTS

It was during the 1980s that I was first introduced to human rights as a framework for practice when working as an advisory teacher within a team responsible for supporting teachers in developing multicultural and antiracist perspectives in schools in Birmingham, United Kingdom, a large and diverse urban school district. At this time the national political climate was not conducive to our work, with the government of the day and the then prime minister, Margaret Thatcher, expressing criticism of antiracist initiatives in education, supported by a media campaign also hostile to such initiatives (Murray, 1986).

Interestingly, I did not learn about human rights education in the United Kingdom, where I grew up and studied to become a teacher, but rather through attending a teachers' seminar in Denmark in autumn 1985, with the support of the Council of Europe. This was my first international conference, and I was shocked to discover a number of Danish colleagues pitying me for living and working in a multicultural environment. They linked the riots that had taken place that autumn in Birmingham directly to the presence of visible minorities, rather than to complex problems of poverty, discrimination, and inequality. Their ideal society was one of homogeneity; a multicultural society was, within this framework of analysis, one that deviated from the norm.

Nevertheless, from this conference, which introduced me to HRE, I saw the possibilities in "rebranding" much of the antiracist work we were doing with teachers as human rights education. After all, it seemed that the UK government, which was overtly critical of antiracism, would not declare itself in opposition to human rights or HRE. So my initial engagement with HRE was strategic.

At this stage, I did not explore the potential of human rights as a framework for addressing a broad range of interlocking dimensions of injustice in education practice; but through my own experiences and those of the young people with whom I was working, I was conscious of the need for a gender dimension to our antiracist practice.

One of the challenges facing the team of advisory teachers to which I belonged was dealing with the guilt generated among some White teachers when facing up to racism in schools and society. Another was the differential experiences of team members in working with schools and school leaders, often dependent on the identity of the advisory teachers concerned and whether they were from a visible minority group. The concept of solidarity, fundamental to the human rights project, helped me to recognize the ways in which all team members could contribute to the struggle for justice in education, regardless of ethnicity or identity. It was also an empowering concept for mainstream White teachers who wanted to promote greater justice through education.

These experiences informed and helped shape my research when 5 years later I embarked on doctoral studies and an academic career. My doctoral project, examining the lives and careers of teachers from visible minority communities, produced rich data that necessarily required me to engage in an analysis that examined interlocking issues of race, ethnicity, gender, and religion (Osler, 1997). At the very time my work was published, Patricia Williams was giving the BBC Reith lectures: *The Genealogy of Race* (Williams, 1997). The stories that she told to highlight the complex ways in which race and racism have an impact on life in the United Kingdom as well as in the United States were liberating, not simply because of her insights into UK society, but because these stories allowed her to discuss everyday realities that were so infrequently aired in a constructive way in the mainstream UK media. The lectures and stories within them confirmed that the realities of race and racist oppression were not something separate from the everyday workings of society.

As Williams's scholarship makes clear, we are not only the sum of our various identities, juggling these in the face of inequality, but are shaped by and bound together and influenced by the structures, institutions, and the wider society in which we study, work, and live our lives. Her stories underline how the various forces of inequality combine to continuously change and re-form their outward shapes, even as we seek to make sense of these same lives. And so I looked afresh at the life stories of the teachers in my study (Osler, 1997) and understood afresh how powerful these remain and how potent narrative can be as a tool both for exposing injustice and, perhaps more importantly, the lessons to be learned through struggles for justice.

Our analysis should not simply address the various identities we adopt, related to gender, sexuality, profession, and so on, but must necessarily explore how institutions and policy work to impact those various identities. In the United Kingdom in the 1990s and beyond, the White mainstream was equated with normalcy. Similarly, the notion of demographic homogeneity was also associated with normalcy, and multicultural communities seen as exceptional, or peculiar to specific cities. In academia, visible minorities had some space to research minorities, but those studies that critiqued mainstream society, its structures, and institutions were vulnerable to criticisms of bias.

This attitude persists in academia, as I found out in 2007 when I attended a symposium of renowned French sociologists meeting to debate racism in French society. It was striking that all present were White, something unimaginable in Britain in a meeting focusing on race. I remarked on this to a colleague, and he expressed a degree of surprise. In his opinion, it would be difficult for non-White French academics to research race since their research would inevitably be seen as biased. So the French principle of color-blindness is clearly applied selectively (Osler, 2010a).

Today, part of my working life is in Norway, where the concepts of equality, tolerance, democracy, and respect for human rights are internalized and accepted as part of the national identity, yet where racial exclusion was part of the historical process of nation-building. The concepts of race and racism are still infrequently discussed in academia. Gullestad (2004) suggests that conversations about racism are viewed as upsetting "the innocent national self-image" (p. 184) crafted in the post–World War II era.

LINKING INTERSECTIONALITY AND HUMAN RIGHTS IN EDUCATIONAL RESEARCH AND PRAXIS

I turn now to explore the possibilities offered by combining Black feminist and postcolonial theory with human rights concepts in order to provide a framework for the analysis and enabling of social justice in and through education. I consider, in particular, intersectionality theory, the concept of recognition, and the "right to narrate" (Bhabha, 2003). I argue that the use of narratives can help bridge the rights gap between a utopian human rights vision and learners' actual experiences.

In teaching for human rights, a key starting point is an acknowledgment of multiple axes of differentiation—including economic, political, cultural, and experiential. It is important to recognize the complexity of subsequent human experiences and societal developments, rather than reducing or artificially separating these dimensions. The concept of intersectionality (Crenshaw, 1989), which signifies the complex interweaving of strands of social life, enables us to better interpret the complex ways learners experience justice/injustice and equality/inequality.

Avtar Brah and Ann Phoenix (2004) understand the concept of intersectionality as

> signifying the complex, irreducible, varied, and variable effects which ensue when multiple axes of differentiation—economic, political, cultural, psychic, subjective and experiential—intersect *in historically specific contexts* [emphasis added]. The concept emphasizes that different dimensions of social life cannot be separated out into discrete and pure strands. (p. 76)

Intersectionality theory complements human rights–based approaches to justice since it gives emphasis to the whole person and addresses the stratification and differentiation within society undermining social justice. It also supports human rights–based initiatives in its concern with social change and social action. It is the intersecting and interweaving of various dimensions and aspects of identity, within a specific location and historical context, that need to inform intersectional analysis, coupled with a deep understanding of the asymmetrical nature of power relationships.

While human rights acknowledge the whole person, the human rights framework does not necessarily invite consideration of how various elements of human identity interact and interweave. Intersectionality encourages consideration of complexity and helps avoid simplistic analyses of injustice. So, for example, a basic rights–based approach may require an individual to select a particular characteristic, say gender, as the basis of discrimination, over other factors, such as religion, ethnicity, or nationality. Intersectionality theory recognizes that it may be impossible to claim that person X is experiencing discrimination simply because she is a woman, and that the category "women" is in fact differentiated. The cause of an individual being disadvantaged in a particular context and at a particular time is the result of a complex combination of factors. Take, for example, the case of an Arab Muslim woman living in a European city, holding EU citizenship but not necessarily recognized as a citizen by her neighbors or coworkers. Her gender, her ethnicity, her religion, and her perceived nationality are not just layered on top of each other but all come into play in a complex way, to deny her rights in the specific economic context and prevailing political climate of city Y. The ways her identity and her opportunities are perceived by fellow citizens, including profeminists, may impact negatively on the range of options open to her.

A key concept within human rights is that of *universality*. Rights belong to all human beings and are derived both from our shared humanity and from human struggle. Although the concept of cosmopolitanism and understandings of the universal have been very influential in early 21st-century scholarly discourses relating to multicultural, international, and human rights education, it has been argued that, in practice, the Enlightenment principles that inform the modern human rights project have sometimes functioned to standardize culture through education at the expense of cultural difference (Foucault, 1995; Popkewitz, 2007). To understand the concept of universality within human rights, it is important to look closely at human rights instruments and their specific provisions as they relate to culture.

The 1948 Universal Declaration of Human Rights proclaims human rights as "a common standard of achievement for all peoples and all nations" and calls for "their universal and effective recognition and observance" (U.N., 1948, preamble). Article 18 confirms that "Everyone has the right to freedom of thought, conscience and religion; this right includes freedom to change his religion or belief " thereby acknowledging that religion, an aspect of culture, should not be seen from the standpoint of an individual's conscience, as something immutable or fixed. Article 27 states that "Everyone has the right *freely to participate* [emphasis added] in the cultural life of the community," again implying individual choice, but other than this there is nothing specifically about how rights are applied in different cultural settings. Article 26, which addresses education, does not specifically mention culture, although it does acknowledge parents' right to "choose the kind of education that shall be given to their children," subject to the general restriction that any right should not be interpreted as implying any activity "aimed at the destruction of any of the rights and freedoms" in the UDHR (U.N., 1948, art. 30).

Schooling, a key means of reinforcing (or potentially negating) culture, is therefore something over which parents are entitled a direct say, according to the human rights framework. Nevertheless, parents are not free to choose a form of education that would deny children their other rights or violate the general principles of justice and equality. Thus the UDHR does not itself suggest standardization of culture. There is a claim about the universal nature of rights, and of universal principles, but the implementation of these rights takes place within a specific cultural context. Rights need to be applied within a cultural context, but the broad human rights principles of justice and equality should prevail. Culture (as a constantly evolving set of practices) does not trump these general principles. Thus all members of any cultural community are subject to the principle of nondiscrimination, and to the principle of equality of dignity.

Mainstream and powerful interest groups generally have few concerns about the homogenizing or standardizing impact of education on culture, but minorities do. By its very nature, culture is not fixed, but fluid and subject to change (Appiah, 2006). Although cultural artifacts may require special protection and preservation, living, evolving cultural practices generally do not. Nevertheless, minorities and indigenous people, in particular, remain vulnerable today to the denial, expropriation, and reduction of their cultures, just as in the past they were vulnerable to the denial of their very humanity. In recognition of this vulnerability, and in response to the struggles of minorities for recognition, the International Covenant on Civil and Political Rights (ICCPR) (U.N., 1966a) accords special cultural protection for minorities under its Article 27.

Some feminist and postcolonialist scholars have also challenged the notion of the universal by seeking to illustrate how discourses promoted by the powerful often serve to regulate the knowledge and values of the colonized (Mohanty, 1984; Spivak, 1999). These critiques remind us of asymmetrical power relations, which need to be considered in any analysis and in curricula addressing human rights, cultural diversity, and justice. There is the risk that if rights and principles are applied without dialogue and without consideration of people's specific social contexts, then human rights, which are designed to be liberating, can become part of a hegemonic discourse, used instead to control.

Asymmetrical power relations need to be explored in contexts where learners may be encountering real difficulties in securing their rights and where their experiences lead them to identify a considerable gap between human rights rhetoric and everyday realities. Power relations also need to be examined in contexts where legal mechanisms for the protection of rights are generally strong, and mainstream populations may have few concerns about their rights. When educating the more privileged, a hegemonic discourse of rights may serve to mask genuine human rights violations among the least powerful members of the same communities, neighborhoods, and nation.

A further key human rights concept is that of recognition. The UDHR opens with the concept of recognition: "recognition of the inherent dignity and of the equal and inalienable rights of all members of the human family" (U.N., 1948, preamble). The concept of recognition of equal and inherent dignity and equal and inalienable rights is fundamental to the human rights project. Article 6 states that "Everyone has the right to recognition everywhere as a person before the law," and Article 7 affirms that this equal recognition extends to equality before the law and protection under the law against discrimination. Yet legal recognition is, I would argue, insufficient in human rights advocacy and human rights education.

According to Bhabha (2003, 2004) and Butler (2006), a postmodern ethics permits us to address the power struggles and asymmetrical power relations in which histories and identities are given recognition. The modern human rights project and legal framework grew out of a period of war and atrocities characterized by processes of dehumanization. Recognition of equal human dignity is, as we have seen, essential to that project. Butler's analysis is in keeping with this; her starting point is that violence stems from processes of dehumanization and lack of recognition.

Schaffer and Smith (2004) also illustrate the centrality of the ethics of recognition and the importance of narrative in strengthening human rights. They acknowledge and explore the real risks of narrative when vulnerable individuals and groups challenge entrenched power imbalances, but they insist that narratives, by drawing on specific localities and differing cultures and traditions of moral understanding, can and do shape and refine the language of rights. Todd (2007, 2009) discusses the challenges of ambiguity and contradiction between the ideals expressed in human rights standards and the reality of learners' lives. She argues that we need a "theoretical framework that faces directly the difficulties of living in a dissonant world" (2009, p. 213). She suggests that without it, human rights education, which is intended to promote justice, may in fact undermine this same purpose.

HUMAN RIGHTS AND IDENTITY

Identity is also a key concept in human rights. Hostility to human rights is often closely linked to people's proclaimed identities, as also is support for human rights. Yet neither culture nor individual identities are static or fixed. All cultures are constantly evolving and individual identities are shaped by a range of cultural and political forces and, indeed, by prevailing political propaganda. I argue that teachers need to be reflexive and aware of their own positionality in relation to curriculum, pedagogy, and the wider power structures in which the processes of teaching and learning take place. Only then will they be able to contribute to enabling rights and social justice for their students, a project, as I have argued in Chapter 2, which needs to be at the heart of education.

As outlined in Chapter 1, since 1948 and the signing of the UDHR, the international human rights project has accorded a central place to education as a means of enabling the full realization of human rights to the world's people. Those who lack education find themselves, in many respects, without the "the right to have rights" (Arendt, 1968). Hannah Arendt coined that term to draw attention to the vulnerability of individuals who find themselves stateless, and thus lacking an authority on which they can call to claim their rights. Human rights, although theoretically universal, are generally unavailable—and in practice hugely constrained—among those who lack a legal nationality, finding themselves in an extralegal space. Those who lack access to education, a right that enables other rights, are also extremely vulnerable. They too find themselves largely without "the right to have rights," dependent on the solidarity of others to assist them in their struggle to claim their rights.

The World Inequality Database on Education (WIDE), developed by the Education for All Global Monitoring Report (EFAGMR), draws attention to unacceptable levels of education inequality across countries and between groups within countries (EFAGMR, n.d.). By combining multiple dimensions of inequality, it can, for example, highlight disparities in educational access between poor, rural women and rich, urban men, within a specific country. The combination of disadvantage due to poverty, location, and gender are not merely cumulative, but these various factors—being poor, living in a rural area, and being female and being situated in a specific location—intersect in complex and intertwining ways to influence an individual's life chances and educational opportunities.

In other words, personal characteristics, such as wealth, gender, and ethnicity, along with circumstances, impact directly on the degree to which children and young people access the right to education. Since access to educational opportunities enables the child to access other rights, denial of educational opportunities further intersects with other characteristics to prevent the child from claiming other rights at different stages in the life cycle, including the right to participate in decisionmaking and other political processes. Intersectionality theory, as Brah and Phoenix (2004) remind us, allows us to acknowledge complexity, and to analyze multiple axes of differentiation, recognizing that various "dimensions of social life cannot be separated out into discrete and pure strands" (p. 76).

With the signing of the U.N. Declaration on Human Rights Education and Training in 2011, the international community has a working definition of *human rights education* (HRE), which we can consider a minimal entitlement for all:

Human rights education and training comprises all educational, training, information, awareness-raising and learning activities aimed at promoting universal
respect for and observance of all human rights and fundamental freedoms and
thus contributing, inter alia, to the prevention of human rights violations and
abuses by providing persons with knowledge, skills and understanding and developing their attitudes and behaviours, to empower them to contribute to the
building and promotion of a universal culture of human rights. (U.N., 2011:
art. 2.1)

Article 2.2 goes on to explain that HRE encompasses education *about*
human rights, education *through* human rights, and education *for* human
rights, as discussed in Chapter 2. The school is an important arena in which
children and young people can learn *about* human rights, including their own
rights and their role in defending the rights of others. Human rights education is essential in supporting learners in understanding their role in shaping
their communities and the wider world and in understanding that solidarity
across difference is essential in struggles both for justice and for the protection of democratic thinking and democratic living. This can be characterized
as education *for* human rights.

The 1989 U.N. Convention on the Rights of the Child confirms the
right, not just to education, but to *human rights education* (see Chapter 2
in this book; Osler & Starkey, 1996, 2010). It has been universally signed
and ratified by all countries except the United States. Significantly, as Sleeter
(2013) has observed,

human rights frameworks are rarely studied in US schools. As a result, among
the general public there is little awareness of the UN Convention on the Rights
of the Child, and even less awareness of the failure of the US to endorse it. Even
teachers generally do not know about the struggle for children's human rights.
(p. viii)

Consequently, many of the struggles in the United States for equitable schooling, including struggles for multicultural curricula and "culturally responsive" (Gay, 2010) or "culturally relevant" (Ladson-Billings, 1995)
teaching have taken place on a local or national stage with little awareness
of how international human rights standards might support these struggles
or, indeed, of parallel struggles elsewhere for equal access for all to quality
schooling. Thus the concept of solidarity with other struggles for justice in
education, as well as opportunities to identify allies elsewhere in the world,
has sometimes been overlooked. A key defining element of quality education
is one where students' rights are guaranteed. In other words, a quality education is where students are educated *through* human rights and where rights
in education are guaranteed.

RIGHTS AND EDUCATIONAL SCHOLARSHIP
IN MULTICULTURAL CONTEXTS

In the United States, contemporary manifestations of multicultural education can be traced back to the civil rights movement of the 1960s and 1970s, a period in which African Americans struggled for fundamental change in U.S. society and particularly for rights and recognition. The concept of rights is often perceived, first and foremost, to be a legal one. Rights are secured through constitutional and legal frameworks and any struggle for equal rights and dignity implies structural change. Yet legal and structural guarantees, although essential, are rarely sufficient to overcome deep-seated inequalities and historical disadvantage. The struggle for rights and recognition also implies cultural change, and this, in turn, implies an educational project. Education has a key role to play in creating a culture whereby human rights violations are not simply addressed through legal mechanisms but are prevented.

For those struggling for civil rights in the 1960s and 1970s, many demands focused on equal access to education in the nation's schools, colleges, and universities. The legacy of this can be seen today in the emphasis attached within the field of multicultural education scholarship to combatting inequalities in educational outcomes through a focus on access and achievement.

In other regions of the globe, and notably in Europe, multicultural education, or what is more commonly referred to there as intercultural education, has tended to focus more on creating inclusive societies through critical examination of identities (including national identities) and strategies to support the integration of immigrant and minority youth (Gobbo, 2011). In contrast to other European nation-states, multicultural education in the United Kingdom tended, as a result of pressure in the late 1960s onwards from minorities—initially from African Caribbean communities—to address the problem of racism and to focus on the educational outcomes of minority students (Figueroa, 2004). Indeed Figueroa (2004) notes the impact of visits to the United Kingdom by U.S. civil rights leaders Martin Luther King Jr. and Malcolm X on grassroots movements to promote multicultural education, develop supplementary schools, and challenge racism within education services. Yet, by the first decade of the 21st century, there was no official multicultural policy initiative in the United Kingdom (Tomlinson, 2009).

Official education policies across Europe, both at national and international levels, during the late 20th century and first decade of the 21st, continue to give higher priority to the integration of minorities than to equitable educational outcomes. In practice, although mainstream society may see changes in food habits, musical tastes, and fashion influenced by migrant and minority ethnic groups, integration is, in both policy and practice, generally understood as a one-way process, with considerably greater official emphasis placed on educational measures for the social integration of minorities, rather than extending levels of understanding and openness of mainstream learners or explicitly combatting racism, discrimination, and intolerance. Effectively, this one-way integration process, which is rarely matched by positive action for the economic or political integration of minorities, may in many cases be one of assimilation.

While Banks (Banks, 2009; Banks & Banks, 2004) suggests a broad consensus among multicultural education theorists about the nature, aims, and scope of the field internationally, he also recognizes its contested nature. In the 7th edition of *Multicultural Education: Issues and Perspectives* (Banks & Banks, 2010) the editors acknowledge the expansion of the dimensions of multicultural education, notably with the addition of new chapters on the intersection of race and gender in the processes of marginalization (Henry, 2010) and on sexual and gender minorities (Mayo, 2010). Grant and Zwier (2011), also presenting a North American perspective, report on efforts within the National Association for Multicultural Education (NAME) to center intersectionality as a frame for research and practice in education, discussing the contentions and concerns this initiative has provoked.

While a number of European scholars, notably minoritized feminist scholars (e.g., Bhopal, 1998; Brah & Phoenix, 2004), are embracing intersectionality in their scholarship, issues of gender, class, and heterosexism are marginal or absent in the way multicultural/ intercultural education tends to be framed in Europe, with such interlocking issues rarely explored together in policy documents and only infrequently addressed in scholarship. Work on students' perspectives (Archer, 2003; Osler, 2010b) and the shaping of students' multiple and flexible identities through the processes of schooling, as well as learners' contributions to a wider social justice project, is one notable exception. Another exception is Zembylas's (2010) complementary work on mainstream teachers' constructions of their own and their students' identities in the Republic of Cyprus, with some teachers reproducing racist, ethnonationalist, and class-based discourses and others attempting to challenge injustices and inequalities through their everyday practices.

Discrimination related to religion has been central to debates surrounding intercultural education and citizenship education in Europe during the first two decades of the 21st century, not least because of the prevalence of anti-Muslim and anti-Semitic discourses (Osler, 2009). Issues of ability/ disability are addressed to some degree as part of a separate educational discourse of inclusion.

Educational scholarship addressing education in multicultural contexts has taken place within a broader European political context often hostile to the concept of multiculturalism. Senior European political figures, including former French President Nicolas Sarkozy, German Chancellor Angela Merkel, and UK Prime Minister David Cameron have attacked multiculturalism (Council of Europe, 2011). Cameron claimed that "state multiculturalism" undermines community, while Merkel asserted multiculturalism has "failed utterly" and that Germans and foreign workers cannot "live happily side by side" (Osler, 2012a). Ironically, neither Germany nor France has ever aspired to multiculturalism, nor has Britain ever developed comprehensive multicultural policies or "multicultural citizenship" (Kymlicka, 1996).[1] What has not been tried cannot be said to have failed. Significantly, these European leaders are criticized for "reacting in a defensive and unimaginative way" to the challenges of the 21st century instead of confronting and challenging populism and extremism (Council of Europe, 2011).[2]

It can be seen that the complexity of issues that have an impact on national and international struggles for justice in education—legal, constitutional, social, and political— together with a complex interplay of identity questions relating to race and ethnicity, gender, sexuality, religion, and other factors, require a framework of analysis that is both comprehensive and sensitive to the interplay of these various factors.

INTERSECTIONALITY, STRUGGLE, AND HUMAN RIGHTS

Drawing on the work and words of Sojourner Truth,[3] the 19th-century human rights activist who struggled for the abolition of slavery and for women's human rights, and other political campaigners struggling for justice and recognition, Brah and Phoenix (2004) show how "identities are processes constituted in and through power relations" involving complexity and multiplicity (p. 77).

The modern human rights project, dating from the mid-20th century and the 1948 Universal Declaration of Human Rights, is based on a concept of rights not restricted to citizens and guaranteed by national governments but a universal entitlement to all human beings, regardless of citizenship or other status. The UDHR sets out a vision. Its preamble claims that universal respect for human rights constitutes "the foundation of freedom, justice and peace in the world." This vision or promise is a utopia, something that is envisioned but does not yet exist. This utopian project drew its inspiration from a desire to overcome and prevent recurrences of the inhumanity and gross injustices of World War II.

Yet the UDHR also recognized how a previous concept of rights tied to national citizenship and accorded by the nation-state was inadequate, not least because war, crisis, migration, and displacement leave many living in nation-states where they lack citizenship rights and are thus unprotected.

Not all citizens of mid-20th-century democracies were equally protected, with clear legal inequalities existing at the time in many contexts between the rights of women and men and according to race and ethnicity. These inequalities were reinforced by racist and patriarchal cultures as well as by legal frameworks. Thus the UDHR proclaimed and envisioned universal rights, but the human rights project relied on subsequent use of human rights instruments as tools to realize these rights in what has proved to be an ongoing struggle. The whole project depends on education and awareness-raising. In practice, a right is only a right if people know about it *and* if they are prepared to struggle for it.

LINKING INTERSECTIONALITY AND HUMAN RIGHTS FRAMEWORKS TO ENABLE JUSTICE

I have sought to argue that just as the concept of intersectionality is used by scholars to inform research analyzing and addressing how multiple axes of differentiation and discrimination intersect—not privileging one axis or one identity over others in this analysis—so the human rights framework offers a way of seeing the world (and education) that does not privilege any one identity but that stresses our common humanity. Both are tools in a struggle for greater social justice. That struggle encompasses both research and action for change.

Human rights have an added dimension in this struggle since they are necessarily cosmopolitan rather than national in their conception, enabling those engaged in struggle in one context to unite in solidarity with others to support their cause. This has been recognized by oppressed groups in many different settings. This chapter highlighted the civil rights struggle in the United States, but other struggles, including that of the African National Congress struggling against apartheid in South Africa and those calling today for a Kurdish homeland also draw on a human rights discourse to achieve support and solidarity for their cause. It is this cosmopolitan vision that gives human rights such potency.

Human rights provide a broad perspective for multicultural learning, opportunities to promote solidarity beyond national boundaries, and a framework that is inclusive of a range of identities. Human rights avoid a singular exclusive focus on the nation, which is a recurrent (and often exclusive) element of most citizenship curricula.

The international human rights project is relatively new—barely 70 years old—and thus is a project in progress and subject to further development. It is important to remember that the concept of universality—that human rights are due to all persons as human beings—does not necessarily imply universalizing processes. Human rights are the minimal requirements on how we should treat and be treated by each other. They can acknowledge commonality as well as difference, but do not imply cultural sameness. Human rights discourses need to be open to critique so that universalist discourses do not disguise or obscure power differentials but take into consideration asymmetrical power relations and the interpretation of human rights principles in different social and cultural settings.

SUMMARY

Human rights are about recognition of our shared humanity and entitlement to human dignity. As human subjects, we can generally agree on the broad principle of universal human dignity, even while we recognize that it is not always upheld. Human rights and human rights education are about translating this shared principle of universal human dignity into action by working for justice. This chapter has stressed the role of power in frameworks of analysis for social justice and human rights, focusing on complexity and on power differentials. I have suggested that, throughout, the teacher needs to be aware of her own positionality. One of the key challenges touched on in this chapter in addressing human rights education in formal education, and particularly schools, is the strongly national focus of public schooling and curricula in various contexts across the globe. This is explored further in Chapter 5. The next chapter illustrates the use of narrative in human rights education and the degree to which it can promote solidarity across national boundaries.

CHAPTER 4

Narrative in Teaching for Justice and Human Rights

Throughout history individual and collective narratives have been used in struggles for justice. This chapter draws on Amartya Sen's (2010) theory of justice and on Homi Bhabha's (2003) concept, "the right to narrate," to examine the potential of narratives in teaching and researching for social justice. The chapter considers the strengths and limitations of narrative as a pedagogical tool in understanding justice, human rights, and inequalities; in stimulating solidarity and our common humanity; and in enabling learners to explore their multiple identities. The chapter includes the life history of one Chinese citizen as an illustrative example to examine the Universal Declaration of Human Rights and its possible meanings for learners in China and globally. Human rights are presented as powerful ethical claims that can be critically examined by learners to consider their rights and responsibilities to others, at scales from the local to the global. The chapter concludes by making the case for human rights as principles for learning and living together in "overlapping communities of fate" (Held, 1997, p. 313) where, regardless of geographical distance, the fortunes of people and countries are increasingly interconnected and enmeshed.

THE POTENTIAL OF NARRATIVE

In struggles for justice across the world, narratives have been used to powerful effect. One example is the antiapartheid struggle in South Africa led by the African National Congress (ANC). In mobilizing support both at home and internationally, the movement's narrative deployed the struggles of individual leaders and the personal sacrifices they made to realize freedom, most famously those made by Winnie and Nelson Mandela following the latter's arrest in 1962 and subsequent trial and imprisonment until 1990 (Mandela, 1994; Smith, 2010). Various other art forms, including theatre, musical productions, and songs, were used to tell the stories of countless other individuals who dedicated their lives to achieving freedom. Today, their stories and those of ordinary individuals coping in extraordinary circumstances are retold in museums, including that of Robben Island, the District Six Museum in Cape Town, and the Apartheid Museum in Johannesburg. As Osler and Zhu (2011) observe,

> The anti-apartheid struggle also developed a collective narrative built upon an entitlement to human rights, equality and dignity, whereby the ANC was [able] to call upon governments, United Nations agencies and nongovernmental organizations from around the world to show solidarity and support for its campaign. (p. 223)

Significantly, following the ANC's victory in the country's 1994 first democratic elections, South Africa established a new constitution based explicitly on the Universal Declaration of Human Rights.

Teachers also use stories to powerful effect, encouraging learners to develop a sense of justice and solidarity with others, sometimes in distant places. So, for example, teachers across the globe tell the stories of inspiring characters, such as Martin Luther King Jr., Mohandas Ghandi, Nelson Mandela, and Aung San Suu Kyi. Teachers may also use films and books to teach about justice and human rights, highlighting other characters, real or fictional, who do not set out to be heroes but for whom circumstances require them to engage in everyday struggles for rights. The use of the narrative method within human rights education is advocated and developed by Osler and Starkey (2010), who draw on three narratives of "unknown" individuals to introduce an academic text on human rights education. Such narratives can inspire learners (both children and adults) to write their own individual and collective stories about struggles for justice, which may challenge existing collective narratives such as those of the exclusive nation-state (Delanty, 2003; Osler, 2011b, 2015a).

Through the use of narrative, teachers can play a vital role in realizing justice and peace in the world, empowering learners not only to articulate their own rights but also advocate for the rights of others. In the history classroom, biographies of human rights defenders can be told in a traditional way or retold from a different standpoint, as Claire (2005) illustrated in her research, drawing on feminist moral philosophy (Noddings, 1986; Larrabee, 1993) and extending Levstick's (2000) work on historical significance. Through the use of story and role play, the young students in her study examined ethical dilemmas and imperfect solutions faced by historical figures struggling for justice, allowing them to consider the (unintended) consequences of decisionmaking, giving attention to the perspectives of women and children.

Nussbaum (2006) drew on the concept of narrative to illustrate how her human capabilities model might be applied in education. Arguing that a neglect of the humanities and arts in education is dangerous for democracy's future, she focused on the capabilities of critical thinking, "world citizenship"

(what Osler and Starkey [2005] referred to as "education for cosmopolitan citizenship"), and imaginative understanding. She observes that through
schooling

> Young citizens . . . learn to ask questions or not to ask them; to take what they
> hear at face value or to probe more deeply; to imagine the situation of a person
> different from themselves or to see a new person as a mere threat to their own
> projects; to think of themselves as members of an homogenous group or as mem-
> bers of a nation, and a world, made up of many people and groups, all of whom
> deserve respect and understanding. (Nussbaum, 2006, p. 387)

Nussbaum drew on the ideas and stories of Rabindranath Tagore to argue and illustrate how the "narrative imagination" is central to realizing such
learning outcomes. Processes of learning in which young people are empowered to ask questions and probe texts, to develop the imagination to identify
with and express solidarity across boundaries, and to recognize themselves as
fellow citizens in a cosmopolitan nation and in a wider global community are
key ones within HRE.

The postcolonial theorist Homi Bhabha (2003) emphasizes the importance of what he terms "the right to narrate," suggesting that the inclusion
of learners' own stories may allow them to find their own places within an
inclusive collective history:

> To protect the "right to narrate" is to protect a range of democratic imperatives:
> it assumes there is an equitable access to those institutions—schools, universities,
> museums, libraries, theatres—that give you a sense of a collective history and the
> means to turn those materials into a narrative of your own. (pp. 180–181)

Bhabha does not claim that schools can act alone. He recognizes that
such an assured, empowered sense of "selfhood" depends on a public culture
in which the rights-holder is confident his or her story will be heard and
acted upon. This, he asserts, depends in turn on civil society's readiness to
defend "the right to take part in cultural life" (U.N., 1966b, art. 15). The
curriculum that follows from this right necessarily includes opportunities to
explore and reflect on various identities and cultural attributes and to create
personal narratives and processes of self-learning. Effectively, narratives can
inspire learners to tell their own individual and collective stories and struggles
for justice (Delanty, 2003; Osler, 2011b).

It is through this use of narrative that teachers can contribute to the realization of justice, peace, and equality as they empower learners not only to
articulate their own rights but also advocate for the rights of others. Bhabha's
insights are valuable to a human rights framework because they give a central
place to the community of learners and to their experiences of justice and
injustice. In this way, human rights enable a broad vision of our common

humanity and our shared struggles, looking beyond the immediate to the global community and at the same time remaining rooted in the everyday experiences and struggles of learners' own lives and those of the community of learners.

NARRATIVES AND SEN'S THEORY OF JUSTICE

Sen's (1992, 2010) theory of justice can inform our understanding of the potential of narratives in teaching and research for social justice. In this, he draws on his earlier work on the "capabilities approach," which seeks to assess how individuals experience justice and injustice, rather than focus on institutions and on the imaginary "just society." In this respect, Sen's theory differs considerably from previous theories of justice, notably that of Rawls (1971/2005). Sen's framework is innovative in that it is concerned with procedural processes in enabling greater justice; his theoretical model departs in this way from other theorists who, following Rawls, seek to imagine a perfectly just society.

By focusing on the remediable injustices that individuals may encounter, Sen argues that his theory is capacious (and incomplete) enough to have some pertinence to policy debates and to research and program development designed to advance social justice. By turning away from the notion of the just society, situated within a particular polity, Sen's theory of justice can be applied at different scales from the local to the global. It supports recognition of our common humanity and responsibility to others in distant places, beyond the limiting framework of the nation-state. It has the added advantage of applicability in different cultural contexts, allowing for comparability. As Chapter 5 will highlight, education systems are profoundly national (and often nationalistic) in character, posing a challenge for human rights education, which is essentially cosmopolitan in nature. Sen's theory of justice provides a framework to those wishing to denationalize school curricula so as to allow learners to find their own places, identities, and narratives within an inclusive collective history. It is these counternarratives that are critical in telling inclusive stories within multicultural communities and multicultural nation-states and that can contribute to a form of multicultural education that may genuinely contribute to greater justice and equality, based on cosmopolitan perspectives and on agreed-upon international principles of human rights.

By adopting narrative as a pedagogical tool, teachers and students open up possibilities to make links between their experiences and those of strangers in distant places, including links between these strangers' struggles for justice and their own. Narratives used in this way can be used to advance justice and human rights through education. They address an affective element within human rights education that may enable genuine engagement with others' lives, extending beyond a cognitive recognition of our common humanity.

It is a combination of the affective and the cognitive that is likely to inspire action for justice and human rights.

GOVERNMENTS, HUMAN RIGHTS, AND DIVERSE CULTURES

As discussed in Chapter 1, there is a tendency in the West to characterize western nations as heavenly and those of the Global South as hellish in relation to their human rights records (Okafor & Agbakwa, 2001). This imagined binary has an impact not only on international relations but also on the perceived need for human rights education. The Chinese government is one that has come under particular criticism in the West. Since this chapter draws on the life history of one Chinese citizen, it is important here to say something about the role of governments in upholding human rights and to explore briefly how human rights apply to the diverse and multiple identities of learners. Since human rights emphasize our common humanity and solidarity across national borders, it seems clear that human rights defenders should be prepared to defend the rights of others and to speak out against abuse, wherever abuses may occur. But the problem of moral superiority, whereby human rights defenders in the West have a clear vision of justice and injustice in other parts of the world, but a blind spot to injustice and oppression at home, needs attention. All governments are responsible for upholding the rights of those living within their territories, and all need to be held accountable. This implies a critical citizenry, prepared to defend the rights of others. Yet governments everywhere fail to guarantee the rights of all and, as a result of their actions or inactions, need to be brought to account.

As ethical claims, human rights are about what *should* be. Governments are generally bound to uphold them through forces of moral rather than legal pressure. The process of implementing international human rights treaties at national levels often leads to changes in the law.

Human rights are sometimes dismissed on the grounds that they do not carry legal force in the same way as constitutional rights, which are enshrined in national legal frameworks. It is, however, important to understand that this can be seen as strength as well as a potential weakness. Before 1948, rights were linked to citizenship or nationality. As the president of the 1948 U.N. General Assembly observed, the proclamation of UDHR marked "the first occasion on which the organized world community had recognized the existence of human rights and fundamental freedoms transcending the laws of sovereign states" (quoted in Laqueur & Rubin, 1979, p. 1). Human rights are inalienable; citizenship can be revoked, and some vulnerable people, including refugees, forced migrants, undocumented migrants, and others caught up in wars and conflicts, may find themselves stateless and/or without documented citizenship. Yet all remain holders of human rights, regardless of their access to rights through nationality.

Human rights are understood as strong ethical claims, which have universal application and have been applied through internationally recognized human rights instruments since the signing of the UDHR in 1948. Nevertheless, human rights have been challenged from a range of different quarters, and therefore I recognize that they should be subject to similar critical scrutiny as any other ethical claims.

At the same time, as someone committed to social justice and human rights, I take human rights at their face value as powerful claims that are often used effectively by those struggling for justice in different parts of the world and in different cultural contexts. I have in this chapter already referred to the antiapartheid struggle and its appeal for international solidarity based on recognition of universal human rights.

Human rights have also been an important force for women's access to justice and equality across the globe. From the late 1980s, women in many different international contexts began to work together as part of a global movement to develop analytical and political tools that today form the concepts and practices of women's human rights, observing that while human rights apply to all by nature of their humanity, in practice women were finding it more difficult than men to assert their human rights within established international mechanisms (Bunch & Frost, 2000; Mertus & Flowers, 2008; Osler & Starkey, 2010). While the universality of human rights is emphasized through legal instruments, their application in specific contexts to particular groups can also be realized through narratives or "personal histories," as Brabeck and Rogers (2000) illustrate with their discussion of human rights work in response to violations against women and children in the United States. They emphasize that ensuring appropriate resources for human rights so that social policy addresses the rights proclaimed in the UDHR "is not the same thing as aid to the poor or social programmes for the homeless," and go on to remind us that "sex discrimination kills women daily. When combined with race, class and other forms of oppression, it constitutes a deadly denial of women's right to life and liberty on a large scale throughout the world" (Bunch, cited in Brabeck & Rogers, 2000, p. 174). They therefore invite educators to help young people, particularly those who live in conditions of poverty and disadvantage, make links between the societal injustices affecting their own communities and the everyday violence and crime that they experience in their own lives (personal histories), not as an individualized experience but as part of a pattern of injustice experienced by the poor in different societies and cultures. In this way, they are encouraging educators not only to consider sociopolitical factors affecting their lives, information about their human rights, and efforts to create systemic change, but also to develop a focus on community well-being, instead of victims and villains, and develop a sense of individual responsibility for the common good. In this way, teachers and students cross boundaries between experiences in the Global North and the Global South.

Since this chapter draws on a human rights narrative from China it seems appropriate to address briefly the question of human rights and "Asian values." Human rights have been universally recognized by the world's governments and by NGOs around the globe. For example, the 1989 Convention on the Rights of the Child has been universally signed and almost universally ratified. Yet leaders in some authoritarian states in East Asia have suggested that human rights may be in conflict with local culture. This was the case in Singapore, for example, following independence from British colonial rule in 1963 and separation from Malaysia in 1965. According to Tan (1994), the school curriculum largely ignored human rights on the stated grounds that Western values encouraged decadence. A discourse of Asian values has circulated, which gives credence to the claim that they derive from Confucianism.

In response, it important to critique the simplistic duality of Asian values and Western values. It clearly masks diverse ways of life in both the West and Asia, and also denies the multicultural realities of modern nation-states. Second, it is important to remember that cultures have never been static and fixed, but fluid, constantly renewing themselves and drawing on different sources for their development. Third, we note that, empirically, a number of East Asian countries, including Japan, South Korea, and the Philippines, have systems of government that guarantee human rights, and a number of others, including the Islamic states of Indonesia and Malaysia, have multi-party democracies. As a Chinese comparative educationalist has observed, following China's participation in the World Conference on Human Rights in Vienna 1993:

> Along with a reassessment of cultural traditions and Western values, a more balanced understanding has been reached by the young generation and the citizenry of the dialectic interrelations of collective and individual rights. . . . Rights are a historical concept that evolves along with societal changes. (Zhou, 1994, p. 86)

HUMAN RIGHTS, NARRATIVE, AND EDUCATION

While human rights are both ethical claims and (sometimes) legal entitlements, they cannot be enforced if they are unknown by policymakers, journalists, teachers, and the citizenry in general. Human rights are usually only realized through a process of struggle. Yet their realization is equally dependent on knowledge of rights. As shown in Chapter 1, education was seen, from the beginning of the universal human rights project, as an essential feature of the project. Since human rights are both ethical claims and may also be legal entitlements, it is essential that learners have the opportunity to study and examine international human rights instruments, including the UDHR.

Narratives have the power to link legal and ethical frameworks with learners' own struggles, and it is for this reason that they need to be placed centrally within HRE. A study of others' narratives can "resonate with the struggles of learners" (Osler & Starkey, 2010, p. 143). When applied to human rights education, narratives permit learners to address their multiple and suppressed identities, examine historical and contemporary inequalities, stimulate empathy and solidarity among all humanity, and demonstrate the import of human rights as principles of living together at all scales from the local to the global in contexts of diversity and in what Held (1997) has characterized as "overlapping communities of fate" (p. 313). In other words, education in general, and human rights education in particular, needs to prepare students to live together in societies whose current fortunes and futures are intertwined and enmeshed (Osler, 2010b; Starkey, 2007).

Flanagan (1992) highlights the power of narrative, pointing out that the "evidence strongly suggests that humans in all cultures come to cast their own identity in some sort of narrative form. We are inveterate storytellers" (p. 198). Narration is one of the most commonly used communication modes. Narratives are said to be able to elicit and disseminate knowledge (Snowden, 2002), encourage collaboration and generate new ideas (Lelic, 2001), and ignite change (Denning, 2001). Moreover, narratives are well liked because they enable materials to be readily accessible, intriguing, and engaging; they foster a sense of our common humanity with the narrator. In this sense, the use of narrative in HRE builds upon the work of those advocating for narrative inquiry, since "education is the construction and reconstruction of personal and social stories; learners, teachers, and researchers are storytellers and characters in their own and others' stories" (Connelly & Clandinin, 1990, p. 2).

One of the key aims of education for social justice is to encourage learner participation and critical engagement with knowledge, ideas, and other learners. I wish to stress three key elements that such learning should include: (1) information about and experience of democracy and human rights in theory and practice (Banks et al., 2005); (2) opportunities to explore and reflect on various identities and cultural attributes, create personal narratives, and develop processes of self-learning (Osler, 2015a); and (3) cooperative practice, teamwork, and the development of collective narratives and study of cognitive models that enable learners as a group to make sense of the world (Osler, 2011a). As is shown in Delanty's (2003) study of citizenship as a learning process, individual and collective narratives enable learners to draw on their own experiences as they create knowledge and explore the relationship between *education* for social justice and *action* for social justice.

Of course using narratives in HRE presents a number of challenges. Teachers and students, asked to present their own family history, may interpret it "within the nation's dominant narratives, rather than using family history as a tool to delve beneath those narratives" (Sleeter, 2015, p. 1). Connelly and Clandinin (1990) warn that "falsehood may be substituted for meaning and narrative truth. . . . Not only may one 'fake the data' and write a fiction but one may also use the data to tell a deception as easily as a truth" (p. 10). Any narrative represents the storyteller's perspective rather than an objective truth and needs to be understood as such; the storyteller may vary the account from one recounting to the next, emphasizing or omitting points according to a variety of circumstances, including the perceived audience. Sleeter (2015) stresses the value of family narratives that emphasize cultural multiplicity and the historic construction of unequal relationships, which may impact on power relationships in contemporary society, shedding light on issues such as institutionalized discrimination.

From a constructivist epistemological stance, narratives are open to different interpretations: "stories are inherently multilayered and ambiguous" (Bell, 2002, p. 210) and "narratives are discursive constructions rather than factual statement" (Pavlenko, 2002, p. 216). Different people may engage with the same narrative in different ways, approaching it from their own positionalities, which are closely tied to their unique life experiences (Bicknell, 2004; Josselson, 1996; Peshkin, 1988). Given that each individual's life experiences are shaped by a confluence of factors including race and ethnicity, class, gender, and sexuality, as well as by the wider social and political contexts and the prevailing power relations, any narrative is likely to be told and retold and rendered diversely by different individuals (Pavlenko, 2002; Riessman, 1991). New layers of meaning and interpretation may lead to the restorying or retelling of a narrative in ways the original narrator may not have intended (Connelly & Clandinin, 1990; Josselson, 1996). In other words, no individual adopts a neutral position; rather, everyone, including the storyteller and the audience, holds a particular standpoint. Every narrative needs to be read with this consciousness. While these issues may pose pedagogical challenges, they do not detract from the value or power of narrative in HRE. Human rights educators need to approach narratives in such a way as to enable learners to understand these epistemological issues and to adopt a critical approach, so as to support students in understanding questions of knowledge and power and support them in their own struggles for social justice, equality, and human rights.

AN ILLUSTRATIVE NARRATIVE: YONGMIN'S STORY

What follows is the life history of one Chinese citizen, who has been given the pseudonym Yongmin. It was compiled by my former student Juanjuan Zhu as part of an assignment for a PhD program at Utah State University, and the account and discussion that follow derive from our joint work (Osler & Zhu, 2011). It is presented here to show how learners might study and critically engage with the UDHR, making links between Yongmin's everyday struggles for justice and human rights and those in their own lives.

Yongmin was born in 1951, just 3 years after the UDHR was proclaimed. He told his story to Zhu on a number of occasions, and parts of it were retold

to her by Yongmin's mother, and others by his wife. Zhu has reconstruct-
ed the narrative below from these various accounts, but does not provide
further details of the context in which the story was told, including precise
places or place names, in an effort to protect the identities of Yongmin and
his family, who remain in China to the present time. The various storytellers
have enabled her to engage in a process of triangulation. This account is
not presented as an objective assessment of the events of Yongmin's life, but
rather as the perceptions of Yongmin and some immediate family members
(his mother and wife) who lived these experiences with him. In this retelling,
translated of course into English, Zhu (and I) concur with Stanley and Wise
(1993) that in any research account the perceptions and biases of the writer
are present (whether they are made explicit or remain implicit). So in this respect we take responsibility for the account as our own, rather than attribute
this precise wording to Yongmin or his family. Nevertheless, the narrative is
presented in the same form as originally told to Zhu.

Yongmin's Story

My name is Yongmin and I was born in a coastal city in East China in 1951.
I'm the sixth of the eight children in my family. Before I was born, my parents used to own a small factory to make bean products like tofu and soy
milk during the period of Chiang Kai Shek's Nationalist regime. However,
as businessmen were ranked the lowest in the traditional Chinese hierarchy,
they could only make a meagre living to raise their then five children, my five
brothers. The small factory was soon confiscated after the Communist Party
overthrew the Nationalist Party and came into power in 1949. My parents
thus became members of the honorable proletariat and served as workers in
a state-owned factory. Three more children were born into the family during
the following 4 years, including me. Life became more difficult as there were
three additional mouths to feed.

But the hardest time did not come until the 3-year great famine set in, in
1959. All I can recall about that period is the endless hunger, the desperate
search for food, and the death of one of my brothers as the result of hunger
and illness. For a family like mine with seven adults (five of my brothers were
over 18 by then) and three children, we were given a ration of about 90 ki-
lograms (about 200 pounds) of rice and wheat flour each month. It might
sound a lot, but given the fact we had nothing else to eat, that amount of
food was barely enough. Each person could purchase only 250 grams (less
than 9 ounces) of pork per month; while eggs, chicken, and fish were only
available once per year. Many times, we ate leaves and wild herbs as our veg-
etables. But that was not the worst. I've heard that people in inland China
starved to death every day.

Hardly had I finished my battle with hunger when another two massive
political movements were launched in China. In the year 1966, the Cultural
Revolution began, and this marked a 10-year period of havoc in China's

recent history. At that time, I was in my 3rd year of junior high. As part of the general social upheaval, the schooling system was paralyzed nation-wide. Teachers were denounced, paraded through the streets, or even beaten at public meetings by some students. Other students either climbed onto trains and traveled to other parts of the country or simply stayed at home. I, together with several of my classmates, once climbed a freight train to Shanghai, where my eldest brother lived. But for most of the time, we just wandered around different parts of the city and played around, as there was no school at all. Honestly, for my entire high school years, I did not receive any formal or consistent education. As a good student who loves reading, I now really regret how I wasted my adolescent years and was inadequately educated as a result of this social turbulence.

Then came the year 1968. At the end of this year, Mao Zedong, who was President (or Chairman as we call him) of China at that time, declared that urban youth should be sent to mountainous areas or farming villages in order to learn from workers and farmers. He aimed to quell the social unrest and help the youth resist bourgeois thinking. As a result, I joined my 16 mil-lion high school peers nationwide in the famous "Down to the Countryside Movement" and was exiled to the less developed rural areas. I should have been sent to Yunnan, a southwest province 2,500 kilometers from my home. But since one of my brothers had been sent there, my mother begged the leaders to let me go to a nearby town where one of my aunts was living.

So, I took a ship and traveled for a whole day, arriving in an area of sparsely populated farmland. There I worked as a farmer for 10 years and was only able to visit my family for a couple of days once a year. I was also denied any further education, because basically, we had no access to and no time for books. But for the end of the Cultural Revolution in 1978 and Deng Xiaop-ing's decision to allow urban youth to return to their hometowns, I would have stayed in the countryside forever.

During my stay at the farmland, I met a girl who had a very similar ex-perience to mine. She was also one of the victims of that chaotic period in China's history. At the age of 15, she was also sent to this remote countryside in place of her elder sister, who had learning difficulties, as part of the Down to the Countryside Movement. She was very talented in singing and study-ing. However, when the authorities discovered that she was a descendent of a landlord in old China, she lost the chance to enter the army or further her education. Instead, she had to work as a farmer, an accountant, and a per-former in the local singing and dance troupe.

We got married in 1979 and moved to the city that was closest to the farmland where we labored. The next year we had a baby girl. She is our only child because like many newlywed couples at that time, we were only allowed to have one child in the family. Later, my wife became pregnant a second time. This time it was a boy. However, due to the one-child policy, we were afraid that we would be severely fined or denied jobs if this baby were born. So my wife had to have an induced abortion 4 months before the due date. At the time, I really wished that we could have kept this boy but given the rigours of life, I am happy with just one child. Both my wife and I have determined to do all we can to give her a better life. We sincerely wish that she will lead a life that is not half as dramatic and arduous as what we have experienced.

Discussion

This narrative of Yongmin's life history, covering the period from the 1950s to the 1980s, reflects a period in China's history during which the government acquired a notorious reputation for its dismissive treatment of human rights (Heater, 2002; Weatherley, 2008). The Chinese government continues to attract criticism from the international community for its human rights record today. Nevertheless, Bjornstol (2009) notes how since 1978 an official policy of reform has led to "remarkable development both in the legal system and in the legal education system in China" with human rights law gradually developing as a legitimate field of study. While legal education is an important field into which human rights need to be incorporated, it is the education of the general population that helps secure human rights in China, as elsewhere. Schools are able to engage with nearly everyone, whereas university law schools educate elites.

It is possible to identify a number of articles in the UDHR that Yongmin's narrative addresses to show how the human rights of Yongmin, his family, and others (such as his teachers) have been violated. These include Articles 3 (the right to life), 5 (cruel, inhuman, and degrading punishment), 9 (protection from arbitrary arrest), 12 (interference with family life), 13 (freedom of movement), 17 (the right to own property), 23 (free choice of employment), and 25 (right to an adequate standard of living for health and well-being).

The events that Yongmin appears to give greatest emphasis in his account are the family poverty into which he was born; the impact of the terrible 1959 famine in which his brother died; the 1966 Cultural Revolution, which led to the end of his education at the age of 15; his separation from his family at the age of 17 and subsequent work as an agricultural laborer; his wife's regret at not being able to follow the profession of her choice; his marriage and subsequent birth of a daughter; and the pressure for his wife to have a late abortion to avoid having a second child and so conform with the one-child policy, for fear of losing their jobs.

In this vividly depicted narrative, the relatively dry material of the UDHR comes to life and takes on real meaning and significance. A study of this life history engages the emotions as well as the intellect, and promotes a sense of solidarity with the struggles of another. Certain articles of the UDHR, which may be somewhat removed from some learners' personal experiences, are transformed from abstractions into an everyday struggle for survival and fulfilment. While discussion of controversial issues and specific interpretations of history do not take place in classrooms in China at the present time (Zhu & Misco, 2014), it is important that students in China also eventually have the opportunity to discuss these aspects of their own history through narratives like that above, rather than read about episodes like the Cultural Revolution and the Down to the Countryside Movement as abstractions in history textbooks.

By combining narratives with international human rights instruments in this way, they become powerful pedagogical tools. Drawing on various individual or collective narratives, teachers can invite their students not only to identify all the articles in the UDHR that are present and recognizable in a narrative, "whether this is through abuse and denial of rights or efforts to act to uphold these rights and demonstrate human solidarity" (Osler & Starkey, 2010, p. 144), but to give them meaning. Students can familiarize themselves with the content of these international treaties; equally importantly, they are empowered to tell their own individual and collective narratives and to defend and claim their rights.

Important in the study of narrative is an opportunity for learners to investigate the wider economic and social processes at work. For example, in investigating Yongmin's account, students can learn about the causes of famine and investigate Sen's (2010) claim that "no major famine has ever occurred in a functioning democracy with regular elections" (p. 342). In contexts where there is public debate and reasoning about such matters, there is pressure on governments to address the question of food distribution and act to protect citizens. A better understanding of the relationship between democracy, open government, and justice is important for the future protection of human rights. Study of human rights equips learners with a language to demand practical redress, sincere apology from those who are responsible, and effective structures and public debate to prevent future violations of rights.

Telling our own narratives and especially those of "invisible" individuals or groups highlights the fact that there are many different histories to be told instead of just one monolithic common national history. Stories told by different people provide spaces for various kinds of discriminations and violations of human rights to be recognized, criticized, and eventually redressed. These narratives fill the blind spots in the dominant discourse and deepen our appreciation of the significance of justice and peace to marginalized groups in various historical periods. Personal and collective narratives developed by teachers and students are a form of "transformative knowledge that challenges the existing and institutionalized metanarrative" (Banks, 2002, p. 11). In other words, personal narratives serve to counterbalance a nationalistic discourse that is characterized by an uncritical identification with a monolithic national culture and history. Numerous research studies examining school curricula in a variety of countries— for example, China (Wan, 2004), France (Osler & Starkey, 2009), Singapore (Baildon & Sim, 2010; Martin & Feng, 2006), Mexico (Ryan, 2006), and the United States (Foster, 2006)—all attest to the dominance of a nationalist discourse that excludes the perspectives of marginalized groups. The use of narrative as illustrated here can serve to present a broader and more open curriculum in which learners have an opportunity to engage with minority perspectives.

It is difficult to find stories such as Yongmin's reflected in China's official history today. Research confirms such stories are not generally present in China's official textbooks and newspapers (Cha, Wong, & Meyer, 1992; Wong, 1992). That period of history is dominated by a powerful monolithic account of the nation's victory over a series of natural disasters and its transformation from an old bureaucratic–capitalistic polity to a new socialist country. Personal tragedies such as Yongmin's have been treated lightly, despite the fact that they are in fact more than personal; Yongmin's story is, in this sense, the story of millions of his compatriots.

A monolithic approach has a negative impact on those whose human rights were violated, but whose sufferings and stories are left untold. Equally significant is the damage this silence inflicts on future generations, who are presented with a very misleading picture; effectively they are miseducated. Genuine multiple individual narratives have given way to a single, celebrated national history. Untold stories, like that of Yongmin, should be told and retold to encourage readers and listeners alike to examine historical wrongs; identify current oppressions; challenge dominant discourses; and engage in an ongoing struggle for justice, peace, and human rights.

Narratives addressing human rights also have the capacity to move us outside of our immediate environment and enable collaboration across national boundaries for dignity, equality, freedom, and peace. As Starratt (2003) observed, "Narrative is a primary vehicle for engaging the imagination in moral reasoning. Not only does it enrich and expand our perspective, it also provides the shared meeting place where people may engage in moral conversation" (p. 211). This is the process of public reasoning that Sen (2010) argues is essential for the realization of justice. Human rights narratives may enable increased empathy for our fellow humans whose lives are different from our own. Through narratives, we identify with those whom we may never meet in our real life, but from whom we may have a lot to learn (Osler, 2010b). Narratives like Yongmin's support the development of solidarity and understanding of the obligations of cosmopolitan citizenship (Osler & Starkey, 2003, 2005; Osler & Vincent, 2002), which is realized in part through a common struggle for human rights.

Others' narratives prompt us to reflect on our own stories and experiences. According to Savin-Baden and Van Niekerk (2007), "Stories are the closest we can come to shared experience" (p. 462). Through reading or listening to others' stories, we are encouraged to tell our own stories and claim our own rights. At the same time, a process of reflection enables learners to better understand their own values, identities, and beliefs in relation to equity, social justice, and democracy.

One narrative was presented here as an illustrative example. Nevertheless, educators can never be overly dependent on one or even a handful of narratives in human rights education. Narratives need to be supported by other pedagogical tools and approaches. Varied sources of evidence, which may present totally contradictory information, provide opportunities for learners to develop skills in research and critical thinking that can be reapplied outside of the learning environment. As narrators or as educators and learners, we each need to develop skills to read these varied sources of evidence from as many perspectives as possible, examining and re-examining the motives of knowledge-creators.

This chapter has aimed to illustrate how individual and collective narratives have potential as powerful tools for human rights education. It has explored some of the tensions in addressing human rights education in cultural contexts where many readers may be unfamiliar, but it has nevertheless sought to challenge the powerful domination of a monolithic national discourse that denies the perspectives of marginalized, oppressed, or hidden histories. Narratives allow us to move outside our immediate environment and find commonalities with those we may never meet but who may prove to be our closest allies in the cause of human rights. In addition, narratives can prompt us to reflect on our own identities, values, and experiences in relation to equity, social justice, and human rights. That said, human rights educators and researchers should also be aware of the potential to enable deepened relations with our fellow human beings and to serve as a springboard for ethical action (Witherell & Noddings, 1991) in the ongoing struggle to realize peace, justice, equality, and freedom in the world.

In Chapter 5 I focus on the nation, arguing that if HRE is to be effectively implemented, teachers need to engage in processes of denationalization and decolonization of the curriculum. These processes further enable the project of promoting multiperspectivity and the inclusion of hitherto silenced voices in the struggle for human rights and social justice.

CHAPTER 5

Human Rights, Education, and the Nation

School systems throughout the world tend to have a strong national focus; and curricula, particularly history education and civics, tend to give emphasis to this national dimension (Reid et al., 2009; Osler, 2009), generally focusing on the mainstream or majority in the nation, frequently occluding and sometimes systematically excluding minority perspectives. In this chapter, my intention is to identify some pointers for those wishing to denationalize school curricula so as to allow learners to find their own places and their own identities within an inclusive collective history.

In this chapter I argue that processes of denationalization or decolonization of the curriculum are critical to the conceptualization of an inclusive vision of the nation, where minorities are properly recognized and able to play a full part in social and political life, and to the successful implementation of education for human rights. Struggles for the full recognition and participation of minorities in society, and for their recognition in school curricula, are not new. Yet there is another pressing issue at the beginning of the 21st century that requires the urgent attention of educators concerned with enabling social justice in and through schooling: This relates to the fragility of democracy and to antidemocratic political movements. Thus I will consider how such forces might be appropriately addressed. In particular, the chapter considers current legal and policy frameworks for HRE and the degree to which these may support efforts for greater justice and peace through schooling.

My arguments are premised on an understanding of human rights and human rights education as cosmopolitan projects, which emphasize our common humanity. I also recognize human rights and human rights education as sites of struggle (Bowring, 2012), which means that I understand my scholarship in this area to be necessarily about realizing greater justice through education. Finally, human rights are always enacted within a specific social and political setting, which means they adopt political meanings. This chapter reflects on the degree to which this may have an impact on their universal nature.

A HUMAN RIGHTS PARADOX

The modern human rights project was introduced after World War II, a period of history characterized by extreme horrors and inhumanity. The preamble to the 1948 Universal Declaration of Human Rights references the "disregard and contempt for human rights [that] have resulted in barbarous acts which have outraged the conscience of mankind" (U.N., 1948). Disregard and contempt for human rights was clearly displayed in Nazi Germany, where between 1933 and 1943 some 2,000 discriminatory decrees consolidated systemic domination and suppression of Jews and the denial of their humanity.

A close examination of the various articles of the UDHR reveals a direct link between the guarantees made in specific articles and Nazi state oppression over a decade (Osler & Starkey, 2010). These restrictions and denials of rights are a clear example of how a nation-state consolidated structural inequality: Between 1935 and 1936 Jewish citizens were deprived of their citizenship and right to vote; denied the right to marry non-Jews; banned from parks, restaurants, and swimming pools; forbidden to own optical and electrical equipment (such as radios), bicycles, and typewriters; and saw benefit payments stopped to large families. A series of rights named in the UDHR respond directly to these violations: Article 15 states that no one shall be arbitrarily deprived of their nationality; Article 16 confirms the right to marry without restriction of race, nationality, or religion; Article 24 guarantees the right to rest and leisure; Article 19 guarantees the right to seek, receive, and impart information and ideas through any media and regardless of frontiers; and Article 22 guarantees that everyone, as a member of society, has the right to social security. In each case, the nation-state is charged with protecting its people from abuses and denials of rights. Effectively, various obligations are placed on the nation-state, through the UDHR, to uphold the rights of those under its protection.

Paradoxically, the state—a powerful actor and one that may effectively deny or abuse the rights of individuals or groups—is made the guarantor of human rights. Although the UDHR and subsequent human rights instruments are traditionally understood by legal scholars as a means of *restricting* the power of the state and preventing it from exercising arbitrary power (Donnelly, 2013), the declaration can equally be seen as a means of *enhancing and strengthening state power* in making it the guarantor of human rights. This point is emphasized by Perugini and Gordon (2015), who highlight how in giving the nation-state responsibility to protect human rights, it was accorded international legitimacy and strength. They suggest that at any specific historical moment, the state can use this power to appropriate the human rights discourse to enhance domination.

Perugini and Gordon (2015) illustrate the paradoxical position of the state through their discussion of the case of Israel–Palestine, arguing that, at specific moments, the Israeli state has used the discourse to assert apparently universal human rights for a specific group of people, namely Jewish Israeli citizens. They argue that Israel, a nation-state that at its foundation was seen by many in western Europe as reparation to the Jewish people for the horrors of the Holocaust and a means of enabling vulnerable refugees to exercise their rights, has, in fact, appropriated the human rights discourse by not applying it universally, but instead restricting it to a specific group of people, Jewish Israelis. They contend that the Israeli state, founded to address a specific human rights challenge, that of displaced and refugee Jews in Europe, has in recent decades adopted a human rights discourse to strengthen its power and pursue policies of domination and colonization, including the right to kill. This is achieved first through labeling the "other" as a threat to the state and then through linking human rights discourses to this threat by presenting Jewish Israeli citizens as vulnerable subjects whose human rights need to be protected.

In this discourse, according to Perugini and Gordon (2015), Palestinians are a threat by their very presence. They need to be displaced and replaced in order to secure the future of the Israeli state. Discriminatory practices such as demolition of Palestinian dwellings and policies that forbid Palestinian construction are justified by reference to the human rights of Jewish Israelis, who are made vulnerable by the presence of Palestinians. In this way a powerful nation-state creates a new narrative in which the position of the colonized and colonizer are inversed, with the rights of the colonized suspended in the name of protecting the nation-state.

By these means, argue Perugini and Gordon (2015), the nation-state asserts the right to dominate. They illustrate how the language of human rights is appropriated to stress, for example, settler rights over those of displaced people who have lost their land. Since the discourse portrays Palestinian Israeli citizens and those living in the Occupied Palestinian Territories of the West Bank and in Gaza as a threat to the Israeli state, this permits the state to restrict, deny, and violate human rights in the interests of the state. Effectively, as in the European colonial era, the rights of one group take precedence; human rights are equated exclusively in this discourse with the rights of colonizers.

This process of "othering" is one in which the colonized are excluded from the category of human rights holder; it is a process of dehumanization. Of course such processes are not unique or peculiar to the Israeli state. Various European nations, during the colonial era, justified policies of domination by distinguishing between the rights of citizens (requiring the protection of the state) and colonial subjects (lacking citizenship, therefore lacking rights). A similar discourse permitted apartheid South Africa to assert its democratic credentials while denying the equal citizenship of non-White members of the community. Effectively, the nation-state, as guarantor of human rights to its people, justifies its own abuse of human rights with respect to minorities (or those it excludes from full citizenship) on the grounds that they threaten or undermine the security of the state, and so curtails their rights in the name of protecting the majority. In the case of Israel–Palestine, Palestinian residents have been forced to leave their homes and villages in the name of protecting settlers. The state's claim is justified on utilitarian grounds, but it overlooks the responsibility of the state to extend human rights protection to all, including minorities and nonnationals. Human rights are used to justify a "human right to dominate" and "human right to colonize" (Perugini & Gordon, 2015, p. 119), leading to dispossession and dislocation of the colonized people.

Such challenges do not detract from the potential of HRE to contribute to greater social justice, but they do require teachers and students to understand human rights as principles for social justice, which are nevertheless implemented within contexts characterized by asymmetrical power relations. Human rights remain potent. Although they are used by state actors to claim power, grassroots groups can also draw on their potency in their struggles for justice. The power of human rights, as demonstrated in earlier chapters, is that they provide such groups with tools and frameworks that permit appeals for solidarity beyond state boundaries. Although human rights are generally guaranteed by states, their potency derives from their international legitimacy and their cosmopolitan nature. This rights framework allows those who individually are powerless, to join in solidarity to claim what the international community has recognized for all and to hold nation-states to account.

ADDRESSING HUMAN RIGHTS EDUCATION WITHIN NATIONAL EDUCATION

Human rights education, conceived as a cosmopolitan project and as a site of struggle, poses particular challenges for teaching and learning in public schools. One challenge is to develop a theory and practice of education for human rights and social justice that meets the needs of multicultural societies, societies that are frequently, and simultaneously, both multifaith and secular.

As discussed above, education across the globe—in particular, school history and curriculum areas such as civics or citizenship education—tends to remain profoundly national in focus (Reid et al., 2009). It might be argued that since the establishment of the United Nations in 1945, with the goal of realizing world peace and strengthening human rights and human dignity, that school systems have been encouraged to introduce more cosmopolitan perspectives. Through the work of UNESCO (United Nations Educational, Scientific and Cultural Organization), efforts have been made to reform school curricula so as to address national and subnational ethnic and cultural conflicts. Indeed, the Charter of the United Nations proclaims that one goal is to enable "We the peoples of the United Nations . . . to practice tolerance and live together in peace with one another as good neighbors" (U.N., 1945). A longitudinal comparative study of over 465 high school civic education textbooks from 1970 to 2008, covering 69 countries, suggests there is an overall move toward greater cosmopolitanism over this period (Bromley, 2009). This study identifies a trend toward universalism and diversity in all areas except the Middle East and North Africa and a significant increase in discussions of human rights in all regions except Asia.

The notion of a cosmopolitan vision in education is not completely new. John Dewey (1916/2002) reminds us that today's predominant national model, based on European mass education systems of the late 19th century, was in fact developed at a time when nationalism was at its height. Before this period, education providers focused on a broader cosmopolitan ideal, emphasizing a shared human heritage. Dewey highlights how "cosmopolitanism gave way to nationalism" (p.108), stressing loyalty to the state rather than to humanity. The new focus was on the education of the citizen of the state rather than the cultured individual. If indeed there is evidence of a trend toward cosmopolitanism in school curricula in the early 21st century, this is but an expression of a cosmopolitan ideal dating back to the Enlightenment.

Osler and Starkey (2005, 2010) challenge traditional citizenship learning, based exclusively on national frameworks (such as the Constitution and constitutional rights) to argue for a form of "education for cosmopolitan citizenship" (Osler & Starkey, 2003, p. 243) underpinned by human rights. Human rights emphasize our common humanity and are essentially cosmopolitan, promoting solidarity with our fellow human beings, regardless of such factors as race, nationality, or religion. In classrooms where there are students who are not nationals and where there may be many who do not aspire to national citizenship, it seems particularly inappropriate to focus solely on the rights and duties of the (mainstream) national citizen. Effectively, this is not a rejection of national citizenship, national rights, or national duties, but one in which the nation itself—and national institutions—are reimagined as cosmopolitan (Osler, 2008).

Certain students who have citizenship status may find it difficult to access citizenship rights, for example, as a result of extreme poverty or if they are from a minoritized community and not recognized as citizens by neighbors. Ruth Lister (1997) warns against a false inclusivity or universalism in citizenship discourses whereby the "white, nondisabled, heterosexual male" is seen as the norm (p. 66). Certainly this is true of citizenship conceived in the civic republican tradition, where citizenship is presented as a fully realized project and the barriers to its full realization go unacknowledged. Similar caution needs to be employed in human rights discourse, and, as Osler and Starkey (2003, 2005) acknowledge, in conceiving education for cosmopolitan citizenship. This model is not without its own challenges (discussed below) but it does invite learners to reimagine the nation as cosmopolitan, aiming to subvert dominant models of national citizenship education.

There are many challenges to implementing human rights education within national school systems. For one thing, schools do not generally stress our common humanity; schools tend to give emphasis to a national perspective. At the beginning of the 21st century, despite (or perhaps in the face of) processes of globalization, the nation-state remains a potent concept as well as a political reality. School systems are pivotal in creating and maintaining the nation-state. Nevertheless, as Kymlicka (2003) reminds us, there is nothing "natural" about the concept of the nation-state, seen as the possession of a dominant national group, which privileges a specific national identity, language, history, culture, literature, myths, religion, and so on.

As discussed above, the state is the protector of human rights but may also be the agency that operates to deny or limit the rights of specific groups or individuals, allocating rights unequally between those subject to its power. Human rights are configured in three ways: serving to offer "*protection from*, *protection by*, and *protection of* the state" (Perugini & Gordon, 2015, p. 28; italics in the original). In other words, human rights exist to protect people *from* excesses of state power; human rights are accessed by people claiming enforcement of their rights *by* the state; and human rights simultaneously enable the protection *of* the state, through a process of legitimization and strengthening of state power.

National education systems (whether operating centrally or mediated by or devolved to a lower tier of government) also serve to confirm and enhance the power of the state. Human rights education as part of national education is likely to emphasize the rights and duties of citizens, and teachers in such systems may feel constrained in discussing how the state in question may deny rights, or in inviting students to examine human rights as a mechanism for restricting state power. Such subjects are seen as political precisely because they invite students to consider questions of power and to examine or question the assumed benevolent nature of state power in democratic contexts. Nevertheless, this potential limitation of human rights education in public school systems should not be exaggerated, since even authoritarian states seldom have total power over teachers or students. It does, however, suggest that a comprehensive program of human rights education in schools should consciously include NGO contributions and perspectives.

THE FRAGILITY OF DEMOCRACY

In the first two decades of the 21st century, the role of religion and the competing demands of secular and religious identities have been playing a key role in debates about the future of multicultural societies. A good illustration of how the principles of equality and justice are applied can be seen in Europe. At the level of the school and classroom one challenge is the reconciling of different worldviews and consideration of how pluralism should be addressed within the public sphere of the school.

In 2010 the Council of Europe's Secretary General Thorbjørn Jagland asked an independent "Group of Eminent Persons," drawn from nine member-states, to prepare a report on the challenges arising from the resurgence of intolerance and discrimination in Europe. The report (Council of Europe, Group of Eminent Persons, 2011) assesses the seriousness of the risks, identifies their sources, and makes a series of proposals for "living together" in open European societies. It expresses grave concerns about far-right activists who have expressed racist and Islamophobic views incompatible with democratic principles. Interestingly—and unusually, for a report published by an intergovernmental body like the Council of Europe—it criticizes senior mainstream politicians for their populist rhetoric, actually naming three (albeit in a footnote): former French President Nicolas Sarkozy, German Chancellor Angela Merkel, and British Prime Minister David Cameron (p. 10, note 1).

The report asserts that identities are a voluntary, personal matter; no one should be forced to choose one primary identity to the exclusion of others. This is in keeping with the perspectives of educational researchers who nevertheless note that, in practice, individuals can be denied full citizenship rights because of others' perceptions of their characteristics or identities related to culture, ethnicity, gender, sexuality, and so on (Banks, 2004; Murphy-Shigematsu, 2012; Osler & Starkey, 2005). The report argues that European societies need to embrace diversity and accept that one can be a "hyphenated European" (Council of Europe, Group of Eminent Persons, 2011, p. 34)—for instance a Congolese-German, a North African-Frenchwoman or a Kurdish-Norwegian.[1] But this can work only if all long-term residents are accepted as citizens (here I use the term sociologically, as a wider category than those holding nationality) and if all, whatever their faith, culture, or ethnicity, are treated equally by the law and their fellow citizens and have a say in making the law.

Expressions of extremism (hate speech, physical violence) curb democratic participation by undermining the psychological and physical security of those under attack. Freedom of expression is not an absolute right. The Parliamentary Assembly of the Council of Europe (PACE; 2000) has noted that in several member states "extremist parties and movements are propagating and defending ideologies that are incompatible with democracy and human rights" (para. 1). PACE (2000) has taken a position concerning "one of the greatest threats to democracy" (art. 3), particularly that posed by far-right groups that encourage intolerance, xenophobia, and racism. According to the Parliamentary Assembly (2003), "*no member state is immune* [emphasis added] to the intrinsic threats that extremism poses to democracy" (para.1). It notes measures that governments can take against such movements and political parties, including withdrawal of funding and, "in the case of a threat to a country's constitutional order" dissolution (para. 13.2d). This is official recognition of democracy's fragility, even in nations that consider themselves exemplars of democratic values.

The judgment that a political party can and should be dissolved if it poses a fundamental threat to a country's constitutional commitment to democracy and human rights was reasserted by the Council of Europe Commissioner for Human Rights Nils Muižnieks in the case of Greece, following a visit in 2013. Muižnieks (2013) focused on the need for urgent action following an increase in racist and other hate crimes. He stressed the need to challenge the immunity of perpetrators of hate crimes, including parliamentary representatives of the neo-Nazi political party Golden Dawn. Given the grave threat, the commissioner concludes that the Greek authorities can legitimately take action against any political party or movement for which there is ample evidence that it advocates and practices racial hatred and violence.[2] In other words, politicians and political parties do not have absolute freedom of expression. A neo-Nazi party that denies the equal rights of minorities and does not respect the country's constitutional commitment to democracy and human rights should not be allowed to continue until it is in a position to take office.

The Commissioner confirms that the European Court of Human Rights:

> has stressed that although the freedom of expression of politicians and political parties deserves a high degree of protection, they cannot advocate for racial discrimination and fuel racism as this goes against the fundamental principles of democracy. (Muižnieks, 2013, para. 58)

The Commissioner called on the Greek authorities to develop and implement initiatives aimed at combatting and preventing racism and extremism, with priority given to actions that raise "*awareness of the dangers of intolerance and racism and enhance human rights education in schools* [emphasis added]" (Muižnieks, 2013, para. 41).

In Norway and across Europe, Anders Behring Breivik's attack of July 22, 2011, in Oslo and Utøya is recognized as an attack on democracy. Seventy-seven people died and many more were injured. Much has been said about the trauma of the Norwegian people following the atrocity. The trauma faced by Norway's minorities as a result of this attack, and as a result of claims (by Breivik and numerous others) about the threat of a Muslim conspiracy in Europe (Feteke, 2012), has received rather less attention.

As Norwegian anthropologist Thomas Hylland Eriksen (2013) has noted, the attacks "revealed a dimension of Norwegian society that was scarcely known outside of the country, and was poorly understood within it." From this point onwards, it was impossible to deny "the existence of an active, militantly anti-immigrant, notably anti-Muslim network, loosely connected through websites and social media" (p. 2).

In Scandinavian countries it appears that the limits of freedom of speech are drawn rather differently from some other western European countries, and in any case the blogosphere is notoriously difficult to regulate. This

Islamophobic element is not confined to Norwegian society, but neverthe-less flourishes there within the context of "a deepening rift . . . about issues of cultural diversity and, in particular, Muslims" (Eriksen, 2013, p. 9). In this context it has become commonplace to assume incompatibility between Islam and democratic values.

A pan-European and troubling aspect of the affair is expressed on the cover of the UK magazine *New Statesman*: "The most shocking thing about Anders Behring Breivik? How many people agree with his opinion" (April 23, 2012). An article explores how certain right-wing British newspapers frequently misrepresent, distort, and even lie in stories about Islam and Mus-lims (Wilby, 2012). The *New Statesman* cover proclaims: "It's time to put mainstream Islamophobia on trial." This is a timely reminder of the need to tackle mainstream Islamophobia, in Europe and beyond, recognizing it as a contemporary form of racism. As Feteke (2012) demonstrates, across Europe neoconservative and cultural conservative commentators, as well as certain politicians from mainstream parties accessing mainstream media, while not supporting the notion of a Muslim conspiracy to Islamicize Europe, never-theless provide arguments that are subsequently used by conspiracy theorists to justify their stance, hate speech, and actions.

This cultural climate has subsequently allowed state actors, including the United Kingdom and Norway, to develop antiradicalization programs that include elements designed to target Muslim youth (Coppock, 2014; Osler, in press). Such programs risk denying children's rights in schools and may take attention away from efforts to close an achievement gap between many such children and their mainstream peers, undermining the identities of Muslim heritage students (Arthur, 2015; Osler, in press). Effectively, they put at risk genuine attempts by schools to create a more socially inclusive society.

In Norway, then prime minister Jens Stoltenberg repeatedly called for "more democracy, more openness, and more humanity" in response to the massacre (quoted, for example, in Orange, 2012). Stoltenberg's call was made to the nation as a whole in the immediate aftermath of the tragedy. He spoke of the "new Norwegian we," echoing then foreign minister Jonas Gahr Støre, when in 2008 he emphasized the need for an expanded conceptualiza-tion of what it might mean to be Norwegian (Osler & Lybæk, 2014). Given the evidence of antidemocratic forces in society and popular expressions of racism, expressed in complaints about "too many foreigners," or "too many Arabs," or "too many Muslims"[3] (Norwegian Broadcasting Corporation [NKR], 2011), it is important to consider what Stoltenberg's call for more democracy might mean for educators' everyday practices both in Norway and in other European settings. I would suggest that it does not necessarily mean more of the same, since efforts to promote democratic practices in schools that are not mindful of today's multicultural realities risk creating learning contexts that purport to be democratic, but which may fail to guarantee the equal rights and entitlements of minoritized learners (Osler, 2014b).

The above case highlights some general principles, applicable not just in Europe but more widely. A call for more democracy in education requires an extension of democratic practices to encompass diversity, recognizing not just visible minorities, but other overlooked identities and histories. Turning a blind eye to intolerance and racism in society does not make it go away. Denying its significance is to misjudge its impact on learners who are subject to discriminatory language, undermining their well-being, sense of belonging, and learning. If we underplay barriers to participation, we also miseducate mainstream students. The message is that minority rights and identities are less important, and students do not need to work to strengthen democracy. In many instances, concern for human rights is reserved for those living in distant places. Learners may fail to recognize that human rights and democracy need to be renewed, refreshed, and guaranteed for all at home.

Genuine democratic learning environments—and democratic decision-making at school—need to ensure that curricula, organizational issues, school structures, and policies guarantee the rights and interests of minoritized students. Furthermore, education for democracy and human rights requires the development of skills and attitudes in all students, both mainstream and minoritized, that equip them to defend democratic principles and to struggle for justice with those who encounter discrimination or exclusion. Solidarity is a key concept in education for human rights and democracy. As argued above, solidarity with people in distant places means little if we are not ready also to defend others' rights in our school, community, and nation.

This section explored the fragility of democracy[4] and the dangers of anti-democratic movements, focusing specifically on pan-European Islamophobic political movements and expressions of extremism and what they imply for education for human rights and democracy. The next section looks in more detail at the theory and practice of human rights education in Europe, focusing specifically on the Nordic region, where political rhetoric and official commitments to international human rights are strong.

HUMAN RIGHTS EDUCATION AND A HUMAN RIGHTS CULTURE

Scholars and HRE practitioners have observed that different models of human rights education prevail, according to the specific social, economic, and political climate (Bajaj, 2011; Flowers, 2004; Tarrow, 1993; Tibbitts, 2008; Yeban, 1995). Although different models of practice exist, the theoretical underpinnings of human rights education remain underdeveloped.

In order to explore some of the challenges of developing HRE theory and practice, I focus primarily on the Nordic region (Denmark, Finland, Iceland, Norway, and Sweden), focusing particularly on Norway, where I work. I have selected the Nordic region as these countries are often cited as exemplary human rights nations. They also—to differing degrees—rely on their human rights credentials in their foreign policy initiatives, engaging in international affairs by trading in an economy of human rights, asserting influence disproportionate to their size or military power.

Although the Nordic region is not presented as representative of the rest of Europe, it does share some common features with other western European nations.[5] Moreover, an analysis of challenges in implementing HRE in the Nordic region may have resonance and implications for other regions and nations in and beyond Europe, particularly those that are established democracies. The region raises questions about the challenges in implementing HRE in countries (in different geographical, social, economic, and political contexts) that have ostensibly strong human rights records.

I argue that critical examination and reflection are required to develop a theory and practice of human rights education, not just in postconflict contexts or in regions where democratic practices are not deeply rooted (see, e.g., Bernath, Holland & Martin, 2002; Reimers & Chung, 2010; Zembylas, 2011; as well as Chapter 6 of this book), but in nations that are proud of their human rights records. I contend that an examination of the tensions and ambiguities that exist between national values and ideals (normally promoted in citizenship education and discussed below), together with consideration of the challenges and complexity of implementing HRE in a prosperous and peaceful region, may support the development of human rights education theory.

The Nordic region is interesting since its population, long portrayed as homogeneous in its makeup, includes indigenous people (the Sami), as well as a number of national minorities (including, e.g., in Norway, the Forest Finns, Kvens, Jews, Roma, and Romani) and migrants. In a number of respects the region has experienced demographic change from the late 20th century onwards that mirrors that of a number of other western European nations.

In the case of Norway, before 1975 most nonwestern arrivals (from Turkey and Pakistan) were labor migrants, but in 1975 the government imposed a general ban on immigration (exempting those from the Nordic region), so that for nearly 30 years non-European Union (EU) migrants could only enter as either refugees or through family reunification.[6] This has meant that since 2004, with EU enlargement, Norway, like other western European countries, has seen significant migration from eastern and central Europe. Between 1995–2011 the number of first- and second-generation immigrants nearly tripled. Numbers have continued to grow, so that by January 2015 there were in total around 805,000 migrants and children born to migrant parents (Statistics Norway, 2015).[7] These are significant numbers in an overall population of 5 million (Eriksen, 2013).

The Nordic countries do not constitute a political entity, yet they have a number of commonalities related to culture, social structure, and history. Although the area is in fact linguistically diverse, the common linguistic heritage of Danish, Norwegian, and Swedish constitutes one key feature of Nordic identity. Importantly, the five countries cooperate politically through the Nordic Council of Ministers (*Norden*, an intergovernmental body); this includes cooperation in the field of education and research. The objective of cooperation in the region (also known as *Norden* in the Scandinavian languages) in the field of children and young people is to create good living conditions and improve children's and young people's opportunities for influence, based on shared fundamental values such as justice, equality, democracy, openness and commitment. Explicitly, within the framework of the Nordic Council, diversity and children's human rights are foundational principles:

> The right to good living conditions and influence should be promoted for all children and young people on equal terms, regardless of gender, ethnic, cultural or socio-economic background, age, domicile, sexual orientation and disability. *This work is based on a rights-based perspective* [emphasis added], and that means children and young people's human rights must be protected and promoted. Efforts directed towards children and adolescents under 18 years must be based on the UN Convention on the Rights of the Child. (Nordic Council of Ministers, 2010, p. 7, my translation)

Alongside a strong Nordic identity, which emphasizes the importance of human rights, are a series of national identities that also give prominence, in official discourse, to human rights. Public policies that support the nation-state, such as those relating to national language(s), national history, national myths, national symbols, national literature, even a national media and national military, and sometimes a national religion, are all in turn supported and reinforced, to a greater or lesser extent, through schooling. It might be expected that these processes of nation-building will be particularly effective in the Nordic countries, which have relatively small populations and where it may consequently be easier to promote and sustain a national myth of homogeneity and distinctiveness of culture. For example, in a discussion of contemporary debates about what constitutes Norwegianness, Vassenden (2010) highlights a national self-image of "a small and fragile nation" and processes by which aspects of peasant culture were reinterpreted and placed in an urban setting during the 19th century, following the dissolution of the Dano-Norwegian union in 1814 (p. 738). He notes how this narrative of national cohesion and cultural distinctiveness was strengthened as a result of German occupation during World War II.

Educators in different regions face specific social dynamics that may support or undermine teaching for human rights. In the Nordic region, as we have seen from the statement from the Nordic Council (Nordic Council of Ministers, 2010), human rights teaching takes place within societies where political and rhetorical commitments to human rights principles are strong.

Intuitively, we might expect such societies to present ideal contexts for human rights teaching and learning. Yet we encounter certain phenomena that may undermine effective HRE in (some) Nordic countries.

There is a tendency for democracy and human rights to be proudly presented as a central feature of a relatively homogenous national culture. National values and human rights values are proclaimed as one and the same thing. A commitment to democracy and human rights is part of what makes one Norwegian, or Danish, or Finnish, and so on. This may lead to a process of othering, whereby "we" as native-born Norwegians or Danes or Finns are seen not to need formal learning in human rights since it is part of our culture, but the "other" (the migrant, refugee, or other outsider) needs to be inducted into "our" human rights culture.

The Danish Institute for Human Rights (DIHR) explains that the preamble to the act on Danish primary and secondary schools states that:

> The school shall prepare the pupils for active participation, co-responsibility, rights and duties in a society based on freedom and democracy. The teaching of the school and its daily life must therefore build on intellectual freedom, equality and democracy. (quoted in Decara, 2013)

The DIHR concluded that although respect for human rights is central to all democratic societies, HRE in fact has a weak status in Danish schools. A study of Danish teachers, carried out on behalf of the Danish Union of Teachers and the DIHR in 2012, found that three-quarters disagreed with the statement: "in Denmark, human rights are so universal that it is not a topic I need to give special attention to in my teaching." In other words, the teachers in the study see the need for human rights education. Despite this, teachers reported that their own teaching of human rights was "indirect" or "implicit" and the subject only addressed spontaneously or as a dimension of another topic, often without the teacher mentioning "human rights" or "rights" (Decara, 2013, p. 44). The Danish Education Act confirms the importance of democratic participation, rights, and duties in education as the basis of democratic society, but this purpose is not translated into practical guidance on the teaching of human rights. The DIHR recommends that what is needed to guarantee a healthy democracy is a national action plan for human rights education that includes professional support for teachers.

A similar situation exists in Norway. In its commemoration of the centenary of women's suffrage the Government of Norway (2013) observes:

> Norway was the first independent country in the world to introduce universal suffrage for both men and women. It is true that there were three states that introduced universal right to vote even earlier—New Zealand in 1893, Australia in 1902, and Finland in 1906—but these countries were not independent and the women could not be elected to political positions.

In such a context, learning about human rights at home can appear ir-relevant. The message given is of an exemplary democratic nation that is well ahead of the game and ahead of other nations (despite what these other nations may claim). There is no concept of women's struggle for recognition. The official view is that the state "introduced" universal suffrage and women took advantage of this gift. The human rights project appears to have been realized.

The struggles of the indigenous Sami people—who have traditionally inhabited areas of Norway, Sweden, Finland, and Russia—to have their very humanity recognized are overlooked in this upbeat account of universal suf-frage in Norway. This struggle has been acutely felt in the area of education policy, since processes of Norwegianification (*fornorskning*), which operat-ed well into the 1970s, served to discriminate, denying and devaluing Sami language and culture (Eriksen, 2013; Lile, 2011). Thus homogeneity was constructed, with teachers and schools complicit in denying and devaluing Sami culture and language. Since 1989, the Sami struggle for recognition has resulted in the establishment of a Sami parliament in Norway[8] and guarantees of specific linguistic and cultural rights.

Today, the Norwegian core and subject curricula express a responsibility to preserve Sami language and culture: "This legacy must be nourished so that it can grow in schools with Sami pupils, in order to strengthen Sami identity as well as our common knowledge of Sami culture" (Norwegian Directorate for Education and Training, 2006). Nevertheless, research on young people's knowledge of Sami history suggests that the curriculum still fails to meet learners' entitlements under the U.N. Convention on the Rights of the Child, Article 29, addressing the aims of education. Specifically, Lile (2011) suggests that Norwegian schools are failing to meet the obligations of the state to Sami children, and to all children, in teaching about diversity. One notable gap in the curriculum is attention to and examination of the ways in which the Norwegian state and Norwegian people may have been complicit in processes of denial and discrimination against the Sami (Osler & Lybæk, 2014). The curriculum is framed so that responsibility for telling Sami history (and the ways in which this interacts with the history of the nation as a whole) is placed within the Sami community, rather than with the broader national community.

The mainstream story of the founding and commemoration of the Nor-wegian constitution, which marked its 200th jubilee in 2014, is likewise si-lent on subsequent struggles or amendments to incorporate minority and indigenous people's rights. That very same Constitution included a general ban on Jews and Jesuits entering the country, which was not lifted until 1851 as a result of a campaign in which Norwegian poet Henrik Wergeland and others were prominent. At this point Jews were accorded the same religious freedoms as Christians. The story of democracy in Norway today, as told on the official commemorative webpages known as "Eidsvoll 1814" (n.d.), is an institutional one presented from the perspective of parliament, in which the only highlighted problems relate to low voter turnout and low levels of support for political organizations. In fact, it was not until the late 1980s that Norway responded to Sami demands that it meet its international obligations for special cultural protection for minorities under Article 27 of the International Covenant on Civil and Political Rights (U.N., 1966a), which the country ratified in 1972. The governmental response was the 1987 Sami Act and a constitutional amendment the following year (Smith, 1995).

I am not claiming that Norway is unique in presenting an upbeat or partial national history, nor in its treatment of indigenous people. Tragically, indigenous peoples across the globe have experienced gross abuses of their rights and denial of their humanity. Barton and Levstik (2013) discuss historical narratives of individual achievement and motivation and "freedom and progress," which they stress "dominates historical representation in the United States" (p. xi). Such dominant narratives impact directly on the ways in which the U.S. civil rights movement is taught in schools. Consequently, it tends to be taught in an upbeat fashion and presented as a successful and complete project. Certainly, this was a message promoted and repeated around the world in 2013 for the commemoration of the 1963 March on Washington and the "I have a dream" speech of Martin Luther King Jr. (BBC, 2013). In this version of history there is no discussion of the deep economic and social divisions that persist in the United States today, or of the ways in which African Americans are disproportionally excluded from political participation due to laws and practices by which the criminal justice system targets young Black men, subjects them to harsher custodial penalties, and once they are labeled felons, imposes a lifetime ban on the right to vote, removing the very rights struggled for in the civil rights era (Alexander, 2012).

Returning to Norway, I do not suggest that this official representation of an ideal Norwegian democracy is accepted by all. Of course there are critical voices dissenting from the official narrative of an unflawed democracy (Eriksen, 2012; Gullestad, 2002) and writing critical and reflexive histories (Schwaller & Døving, 2010). My point is that, when the dominant story taught at school (in the United States, Norway, or anywhere else) portrays an uncritical, sanitized version of "we the nation," this poses a problem for HRE at home.

If sanitized versions of history are taught at school then the story of past struggles can be erased from the public memory, at least among mainstream students. It is left to minoritized communities to tell an alternative story. The possibility of HRE as a site of struggle, within the nation as well as internationally, is lost. HRE *may* encourage solidarity with oppressed people elsewhere when students learn about violations of rights (and possibly struggles for rights) in other nations. It is more likely to be the story of less fortunate people in distant places who lack the rights that we enjoy, resembling a missionary story from the colonial era. At best, this type of HRE may encourage commitment to others' struggles for justice. At worst, it may lead to feelings of moral superiority, as Vesterdal (2016) has observed, with learners failing to reflect critically on their own society's human rights record. A key question remains: What is the value in expressing concern for strangers in distant places if an individual is blind to others' experiences of injustice and their lack of rights within the same neighborhood, community, or nation?

Indeed, HRE may be used in schools not to promote social justice but to encourage conformity and obedience. It may be used as part of the modern civilizing mission of schools, replacing 19th-century missionary Christianity with 21st-century human rights to ensure conformity. Colonial education in 19th-century India was built on an assumption that Indians, as an inferior people, "had to be made similar and hence equal, by being civilized" (Mann, 2004, p. 5). The mission in the colonies was extended to working-class poor and indigenous children in Europe, so that the underlying purpose of schooling for working-class children in industrial cities such as Manchester, the schooling of farm laborers, or the schooling of indigenous children, was to pacify and civilize them and remove cultural preferences and traits (e.g., nomadic lifestyles) that would make them more difficult to manage or rule, or interfere with the rights of the dominant group who might want to farm or otherwise exploit ancestral lands. Such schooling was not designed to extend full and equal opportunities with the powerful and more privileged, but to make such populations effective workers or servants.

There is a risk that certain forms of human rights education, which ignore power relations, may not enable greater justice but be part of a 21st-century civilizing mission. This may be achieved through a variety of means. It may involve reinforcing the values of the powerful in the name of the nation or as "national values" ; disciplining groups of students whose values might be different from the mainstream; using human rights as a way of managing student behavior and achieving compliance; insisting on blind obedience to the law or school rules; and encouraging children (particularly working-class, indigenous, migrant, or colonized) to deny aspects of themselves, their cultures, and their languages, which distinguish them from the mainstream.

A further question relates to the relationship between human rights education and ongoing struggles for justice. If human rights education is to be effective, and linked to social change, then to what degree is it important that both teachers and learners consider and interrogate individual and community complicity (at the level of the school, the neighborhood or city, the nation and internationally) in sustaining inequity and injustice? In such cases, complicity may often mean doing nothing. Not speaking out and not acting reinforces current inequalities and injustices.

LEGAL AND POLICY FRAMEWORKS FOR
HUMAN RIGHTS EDUCATION

A sound legal framework is essential to enable a nation to meet its international commitments to human rights within education, but it is insufficient. The Danish Institute for Human Rights (DIHR) has called for an amendment to the Education Act on primary and lower secondary schools, so that "human rights" are explicitly addressed in the Education Act. DIHR notes that in both Sweden and Norway "human rights" are inscribed in the preamble to the respective national education acts, as they are in Finland in the goals for the decree on national objectives for basic education (primary and lower secondary) (Decara, 2013).

The DIHR-commissioned study revealed that both teachers and teacher educators believe they lack understanding of a theoretical basis for adapting HRE to school students at various ages (Decara, 2013). In the Norwegian Education Act, which applies to primary and secondary education and vocational training, human rights values underpin the curriculum, and democracy is both a *process* (relating, for example, to relationships between parents and school and to children's role in decisionmaking) and an educational *outcome* (Education Act, 1998). The act states:

> Education and training shall be based on fundamental values in Christian and humanist heritage and traditions, such as respect for human dignity and nature, on intellectual freedom, charity, forgiveness, equality and solidarity, values that also appear in different religions and beliefs *and are rooted in human rights* [emphasis added]. (Education Act, 1998, revised 2008, para. 1-1)

Human rights underpin the curriculum yet remain tied to specific traditions: Christian and humanist. The formulation "Christian and humanist values" is repeatedly used in the act, and although the curriculum objectives acknowledge other (unnamed) religions and beliefs, any learner who does not identify with either Christian or (Western) humanist traditions may feel excluded from the human rights "we" (Osler & Lybæk, 2014). A further difficulty is that there is, to my understanding, no proper conceptual distinction between human rights and democracy in the legal and policy frameworks of education.

In fact, this expression of curriculum objectives within the Norwegian Education Act is something of a compromise. The 2008 revision of the curriculum objectives (or "purpose clause," as it is known) aimed to respond to the concern for qualitative equality between Christianity and other religions and philosophies, following a legal challenge by groups of secular parents. Judgments were made against Norway in the U.N. Human Rights Committee (*Leirvåg and other v. Norway*) in 2004 (UNHRC, 2004) that the country's mandatory religious and ethics curriculum education was not delivered in a neutral and objective way.[9] The European Court of Human Rights (*Folgerø and others v. Norway*) likewise judged in 2007 that this curriculum was in contravention of Article 2 protocol 2 of the European Convention on Human Rights.[10] It would seem that HRE in Norway should not be justified solely by appeals to culture or tradition (Christian, humanist, or otherwise) or even by reference to the state's international commitments. Teachers and teacher educators, like those in Denmark, also need a theoretical basis, together with training and support, that will enable them to apply HRE to students at different stages of their school careers.

In Norway there is no named common core subject of human rights education or education for democratic citizenship. Human rights are one of the elements of the curriculum in the lower secondary school, but they form one among a number of topics to be addressed. Students in upper secondary school can opt to study human rights; generally, if there are sufficient numbers interested, the course will run. A further complexity in Norway is that prior to 2014, policymakers and political decisionmakers did not stress the need to strengthen HRE within the school curriculum,[11] since students appear to score well on international tests measuring democratic values (Mikkelsen, Fjeldstad, & Lauglo, 2011). In fact, they score well on abstract items relating to equal rights in principle, but their scores reflect a more skeptical attitude when considering the rights of minorities (Osler & Lybæk, 2014). Decara (2013), reporting on a 2012 study from Aarhus University, notes a similar response pattern in Denmark, with lower secondary students largely positive about equal rights in principle, but with boys, in particular, showing greater skepticism when questions relate to equal rights for minorities and to gender equality. In 2014 a clause in the revised Norwegian constitution establishes education underpinned by human rights as a constitutional right.

Nevertheless, it is left to individual school principals and to teachers themselves to apply human rights and democratic values in their day-to-day teaching and within their subject specialties. Students' learning about democracy and human rights is likely to depend on the focus of the school principal and on the individual teacher's strengths and interests. It is then difficult to determine whether students are in a position to claim their entitlement. Although students may learn about democracy, they are not necessarily guaranteed opportunities to apply their knowledge. Consequently, they may believe in abstract ideas, like equality, but may not necessarily argue for equal rights, such as freedom of religion, for those different from themselves. For example, more than 56% of 9th-grade students in a national study (sample size 3,300) failed to appreciate a racist dimension to a ban on building mosques in Norwegian cities (Mikkelsen et al., 2011, p. 15).

An important and perhaps connected concern is the use of the terms *race* and *racism* within a Scandinavian context, both within the academy and beyond. In the field of education research in Norway, with some notable exceptions (Brossard Børhaug, 2012; Svendsen, 2013), there appears to be a general silence around both terms. Bangstad (2015) argues that not only has Norway had a rather weak tradition of social science scholarship on racism, but there has been a "conscious effort by numerous Norwegian academics and public intellectuals to restrict its meaning," avoiding reference to both race and racism in recent decades (p. 49). On two separate occasions, in professional contexts within and beyond the academy, I have been discouraged from using each of these terms: *race* (*rase*) because "it's not a nice term in Norwegian," and *racism* because "if you say it in a lecture, people will stop listening." Raising this issue with a Swedish colleague at a conference on education and cosmopolitanism in Sweden, he effectively closed further discussion by advising these are not topics for polite conversation in Sweden either.

This Nordic reticence stands in contrast to a significant body of research on race and racism in education in North America, where scholarly activity across a range of disciplines, notably sociology, law, and women's studies (for example, Alexander, 2012; Crenshaw, 1989; Hill Collins, 1990; hooks, 1981), finds parallels in race and education (e.g., see Au, 2009; DiAngelo & Sensoy, 2010; Grant & Sleeter, 1986, 1988; Ladson-Billings, 1995). In Europe similar relationships exist between the wider field of race-related research (e.g., Hall, 2002; Parekh, 2000) and educational research (e.g., see Bhopal, 2004; Bryan, 2009; Gillborn & Mirza, 2000; Osler, 1997), yet scholars have observed, in the case of the United Kingdom, a declining policy focus on multicultural education (Figueroa, 2004; Tomlinson, 2009) since the mid-1980s, which has led to less attention to race and racism in education and fewer resources to race-related research in education.

To understand this near silence within educational research (and within teacher education) in Norway, it is important to reflect on historical developments and contemporary popular usage of these terms and concepts. Norway became an independent nation-state in 1905, after being the junior partner in a union with Sweden for just over 90 years. Before that, Norway was under the Danish crown for 400 years. The relationship with Denmark is commonly conceived as colonial in nature, but not the union with Sweden, during which Norway had its own constitution and parliament. Following independence in 1905, the new nation-state enjoyed just 35 years of freedom before the World War II Nazi German occupation of 1940–1945.

The four Nordic countries of Denmark, Finland, Norway, and Sweden all introduced eugenics and sterilization laws in the 1930s. Remarkably, some of those laws stayed on the statute books until the mid-1970s. From 1934, Norway's law came into effect with some 1,000 Norwegian women believed to have been sterilized in a project that appears to have linked the welfare state and sterilization in a ghastly endeavor of social engineering (Turda, 2007).

Eriksen (2013) notes that Norwegian resistance during the period of occupation was "mainly nationalist in character, and did not visibly engage with the issue of genocide against Jews and other minorities. Unlike in Germany, 'ethnic undercurrents which formed part of Norwegian nationalism before the war were not dealt with critically in the aftermath of the war and were allowed . . . to thrive' " (p. 4).

Today's silences around questions of racism are paralleled by silences relating to recent history, silences that, if broken, disturb the narrative of a human rights–focused and peace-loving Norwegian nation. If we recognize the social construction of race—and, in particular, the specific social-historical contexts in which racism operates—we need to find a way of analyzing its impact on social relations. If the word racism is reserved for expressions of hate speech or physical violence, but institutional or structural racism and processes of racialization remain hidden, racism itself goes unchallenged.

Gullestad (2004) argues that "anthropologists potentially have much to gain from the more explicit discussions of racialization (the categorization of people on the basis of characteristics assumed to be innate) and racism" in Norway (p. 117). I would echo her observation for the fields of education research, policy, and practice. If we lack a language in which to debate and analyze aspects of inequality and injustice, this hinders both our understanding and the development of effective strategies to overcome inequalities. Silences around race and racism, and a failure to study processes of racialization as part of the professional training of teachers, remain a key challenge to the human rights education project in Norway, as in many other contexts in Europe (and beyond). The process of creating such disturbances is vital in creating spaces where teachers and learners can consider individual and community complicity in inequities and injustice, so permitting action for change.

As we have seen, even in contexts where democratic practices are deeply rooted, tensions between national values and ideals on the one hand, and ways in which the curriculum is constructed to include or exclude minority groups on the other, may serve to undermine effective HRE. In particular, the history curriculum and the ways in which the nation is shaped through history education (Osler, 2009, 2016), may impact negatively on HRE practices.

Chapter 6 will examine teaching for justice and human rights in the contrasting context of postconflict societies, drawing on research in the region of Iraqi Kurdistan that focuses on teachers' understandings of their professional roles and the potential for education to enable greater social justice. It will consider what human rights educators in established democracies might learn from postconflict societies.

CHAPTER 6

Human Rights, Peace, and Conflict

Since the early 1990s my work has taken me to a number of conflict-ridden regions and to places where people are working to address past conflicts and violence that continue to impact on their everyday realities. In these situations, whether I have been engaged in research, teaching, or other kinds of projects, I have entered into dialogue with policymakers, government ministers, university colleagues, teachers, education administrators, community activists, students, business people, and international aid workers. It has repeatedly struck me how policymakers, researchers, and educators in relatively peaceful societies might learn from their experiences and be informed by their insights into strengthening human rights through education.

The utopian vision of the Universal Declaration of Human Rights of "the inherent dignity and of the equal and inalienable rights of all members of the human family . . . [as] the foundation of freedom, justice and peace in the world" (U.N., 1948, preamble) is often far removed both from people's everyday realities and from media images they receive from faraway places. The human rights project is cosmopolitan, expressing human solidarity across nations, yet studying the situation in some regions can feel oppressive and be potentially disempowering to learners.

As discussed in Chapter 1, when teachers focus exclusively on human rights abuses in distant places, this may prove to be inadequate preparation for living in an interdependent world, since it is likely to mask other human rights challenges closer to home. At worst, it may actually foster a sense of superiority and indifference to the rights of the "other," who is portrayed in a dehumanizing way. A sense of indifference may indirectly support continued hostility, war, and violence. In this chapter, I present the voices of educators from one conflict-ridden region, that of Kurdistan–Iraq, to highlight a more complex and nuanced picture of their struggles for justice, peace, democracy, and human rights. I suggest that recognition of complexity, as well as exploration of our common challenges, is more likely to engender a sense of solidarity.

In December 2010 the world witnessed the beginning of a wave of demonstrations and popular uprisings across the Arab world. One common feature of these uprisings was civil resistance. A key slogan across the region was *"al-shab yurid isqat al nizam"* (the people want to bring down the regime). Despite popular demands for greater democracy, the region remains conflict-ridden. At the time of writing, the war in Syria continues to rage, with considerable impacts beyond its borders, in the region and further afield. Significant numbers of refugees and displaced people are seeking asylum in neighboring countries and beyond. My focus is not to analyze the complex causes of conflict, but to draw on the experiences of educators in the neighboring jurisdiction of Kurdistan–Iraq to consider the type of education needed to build and sustain democratic practices, in the expectation that their understandings might enable future generations to benefit from recent and ongoing struggles for justice and peace.

The research took place from 2011 to 2014 and draws on the perspectives of teachers and education administrators working under the Kurdish Regional Government (KRG). Before focusing on this case, which engages with the dissonance between declared commitments to human rights, justice, and peace and some of the everyday practices of schools, I address some key human rights concepts and some theoretical possibilities of "education for cosmopolitan citizenship" (Osler & Starkey, 2003, 2005).

COSMOPOLITANISM AND CITIZENSHIP

The human rights project is cosmopolitan, since it requires human subjects to acknowledge, and where appropriate to defend, the dignity and rights of fellow human beings across the globe, who are characterized as members of the same "human family." The key principles underpinning the UDHR are expressed diagrammatically in Figure 6.1, showing the relationship between the central goal of justice and peace in the world and other key human rights concepts. Figure 6.1 illustrates that the realization of justice and peace lies at the heart of the human rights project. Around the outside of the diagram are the four concepts of solidarity, universality, reciprocity, and indivisibility, which frame the project. Within the human rights framework are other concepts, which are principles for human rights practice. These principles permit dialogue across difference: dignity, equality, security, democracy, participation, and freedoms.

Solidarity

Rights demand human solidarity, as examples provided in earlier chapters of this book have sought to illustrate. Individuals need to recognize and defend the rights of strangers, including people with different cultures and belief systems. As explored in Chapter 5, solidarity needs to extend beyond the borders of the nation-state. Solidarity also applies among nation-states: Of the

Figure 6.1. Key Concepts in the Universal Declaration of Human Rights (1948)

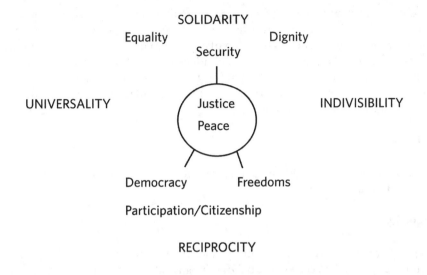

Source. Teachers and Human Rights Education, A. Osler & H. Starkey, 2010, Stoke-on-Trent, United Kingdom: Trentham.

193 members of the United Nations, two-thirds are classified as developing nations, likely to need the support of others in their efforts to guarantee the rights of inhabitants, notably their socioeconomic rights.

Universality

Rights are the entitlements of all human beings, without exception. The concept of universality is central to human rights; rights belong to all members of the human family, regardless of their citizenship or other aspects of identity. Universality of rights implies the principle of nondiscrimination, with steps taken both to remove barriers to rights and to put in place legal frameworks to protect vulnerable groups.

Reciprocity

My rights cannot be secured unless you are prepared to defend them, and vice versa. Inherent in the concept of human rights is the notion of responsibility. All have a responsibility to protect the rights of others. Nevertheless, an individual's rights are not dependent on their behavior.

Indivisibility

Rights are indivisible; they come as a package, they are not offered as a menu, from which individuals or governments can select. This is not to deny tensions between rights, such as freedom of expression on the one hand, and the right to a fair and public hearing by an independent tribunal, in the case of a criminal charge, on the other. This means the freedom of the press is not limitless, and newspapers do not have the right, for example, to publish material that might prejudice a fair trial.

Dignity

The concept of human dignity is foundational and is the basis of human respect and human interaction.

Equality

Equality refers to equality of dignity, and includes the principle of nondiscrimination. All are accorded equal dignity and all have equal entitlement to rights.

Security

Security, both physical and psychological, is essential for guaranteeing rights, at all scales, from the personal to the global. Violence in its different forms—whether interpersonal violence between students in school, expressed in bullying or racist or homophobic insults, or within or between nations, such as interethnic conflict, aggression, and war—effectively serves to undermine the human rights project of peace and justice in the world.

Democracy and Participation

Human rights and peace can only be fully realized when individuals have an opportunity to participate in decision making, and this implies democratic practices at all levels. This involves a readiness to critique and challenge a democratically elected government when it fails to observe human rights standards. At the Deng Liberty Foundation's human rights education award ceremony for teachers in Taiwan, board member Ronald Tsao said that when people are aware of human rights issues, "they will know what to do when a democratically elected government goes astray." Fellow board member Lee Min-yung observed: "A lot of controversial political issues occur in Taiwan because people do not learn enough about protection of human rights at school" (Loa, 2010). Both recognize that knowledge about human rights is essential. A democratic governmental system does not automatically guarantee the realization of human rights, but it does enable a process of accountability. This accountability depends on a citizenry educated in human rights. Authoritarian regimes, by contrast, do not expect to be held accountable by citizens. Nevertheless, citizens may challenge this and seek solidarity from others in the wider global community.

Freedoms

These freedoms are freedom of expression, freedom of religion and belief, freedom from want, and freedom from fear. They are all essential features of democratic participation; while the first two protect political and cultural expression, recognized features of democratic life and critical to the protection of minorities, the latter two are prerequisites—no one can participate fully if they are hungry or homeless, or if their safety is not guaranteed.

It is insufficient for young people merely to be educated about human rights and democracy; they also need the opportunity to practice democratic participation skills. Both human rights and democracy are strengthened in school contexts where young people have access to knowledge about human rights and child rights and where students feel they have genuine opportunities to participate and to advocate for justice and equity (Carter & Osler, 2000; Osler, 2010b). Advocacy may involve critique of government policy, even in apparently exemplary human rights states.

In our globalized world our lives are interconnected with those of strangers in distant places. Our actions and behaviors, and the decisions of the government we elect will have an impact, not only on our own lives but also on theirs. Our local communities are increasingly diverse, and we live alongside people with many different belief systems. Cosmopolitanism requires us to engage with difference, rather than create the illusion that it is possible to live parallel lives. Appiah (2006) characterizes this day-to-day process of living together with people holding different values and beliefs as a pragmatic one: "We can live together without agreeing on what the values are that make it good to live together; we can agree about what to do in most cases, without agreeing about why it is right" (p. 71). Human rights provide us with some broad principles within which we can work and engage with each other, and which we can apply in efforts to resolve problems when we cannot easily agree on what to do.

Citizenship education is most commonly perceived in terms of preparing young people for the rights and responsibilities of adult citizenship of the nation-state. There are a number of difficulties with this, not least that it fails to fully recognize young people as rights-holders and as citizens in the present, rather than citizens-in-waiting (Verhellen, 2000). Another difficulty lies in the fact that in a global age, with complex migration patterns and naturalization processes, not all learners will be nationals of the nation-state in which they are schooled, or necessarily aspire to national citizenship. To teach exclusively for national citizenship, focusing on the rights and duties of nationals, may be counterproductive, if the intention is to promote cohesive communities, for such students will quickly feel excluded. Further, much of what is promoted as education for national citizenship encourages learners to identify first and foremost, and often uncritically, with the nation-state. It assumes that the democratic project is complete, rather than acknowledging formal and informal barriers to full participation on the basis of gender, ethnicity, or other aspects of identity. A framework that acknowledges such barriers allows for the possibility of challenging injustice and for creating spaces where various individuals and groups (including those outside of the mainstream) can contribute to the development of a more inclusive society.

Education for national citizenship that demands blind allegiance or love of country can also be counterproductive. It demands an unquestioning loyalty, rather than critical patriotism, which would involve efforts to achieve a more just society and inclusive democracy. It is important to reflect on patriotism, given the concerns of many political leaders to emphasize the role of education in developing a sense of national belonging. As we have seen in Chapter 3, patriotism within a pluralist society can be conceived of as a *commitment to a political community* and a readiness not to undermine its integrity (Parekh, 2000). It does not demand, neither does it rule out, intense affective ties. The role of schools in fostering political commitment is complex. Any attempt to foster emotional attachment in learners is not a one-sided process in which the student (or teacher) is passively accepting a feeling of concern for the nation. Each individual is negotiating and interpreting the curriculum. Even quite young students are able to understand the notion of critical patriotism, whereby an individual cares enough about the country to criticize what is wrong (Osler, 2010b). Nevertheless, the impetus for citizenship education that encourages affective ties to the nation is likely to be somewhat different in emphasis among people in established nation-states and among people, like the Kurds, who aspire to a national homeland fully recognized by the community of nations.

Education for cosmopolitan citizenship (Osler & Vincent, 2002; Osler & Starkey, 2003, 2005) is based on shared human rights and permits learners to reflect on and practice citizenship at local and community scales, as well as at the national, regional, and global scales. It is inclusive, rather than exclusive: While not all learners may be national citizens, all are holders of human rights. So, for example, across Europe, all individuals living within any nation-state can seek redress under the European Convention on Human Rights if they believe their rights have been infringed, whether or not they are citizens of the country in which they are living. Although governments have a responsibility for protecting human rights, human rights are not dependent in this respect on holding national citizenship.

HUMAN RIGHTS, PEACE, AND LEARNING TO LIVE TOGETHER

As I have shown, the UDHR is a moral commitment by the world's governments to uphold and promote human rights and peace. This commitment has been reaffirmed and reinforced through many subsequent agreements including the U.N. Conference on Environment and Development (the Earth Summit), Rio de Janeiro, 1992; the World Conference on Human Rights, resulting in the Vienna Declaration and Programme of Action, Vienna, 1993; the World Summit for Social Development, Copenhagen, 1995; and the Habitat II conference in Istanbul, 1996. Effectively, the international community recognizes the interrelationship between human rights, peace, and development in deliberating a range of issues relating to social and economic development and the environment.

Human rights can be understood as principles for living together, and are effective for establishing minimum standards for living together with a range of communities, including the community of the school. The UDHR and subsequent human rights instruments can be read both as inspirational or utopian rhetoric and as realistic principles for challenging oppressive laws or state practices, in other words, as an agenda for action.

This chapter has focused so far on the potential of human rights as principles for promoting justice and peace in the world through the processes of schooling. Teachers, equipped with knowledge and understanding of human rights, have the potential to transform citizenship curricula. Significantly, such teachers are also well positioned to take steps toward realizing a broader utopian vision of justice and peace in the world. I turn now to the case of Kurdistan–Iraq, which has been a conflict-ridden area for many decades. Human rights education is frequently introduced in postconflict societies, often with the support of international organizations, with the expectation that it will support a transition to peace and democracy.

EDUCATION REFORM AND CONFLICT IN IRAQI KURDISTAN

The 2005 Constitution of Iraq established Iraqi Kurdistan as a federal entity under the unified Kurdistan Regional Government (KRG) administration. The official name of this area of Iraq is the Kurdistan Region, and I will generally refer to it here simply as Kurdistan.[1] In 2009 the KRG, which had focused on developing Kurdistan's economy and infrastructure, turned its attention to educational reform. The reform extended the number of years of compulsory education from 6 to 9, introduced new learning objectives, and placed greater emphasis on human rights and democratic citizenship, making a specific commitment to gender equity.

Education policy is a dynamic process in which teachers, administrators, and students are actors. These various actors can support, subvert, or undermine the original goals of policymakers, both unintentionally and de-liberately. The program of research I report on therefore extends to an ex-amination of the perspectives of teachers, school administrators, and school inspectors. Here the focus is on educators' perspectives and on their under-standings of democracy, development, and human rights, specifically human rights education and gender equity. These perspectives are critical to an un-derstanding of the impact of reform, particularly its impact on young people, schools, families, and communities. If the KRG is to be effective in enabling democracy, development, and equity through education, professionals' expe-riences, needs, and understandings need to be taken seriously. Their insights may support the identification of appropriate strategies to strengthen demo-cratic dispositions among the young. And it is my contention that they may also inform thinking about education for democracy and human rights in long-standing democracies.

Iraqi Kurdistan experienced considerable conflict and instability in the latter 20th century and early years of the 21st, resulting in a severely dam-aged infrastructure. The conflicts included a long history of border disputes with Iran, the Iran–Iraq war (1980–1988), and the Anfal genocidal cam-paign against the Kurds (1986–1989) led by the Iraqi military under Saddam Hussein. The year 1991 saw the Gulf War, followed by the Kurdish uprising, resulting in mass displacement and a subsequent humanitarian crisis. The uprising was followed by a brutal crackdown on the Kurdish population, the later withdrawal of the Iraqi administration and military, and an Iraqi internal economic blockade. Between 1990 and 2003 the region also suffered the consequences of U.N. sanctions and an international embargo against Iraq (McDowall, 2003; Yildiz, 2004).

From 1991, the region gained ad hoc autonomy (Stansfield, 2003), and in 1992 a regional government was established, following a closely contested and inconclusive general election. But rivalry between the Kurdistan Demo-cratic Party (KDP) and the Patriotic Union of Kurdistan (PUK) resulted in a de facto partition of the region (McDowall, 2003). By 1994, power-sharing agreements between the parties had broken down, leading to civil war, referred to in Kurdish as "brother killing brother" (*brakuzhi*). Open conflict between the KDP and the PUK was brought to an end under the 1998 Washington Agreement. Nevertheless, the civil war and conflict between the two dominant parties have shaped contemporary Iraqi-Kurdish politics (Stansfield, 2003).

Following the 2003 invasion of Iraq and subsequent political changes, the 2005 Constitution of Iraq defines the internal political, socioeconom-ic, and judicial autonomous governance of Kurdistan. The KRG's federal region, comprising three governorates—Erbil, Sulaimaniyah, and Duhok—borders Iran to the east, Turkey to the north, Syria to the west, and the rest of Iraq to the south. Erbil is the region's capital city. The region continues to feel the impact of instability in neighboring jurisdictions as well as ongoing tensions with the Baghdad government, fueled by concerns over disputed areas, including Kirkuk. An opposition movement called *Gorran* (Change) challenges the power-sharing arrangements, placing substantive democracy on the political agenda.

It is within this complex postconflict context that education reforms are being implemented. In the immediate preconflict era, Iraq had a leading regional position in school enrollment and completion rates (UNESCO, 2011). But Iraqi Kurdistan's educational infrastructure was adversely affected by the conflicts. Some 20 years after the civil war, there remains considerable pressure on the system, with insufficient school buildings and continuing and notable disparities in basic facilities between urban and rural areas. There remain considerable challenges in providing appropriate facilities for students in a fast-changing socioeconomic and political context.

The challenge facing policymakers is not only to make good the damaged educational infrastructure and ensure that schools are staffed with effectively trained teachers; it is also to ensure appropriate educational measures to support other societal priorities, such as anticorruption measures and guarantees for the rights of women and minorities. Education needs not only to prepare young people for successful economic integration but also to play an active role in shaping society in accordance with democratic ideals that embody equity and social justice. In other words, the education system, and schools in particular, have a central role to play in strengthening democratic development and human rights.

The conflict had a disproportionate impact on women and children and on their educational opportunities. Before the conflict, girls across Iraq already had lower school enrollment and attendance rates than boys (UNESCO, 2003). Following the conflict, the majority of internally displaced persons were women and children, with some 50% of the most vulnerable children unable to access schooling (UN-Habitat, 2001; United Nations Development Group/World Bank, 2003). In this respect, Iraq, including the autonomous region of Kurdistan, reflects a wider regional and global picture of discrimination and disadvantage faced by women and girls. Security problems may place girls at a greater risk of gender-based violence (Harber, 2004) in traveling to school, further impacting on school attendance.

In 2000 the world's nations made a promise to free people from extreme poverty and multiple deprivations. This pledge was formulated into eight Millennium Development Goals (MDGs). Two goals specifically addressed gender equity in education, recognizing that challenges remain at different points throughout the system. MDG 2 was to promote universal primary education and MDG 3 was to promote gender equality and empower women (U.N., 2015). Girls from the poorest households face the highest barriers to education, with subsequent impacts on their ability to access the labor market.

Effectively, education is recognized as a prerequisite for sustainable human development (Matsuura, 2004; UNESCO, 2015). These initiatives are concerned with enacting international human rights standards on gender equality, including the Convention on the Elimination of all Forms of Discrimination against Women (CEDAW; U.N., 1979, art. 10) and the Convention on the Rights of the Child (CRC) (U.N., 1989, arts. 2, 28).

The MDGs sought to realize both gender parity in education through *formal equality* (parity in access and participation rates) and *substantive equality* (equal opportunity *in* and *through* education) (Subrahmanian, 2005). In Kurdistan, some steps have been taken to guarantee formal equality in access and participation rates. Since 2006, the KRG has put arrangements in place to enable students who were not enrolled at the standard age, or who had their education disrupted, to continue or restart schooling through accelerated learning programs. The reform states: "Students should not be younger than 9 for boys starting at grade 1 and not older than 20 whilst the girls should not be younger than 9 starting at grade 1 and not older than 24" (KRG, 2009, 13, art. 15). It recognizes the traditional disadvantage that girls experience (Griffiths, 2010; UNICEF, 2010; UNESCO, 2011) and thus creates some flexibility by extending the age range within which women can complete schooling.

This chapter focusses on the contribution that HRE might play in realizing *substantive equality*, in and through education, by examining professionals' understandings of human rights and HRE. The right *to* education is insufficient in realizing gender equality since this is concerned largely with equivalence in enrollment and completion rates between girls and boys. By focusing on rights *in* education (guaranteeing achievement and learning outcomes) and rights *through* education (the ability to utilize knowledge and skills to claim rights within and beyond the school) it is possible to focus on girls' empowerment (Wilson, 2003) and greater equity in school and, potentially, in the wider society. This means recognizing and overcoming inequalities and instances of discrimination via an examination of learning content, teaching methods, assessment modes, management of peer relationships, and learning outcomes (Chan & Cheung, 2007). The realization of substantive equality requires attention to the ways in which both girls and boys are educated.

DIVERSITY AND GENDER IN IRAQI KURDISTAN

It is widely recognized that schools both produce and reflect broader social norms and inequalities, related, for example, to poverty, structural inequalities, historical disadvantage, institutional discrimination of women and minorities, gender-based violence, and traditional practices that harm or impact unjustly on women and girls (Tomaševski, 2005). What follows is an outline of Kurdistan–Iraq's demographic features. Struggles for rights take place within a multicultural setting and within communities characterized by gender inequalities and growing economic disparities.

One challenge is the successful accommodation of diversity. Although Kurds form the majority population, the region is characterized by long-standing religious, ethnic, and linguistic diversity. The Kurdish majority has lived for many centuries alongside smaller numbers of Assyrians, Chaldeans, Turkmenians, Armenians, and Arabs. According to the KRG, the region has a population of around 5 million, of whom more than 50% are younger than 20. There has been no census, so it is not clear what proportion of the KRG-administered population considers themselves Kurdish. Estimates suggest Iraqi Kurds may comprise as much as 25% of the total Iraqi population (Yildiz, 2004).

There is also considerable religious and linguistic diversity in Kurdistan. The majority of inhabitants, including Kurds, Iraqi Turkmenians, and Arabs, are from the Sunni Muslim tradition. Within this grouping, there is further diversity with some individuals being observant and others adopting more secular positions. The region also has populations of Assyrian Christian, Shiite Muslim, Yezidi, Yarsan, Mandean, and Sahbak faiths (Begikhani, Gill, & Hague, 2010). Official KRG languages are Kurdish[2] and Arabic.

Diversity is highly politicized since territorial disputes between the federal Baghdad and Erbil regional governments, including Kirkuk, require political solutions that guarantee the protection of minority rights and interests. This diversity demands pragmatic solutions in the public sphere, including schools, where learners' rights and societal outcomes may be weighed against each other. For example, a choice to guarantee linguistic rights through separate schooling for specific language communities impacts on the ways in which young people are prepared (or not) for living together.

The region's diversity has also increased as a consequence of inward migration, with the protection of migrant rights adding to the complexity of the picture. At the time of the research reported in this chapter Kurdistan–Iraq's rapid economic development was attracting labor migrants from around the globe and irregular migrants (including victims of trafficking), whose undocumented status leaves them vulnerable (International Organization for Migration [IOM], 2010a). Many were new populations drawn to Kurdistan because of instability elsewhere in Iraq, while others were former inhabitants who had fled from past conflicts. They include internally displaced persons (IDPs) drawn from other parts of Iraq, refugees and migrants from neighboring countries, and returnees, including highly educated elites, from the wider diaspora. In 2012, at the point of our research, the KRG appealed to the International Organization for Migration (IOM) for more help in dealing with the needs of refugees fleeing war in Syria.[3] While some Syrian refugees are accommodated in camps, others are spread across the region, supported by families and communities (IOM, 2012). Midway through 2015, the United Nations High Commissioner for Refugees (UNHCR) reported nearly 252,000 registered Syrian refugees (over 89,000 households) in camps in the KRG (UNHCR, 2015).[4] At about the same time the U.N. Humanitarian Coordinator for Iraq reported to the European Parliament that across the whole of Iraq, over 8 million people required life-saving assistance as a result of the violence between government forces and the Islamic State in Iraq and the Levant (ISIL) (U.N. Iraq, 2015). Child refugees outside the camps may lack appropriate papers to access schooling.

Gender equity is a key issue in Iraqi Kurdistan, where society is characterized both by patriarchy and postconflict dislocation (al-Ali & Pratt, 2011). Three interrelated challenges to realizing gender equity and the human rights of women and girls are: violence against women; traditional inheritance laws (Sharia law and traditional inheritance practices across faith communities that favor men); and low rates of school attendance among girls (Ahmad, Lybaek, Mohammed, & Osler, 2012).

Some efforts have been made to tackle gender-based violence, by both local women's organizations and international NGOs, resulting in the establishment of women's shelters to support victims of domestic violence (Begikhani et al., 2010). There has also been some discussion in local media of a societal failure to support such women who, although protected by law, remain vulnerable.[5] (Ahmad et al., 2012)

Under Islamic (Sharia) inheritance law, women are entitled to one-third, while their brothers receive two-thirds. Nevertheless, it is often difficult for women to claim their inheritance, even when courts rule in their favor, since traditionally, married women are expected to receive support from their husbands. Consequently, many families, particularly in rural areas, consider it shameful to allow daughters to inherit property. Effectively, women and girls rarely receive the unbalanced division of property provided for under Sharia law.

At the time of the research, female school attendance was rising, with the Duhok governorate recording one of the highest levels of attendance and lowest differentials between boys and girls, both in Kurdistan and across Iraq (Griffiths, 2010; UNICEF, 2010). Local women's rights NGO Harikar (2011) reports that rural parents are more prepared to send their daughters to school where there is a woman teacher and quotes an education supervisor as confirming that in Duhok governorate the number of female teachers now exceeds the number of males (Ahmad et al., 2012).

In Kurdistan, where deeply rooted inequalities persist between children, it is critical that the type of human rights education offered at school is appropriate to their needs and supports them in claiming their rights. Acknowledging and addressing the roots of inequalities within and beyond school is essential, whether they arise from gender-based discrimination or from discrimination based on ethnicity, religion, or other differences. Thus equalities in education require more than merely translating international instruments into national policies or implementing educational reforms.

They imply a holistic approach that includes policies and practices inside schools to empower students. In addition, they imply opportunities to transform knowledge into the application of rights both in and beyond the school (Stromquist, 2006). Such a holistic approach to quality education requires a sincere commitment and active engagement from both policy-makers and civil society (Wilson, 2003).

METHODS AND FIELDWORK

Educators' perspectives on the potential of HRE to contribute to social justice, democracy, and development in Iraqi Kurdistan were gathered during fieldwork visits to two Kurdistan Region governorates—Erbil and Duhok—between 2010 and 2012, and a third visit to assess refugee needs in 2014. In Duhok I was part of a research team that observed classes and later conducted interviews with teachers whose classes we observed.[6] In Erbil, graduate student Chalank Yahya interviewed a range of education professionals, including teachers, a school principal, and education inspectors. What is reported here draws on our collaborative work (Osler & Yahya, 2013).[7]

In total, 15 educators (7 female and 8 male) agreed to act as research respondents. The fieldwork is informed by a study of documentary sources, notably the reform of the basic and secondary schools (KRG, 2009) and the human rights text books (Rauof, 2007), of which translations were made. All interviews were conducted by a researcher familiar with local cultural norms and practices. Interviews were conducted in either Arabic or Kurdish, transcribed, and then translated into English. The Duhok teachers were working in two schools as part of a 2-year study (Ahmad et al., 2012). The Erbil respondents were a convenience sample, identified through personal contacts and snowballing. A number of common themes became apparent across the two geographical locations.

EDUCATORS' PERSPECTIVES

Educators discussed their understandings of HRE and, specifically, their observations on diversity and gender equality. Since teaching was taking place within the context of education reform, respondents also reflected on this, with some respondents focusing on pressing social issues, and others on teaching strategies and the relationship between student-centered teaching and education for human rights, citizenship, and democracy. All names are pseudonyms.

UNDERSTANDINGS OF HUMAN RIGHTS EDUCATION

Some educators linked the need for HRE to the Kurdish struggle for political recognition. They focused on the need for children to know Kurdish history and to understand the fragility of society when the rights of minorities are overlooked:

> Of course, human rights and HRE are very important to know about and be aware of. Especially in our society and due to past experiences of conflicts and violations, we need to be educated about our rights. . . . Each of us needs rights and also to understand our rights and how to claim them. However, HRE as a subject in our education system does not have as much emphasis as it should. We lack expertise in this discipline and we do not have specialized teachers. . . . For the time being, social studies teachers are required to teach this subject. (Payman, school inspector)

Thus, despite the emphasis on HRE in the 2009 curriculum reform, the subject lacked specially trained teachers. Respondents confirmed our impression that textbooks (particularly for older students) are dry and uninteresting, containing long extracts from international instruments, such as the UDHR, but with little guidance on how they might be made accessible or relevant to students. They identified an emphasis on knowledge, rather than values:

> The content is very dry and very limited. It would have been better if HRE was not simply regarded as just another curriculum subject, examined to test students' knowledge. (Ahlam, high school teacher)

> This subject should be designed and taught in all grades, according to the students' age and needs. For example, as a child in grades 1–6, you have specific rights/needs that need to be provided by school and society. If they don't learn about human rights and entitlements at a specific age, then they will not understand or be aware they have these rights. . . . It's important for them to be . . . able to demand them. (Kawthar, school inspector)

Generally speaking, educators placed considerable emphasis on the place of human rights in creating a just and sustainable society. They stressed the importance of human rights but expressed concerns both about a general understanding of human rights in contemporary Kurdish society and about their own and other teachers' lack of appropriate training:

> When it comes to the subjects of human rights education and democracy, I do not have very close knowledge of them. Only that my daughter

has taken these subjects and, from my perspective, it's important to teach these subjects to school students. (Kamaran, school inspector)

In general, not only in Kurdistan, but across the Middle East, we're not aware of our rights. We don't really understand what is meant by human rights. So a good awareness campaign is needed. (Kawthar, school inspector)

I don't think the subject [HRE] is given the attention and development it deserves. . . . It should be included in all grades . . . as it's very important for our teachers and students to behave according to human rights standards. . . . Most importantly, it's insufficient to learn about human rights as a paper exercise, there should be genuine opportunities to practice them. (Asem, Arabic teacher)

Despite the fact that Kamaran was a school inspector, responsible for nine schools, he admitted he knew relatively little about HRE and citizenship as taught in those schools, although he considered these areas to be important. This viewpoint is echoed by others, who criticize the minimal coverage of human rights in the curriculum and stress the limited societal knowledge of the field. There was a general impression that while human rights are important they were poorly understood.

A number of respondents suggested that for HRE to be relevant, both children and adults need to be in a position to *claim* their rights. Among several respondents, there is an implied criticism of the Kurdish administration for not fully securing the rights of citizens and enabling them to practice these rights.

Children learn about authority, but the obligations of authority figures (parents, teachers, government officials) to uphold children's rights were not addressed, perhaps reflecting government's resistance to criticism. Kawthar observed:

It is not enough just to teach our children about rights in books; as individuals, we also need to be able to practice these rights outside schools. However, in reality, there are many rights that we know of and yet cannot claim. It would be better that these subjects are taken up to the political level and enacted through laws. (Kawthar, school inspector)

In some institutions HRE was so low-status that schools might adopt corrupt practices to hide the fact they were neglecting the subject.

Some HRE teachers . . . make the lesson available for other subjects, such as English or mathematics. . . . In such cases, HRE topics will be limited to a few classes before the exams and all students will be graded as if they have mastered their rights very well! (Fawzi, high school teacher)

PRACTICING HUMAN RIGHTS EDUCATION

In order to bring the subject alive, a number of respondents suggested more active learning methods, including group work, the use of stories, and the involvement of NGOs:

> [With active methods] the student will understand the topic and s/he will never forget it because s/he takes part in explaining, presenting and discussing. (Tara, primary school treacher)

> When I use role play, the student takes over the role of the teacher and explains the topic. This makes them feel responsible and will improve performance. (Loreen, primary school teacher)

Foad, who worked as a school principal and school inspector, observed how some teachers feel HRE should not be examined because a student should not fail in something as fundamental as human rights.[8] He strongly opposed this argument, pointing out the importance of the subject content and the recognition that testing gives.

TEACHING RIGHTS WHERE RIGHTS ARE DENIED

One specific challenge raised by educators was that of teaching rights in contexts in which rights are denied, both in society and in school. Efforts to reform the education system have occurred rapidly, and in many places school building programs and the provision of basic facilities have not kept pace with demand.

> Right now, the [education reform] process is being implemented with many shortages, which has caused chaos and confusion among professionals, students, and their families. . . . You hear now of the current student demonstrations that are going on in various towns/regions in Kurdistan. This is because of lack of understanding and [failings in] the system. . . . Consequently, we have been witnessing school children demonstrating on the streets for some years. (Payman, school inspector)

One school principal spoke of being instructed by his superiors to drop an investigation into a teacher's professional behavior, and to turn a blind eye to equality and justice. Turning a blind eye feeds into an everyday culture of corruption (what our colleagues in the region termed *wasta*[9] in Arabic):

> Human rights norms should apply to staff as well as students. Very often, you are forced to drop taking it to the next level because someone on a higher level instructs you to do so. This contradicts genuine implementation of human rights rules and equality. (Sarkawt, acting principal, rural school)

Equally, professionals felt it important that HRE was not restricted to children but extended into communities. One suggested that HRE has been introduced merely to conform to international standards, rather than with commitment and clearly articulated social justice aims:

> I don't think HRE fits with our reality. Our society is still based on a tribal/agricultural system, which is not ready to digest the message behind human rights norms. . . . I think it has more of a political benefit than a genuine social one. It's more to show to the West that we adhere to human rights norms and have included that in our schooling, without first focusing and addressing real societal problems and injustices. (Sawsan, social studies teacher)

> In order to make HRE content more meaningful, we need to add more practical activities. For instance, bring pupils to universities, visit different NGOs, and show documentary films . . . and stories about human rights. . . . It's important to make a link between HRE and the existence of [human rights] organizations so students are aware of the need to address human rights issues in our region. (Fawzi, high school teacher)

> HRE teachers need to be continuously trained. . . . It would be good to have HRE professionals from local universities and even abroad to provide teacher training. (Azad, school inspector)

While the examples discussed above relate largely to broader societal denials of rights, another challenge was responding to children who have personal experience of human rights violations. The example below illustrates how making HRE relevant to children's everyday lives may empower teachers to address sensitive questions of child abuse. It also illustrates how giving the child the right of expression in class (participation rights) may serve to guarantee children's protection rights:

> Sometimes, students give examples of human rights violations they themselves are . . . experiencing at home, such as parents beating them

or verbally undermining their personality. . . . I give my students freedom to participate, including time to reflect upon the topic and discuss
examples. . . . Sometimes, a student will come to say they have understood the content, but this is not practiced at home. In such situations,
we inform the principal and school board, investigating the home situation and inviting parents to school to talk. . . . HRE can contribute
in building up the student's personality. Many young learners are not
taken seriously at home. Their rights may be neglected, denied, or even
violated. Some may grow up in fear, not daring to speak up. (Sherko,
primary school teacher)

HUMAN RIGHTS EDUCATION, GENDER, AND DIVERSITY

Our respondents tended to prefer talking about gender issues rather than
ethnic or religious diversity when discussing social justice. Although a number of respondents made direct reference to past conflict, few elaborated on
it. One teacher adopted what we have termed a "paradise narrative" (Ahmad
et al., 2012) whereby she denied Kurdistan's decades of violence:

> In our society coexistence stretches from time immemorial. There's no
> discrimination between nations, races, and religions, and history tes-
> tifies to this. . . . We have always been brothers who love and tolerate
> each other, in class, in the neighborhood, in the village and in the city.
> (Tara, primary school teacher)

Such claims form part of a wider political discourse in Kurdistan–Iraq
in which the recent conflict among Kurds is denied. This discourse, while
undoubtedly part of the rhetoric of Kurdish nationalism and shared political
destiny, remains deeply problematic within the context of schooling, since
it denies the realities to which children will be exposed, namely, family and
community narratives of conflict and ongoing inequalities.

By contrast, other teachers responded pragmatically to diversity. Halat
proposed asking children questions to find out what they knew about their
multicultural, multifaith society and about different religions and cultures
"because the more information a person has the stronger their personality
and ability to express themselves."

Kamaran spoke at length about his understandings of schooling and gender equity and teachers' responsibilities within this:

> There is no doubt that our society is a closed society, strongly based
> on customs and traditions, where religion also plays a vital role. The
> only way, in my view, to bring these two sexes closer to each other and
> enhance gender equality is via school. Our society is a male-dominated

society. Men have the power and women are looked down on to a certain degree. . . . Schools play an important role in enhancing general knowledge about gender equality and its advantages in society. . . . I try to encourage a sense of responsibility in every teacher and stress each individual's role in changing cultural norms to incorporate gender equality awareness.

Nevertheless, like a number of other professionals, he did not underestimate the scale of the challenge or the conservative forces undermining equality initiatives, recognizing that schooling needs to be complemented by a comprehensive awareness-raising strategy and legal reform:

We need to acknowledge the fact that tribalism plays a big role in our Kurdish society, in combination with traditions and religion, which all work against the idea of gender equality. Women are viewed as second-class citizens and sometimes used as a commodity to be exchanged in marriage. (Kamaran, school inspector)

Most respondents felt that schools had a key part to play in realizinggender equity, although few were able to articulate the precise contributionof HRE. While a few had personal reservations about co-education, many recognized the lead role of schools in shifting attitudes over time and in building community confidence concerning mixed-sex schooling:

School has a major role in establishing positive gender relationships because if from very early stage children get used to studying and playing together . . . it will become normal for girls and boys to interact, communicate, and study together. (Kawthar, school inspector)

Families were sometimes seen as an obstacle, rather than as partners. Sherko suggested:

Gender equality has to start at home. Parents need to treat their boys and girls equally without any differences. . . . But parents interfere in school business. . . . Very often we hear parents complain about the fact that their daughter is placed next to a boy in class. (Sherko, primary school teacher)

Our culture isn't ready yet to mixing the two sexes at this sensitive age [teenage]. I can bring you to a mixed-sex school and just look at the classroom walls! There're filled up with love messages between boys and girls. . . . They do not understand yet how to treat each other respectfully as a sister–brother or as friends. Consequently, the number of mixed-sex schools is decreasing day by day. Teachers are sometimes

unable to control the situation and many parents are against the idea of
sending their daughters to a mixed school, even if it's close to home.
(Azad, school inspector)

Mixed-sex schooling should begin in preschool. In the secondary
school or college, it is already too late. . . . Ours, the only mixed-sex
school in this district, will close next year and boys and girls will be separated. . . . There are no big differences in gender relationships between
rural and urban areas. On the contrary, in some rural areas, girls and
boys are freer to interact. For example, in the spring it's normal for a
group of girls and boys to have a picnic together. Agricultural work has
made interaction a regular habit. Although we find more educated people in urban areas, gender relations there are not as free as one might
imagine. (Hassan, principal, rural school)

Hassan was not alone in noting anomalies in gender relations, whereby
in certain contexts, boys and girls are free to mix:

We still have many families that are against the idea of sending their
children to a mixed sex school. . . . This is a matter of getting used to
the idea. In our Kurdish culture, it is not acceptable for a girl to look
at a boy . . . yet it's normal at a wedding to dance hand-in-hand with
a strange boy. The latter practice is common and culturally acceptable.
(Fawzi, high school teacher)

Yet it appears that educators were in some cases perpetuating problems
by their own reluctance to engage on the basis of equality with their oppo-
site-sex colleagues, preferring the familiarity of same-sex social relationships:

There are many schools, where the female and male teaching staff
have two separate teachers' rooms. If this is still the dominant mode
of thinking among teachers, how can they address gender equality
with their students or support interaction between the sexes? (Payman,
school inspector)

Our visits to schools confirmed Payman's observation. Teachers argued
for more cooperation and shared engagement in learning activities between
girls and boys, yet opted to use separate male and female staffrooms, not
modeling the behavior they sought.

RELIGION, VALUES, AND GENDER

Fawzi told a shocking story of a student who committed suicide after her
brother prevented her from joining classmates on a school visit. He suggested

that the case raised fundamental questions about societal recognition of girls' capabilities, as well as questions about home-school communication:

> Yesterday, a young female student, aged between 16 to 17 years, committed suicide by burning 65% of her body. She did it because her brother didn't allow her to join her class in an out-of-school visit. . . . This is . . . a classic example of a lack of communication and cooperation between schools and families in grasping curricula activities. . . . Gender equality is tied to cultural understandings of girls' and boys' roles, and this is not based either on religion or science. . . . It's an example of false perceptions of girls' potential and behavior. (Fawzi, high school teacher)

Fawzi also expressed concerns both about the power of tribalism and the influence of mullahs in preventing the realization of gender equity:

> The biggest limitation is the tribal mindset controlling society. Society isn't open to the modernization we so strongly need. . . . Another important concern is the lack of well-educated religious personalities. . . . We have many mullahs that play an important role in society, but very few that are sufficiently well-educated to understand the real meaning of the Qur'an. Our religion allows equal rights for women and men, but this isn't properly understood. To be honest, we need a mindset ready for religious reformation, according to societal needs. This is allowed in Islam. I'm not talking about reducing prayer from five times a day to three, but we need to understand that time when our Prophet was living is very different from today's age. (Fawzi, high school teacher)

Sawsan, herself a Christian, agreed:

> [We need to] link gender equality to our religious ideals, which stress equal treatment. Even Islam highlights the need for gender equality. I was just now teaching history and our topic is the history of Islam, where the Prophet Mohammad highlights gender equality. (Sawsan, social studies teacher)

Finally, it appeared that few, if any, educators appeared familiar with the U.N. Convention on the Rights of the Child and did not realize that child rights were absent from the textbooks reviewed. Although educators appeared more comfortable discussing gender than ethnic diversity, a number insisted that any class discussion with students that might be construed as political, religious, or gender-related, remained problematic:

> Misunderstandings happen very easily in our community . . . if we talk about political, religious, or gender-related issues. Class discussion may

be counterproductive. For example, if we talked about Valentine's Day in class, it may lead to misunderstanding . . . even their families might interfere. . . . So you consciously avoid opening any gender-related topic in the classroom. (Ahlam, high school teacher)

WAYS FORWARD

A key strength of the Kurdish educators was a general commitment to social justice and children's well-being. The challenges were considerable, with inadequate training and a prevailing social climate where considerable inequalities persist between women and men. Nevertheless, teachers were often advocates for children's rights.

The curriculum focus is knowledge *about* rights, yet there is a gap between the ideals expressed in international instruments and reiterated in the political rhetoric, and the everyday realities of teachers and children. Teaching about human rights in school takes place in contexts where children's rights (particularly those of girls) are denied, and in family and societal contexts where powerful conservative and patriarchal values prevail.

Importantly, teachers need training in active methods, and opportunities to discuss tensions between rights and cultural norms and how to support children in claiming rights. There also needs to be awareness-raising for parents and community members, focusing on basic human rights standards in children's daily lives. Teachers need high-quality textbooks and further consideration to be given to the assessment of HRE, so that books, pedagogy, and assessment procedures support stated policy goals relating to human rights and gender equity.

Students are likely to feel disempowered if, despite the human rights they learn about, societal conditions undermine these rights. They need opportunities to experience rights within the community of the school. Within a conflict-ridden society such as Iraqi Kurdistan, a particular focus is required on education *for* rights and on learner empowerment. This implies skills training and creating a sense of solidarity between the genders and across ethnic and religious groups so that learners are encouraged to show responsibility toward and defend the rights of others, particularly those different from themselves. It is this that constitutes "education for cosmopolitan citizenship" (Osler & Starkey, 2005).

The educators addressed the key concept of solidarity and its place in realizing rights. The KRG promotes Kurdish solidarity, countering other solidarities that may undermine rights, such as tribalism. However, an appeal to Kurdish nationalism and identity, while serving political ends and encouraging unity, has its limits, since not everyone will identify as Kurdish, and diversity is extended with inward migration and, with increased insecurity and threat of war, significant numbers of internally displaced people and refugees.

Powerful conservative forces, including religious and tribal authorities, combine to undermine gender equity. While gender proved to be a sensitive area for discussion, religious and ethnic diversity was often completely off-limits. Effective HRE requires more than translating international instruments into national policies. HRE needs to include school-level policies and practices that empower students and provide them with a language to discuss sensitive issues.

It is the responsibility of government to uphold human rights, and this is where educators saw a gap between rhetoric and reality in children's lives. They observed that HRE in school is taking place in a vacuum, without sufficient attention to measures beyond the school to raise awareness about the rights of girls (and minorities). Since governments rarely emphasize their own responsibilities or processes of accountability, HRE may best be realized in cooperation with civil society, with teacher training implemented in cooperation with local and international NGOs. This should enable the best use of human resources, especially women's and girls' contribution to strengthening democracy and development. It might also indirectly counter conservative forces who suggest that women's human rights are counter to religious teaching.

It appears, from the complex perspectives of the Kurdish educators, that education *about, in,* and *for* human rights has the potential to strengthen gender equity, challenging patriarchal values and tribalism from the grassroots. This holistic approach to HRE might also inform those seeking to implement HRE in established democracies.

HRE will not be effective without effective political leadership and legal provisions across a range of policy areas. In a multifaith society that also includes secular perspectives, and particularly in postconflict contexts, recognition of the universal nature of rights and the obligations that this places not only on governments but also on civil society has the potential to promote solidarity and cohesion across cultural and religious boundaries. It is this solidarity that is critical for a just and peaceful long-term future.

Chronic insecurity and the threat of war again hang over the region at the time of writing. Security, as we have seen, is a basic HRE concept and a prerequisite for guaranteeing of human rights. One powerful tool for change worldwide, which the Kurdish educators did not refer to, and one that has considerable potential for HRE in schools, is the Convention on the Rights of the Child. Chapter 7 examines the CRC and child rights in education.

CHAPTER 7

Child Rights: The Heart of the Project

No longer can it be claimed, as Hillary Rodham Clinton did back in 1973, that "Children's rights is a slogan in search of a definition" (Rodham, 1973).[1] Attitudes toward children, and our understandings of childhood, have changed considerably. This change is due, in no small part, to the 1989 U.N. Convention on the Rights of the Child (CRC), which has been almost universally ratified and has had a direct impact on policymaking across the globe.

While children are commonly recognized as vulnerable subjects in need of special protection, they are today also more commonly recognized as fellow citizens with participation rights, rather than "citizens-in-waiting" (Verhellen, 2000). The CRC is significant, not least because it addresses *participation* rights, as well as rights of *provision* and *protection*. In other words, it integrates civil and political rights with social, economic, and cultural rights in one instrument.[2] In reality all these human rights are interlinked: For example, accessing the right to education may be critical in securing work; without basic education and literacy, it is likely to be harder to engage in political activity or to exercise the right to freedom of expression. So political and civil rights, as well as other social, cultural, and economic rights are linked to the right to education. For this reason it makes sense to refer to "civil, cultural, economic, political, and social rights" when considering the rights of all human beings, including children.

The CRC recognizes children and young people under the age of 18 as rights-holders who are entitled to political rights, including the right to exercise such rights in their schooling. The project of enabling human rights and social justice through education is dependent on a deep understanding and application of children's human rights, particularly their participation rights, by policymakers and by teachers and other professionals working in school settings.

One key principle in the CRC is that of the best interests of the child. The principle predates the CRC, but its modern interpretation is central to understanding children's rights in education. Realizing the best interests of the child necessarily involves the participation of the child and giving consideration to the child's view in decisionmaking processes. Adults seeking to apply the best interests principle and to foreground the child's best interests in school settings need to ensure that schools are conceived, first and foremost, as places where children are recognized as fellow citizens who have agency in learning processes and in shaping their own futures.

This chapter explores how children's participation and engagement in decisionmaking processes that affect them is a means of protecting their human rights and realizing greater social justice. Children's participation is central, since it can support efforts to overcome a number of barriers to ensuring quality education. The participation of children and young people and their expression of their views in decisions that affect them does not simply have a utilitarian purpose but is itself a right articulated in the CRC Article 12. To illustrate this point, I begin by presenting a short account of my own early schooling. The events that I describe were taking place before child rights were broadly recognized, but at the beginning of an era—the 1960s—when there was widespread awakening of civil rights and women's rights. At that point in history the child rights "slogan" was being used by some adults (Osler & Starkey, 1996) even if, in reality, children's rights were not being advanced.

CHILD-CENTERED EDUCATION?

I grew up just outside London and was fortunate enough to attend a newly built school, serving a new town with a young and rapidly growing population. I started school just a few weeks before my fifth birthday. We had bright and airy classrooms, extensive playing fields, and large playgrounds. This was in direct contrast to many of our contemporaries, whose schools were housed in late 19th-century Victorian buildings, many of which had seen minimal improvements since the time they were built. The views from our classroom windows extended beyond the grounds, not to the new housing developments into which families were moving from London, but to woods and fields. The teachers would take the young children for nature walks.

Our bright new school was part of an initiative to invest in education in postwar Britain. It is said that between 1950 and 1970 there was a new school built in England every day (Saint, 1987), and Hertfordshire, where I lived, exemplified this in its innovative school-building program. The architecture and furnishings were experimental, with the interiors resembling some of the most attractive classrooms designed in the early decades of the 21st century. Our classrooms were large, and consisted of two adjoining squares, one equipped with hexagonal tables where children worked in groups, and the other furnished with toys, games, a classroom library, and some facilities intended for younger children, such as a sandbox. The assembly hall doubled as a gym, and music, physical education, and creative arts were important parts of the curriculum. The teachers were generally energetic and, as is clear to me now, aiming to implement child-centered and progressive methods, which the school architecture was designed to support.

I was a keen, enthusiastic student, eager to learn to read. Yet there were daily practices that had a negative impact on my curiosity and excitement in the early years and, later, on my sense of well-being at school. We started reading with the then ubiquitous Janet and John scheme, a look-and-say method with bright pictures of cheerful gender-stereotyped children in a traditional, White, middle-class nuclear family. This family in no way resembled my own, yet I learned quickly. The content of these books were not as exciting as I had anticipated, but this did not matter too much, for once students had completed them, they were able to select more interesting "free choice" books and stories.

Unfortunately, before a student could progress from one book to the next, each was required to stand in line at the teacher's desk and, in turn, re-read the text aloud. Clearly, this system was designed to monitor and record progress, but I recall a long wait each lesson, a time-wasting process, when there were so many other available books to explore. I remember asking, on one occasion, if I might move to the next book without reading out loud, or if I might look at another book while standing in the line. The firm "no" gave me the distinct feeling I was not trusted and reinforced the message that for competent readers, reading lessons consisted largely of lining up, not enjoying books.

By the time of my sixth birthday, I had learned that, for students, a lot of schooling was about filling up time aimlessly. No doubt my teacher was highly organized and skilled in managing a large group of young children. Nevertheless, since little attention was given to children's perspectives, it was difficult, if not impossible, for her or any other adult to establish if they were really acting according to the principle of the child's best interests. Treating all children identically did not ensure equity then, any more than it does now, but simply frustration and disappointment. The concept of child-centered education that prevailed was one in which benevolent adults decided the best interests of the child and where differences were overlooked in the name of equality.

Yet a far worse feature of my early schooling began a few years later, at the age of 9. Two of my classmates, twin brothers, consistently arrived late. I don't know whether anyone sought to find out the underlying cause, although when I discussed it with my mother she explained that their family circumstances had changed and that they were living with their father and stepmother. In any case, our new classroom teacher gave the twins a warning about lateness. This appeared to have little impact on their morning routine. So, every day for 2 years, as I recall, our class began each morning with the ritual of each twin in turn being beaten with "the slipper," a running shoe. I'm not clear what impact this had on the two boys, but it became a routine I grew to dread, and one that dented my enjoyment of school. My school survival strategy was outward conformity to every rule, only participating or venturing an opinion if invited. I suspect I was not the only student for whom fear of disapproval and punishment dominated every classroom activity for those 2 years.

Regrettably, such practices do not belong to the distant past. It is not so long ago that corporal punishment at school was finally outlawed in the United Kingdom. The CRC (Article 37) states that no child shall be subjected to cruel, inhuman or degrading treatment or punishment and that school discipline should be "administered in a manner consistent with the child's human dignity" (Article 28). In 1987, corporal punishment was finally prohibited in publicly funded schools in the United Kingdom and in those private schools receiving government subsidies, although well before this, individual teachers were banned from carrying out the kind of public punishments we witnessed. It was subsequently outlawed in other private schools in 1999 (England and Wales), 2000 (Scotland), and 2003 (Northern Ireland). Yet, as recently as 2005, there was an unsuccessful challenge to prohibition of corporal punishment by the headteachers of private Christian schools.[3] Various international human rights bodies, including the U.N. Committee on the Rights of the Child (2006), the Parliamentary Assembly of the Council of Europe (PACE; 2004), and the Inter-American Commission on Human Rights (2009), have stated that physical punishment of any kind is a violation of children's human rights. It is virtually banned in most of Europe and in South Korea, and outlawed across Canada, South Africa, and New Zealand. Even in countries where corporal punishment is outlawed, its practice often persists, formally or informally, where children lack a voice and where parents may condone it.

It is in mundane, but unchallenged, everyday practices that schools may undermine children's human rights, particularly children's right to participate. Schools, which are potentially a key means of enabling the utopian human rights vision, may unwittingly reinforce existing inequalities, neglect the perspectives of those they claim to serve, and be tools of violence against children.

CHILD RIGHTS AND VIOLENCE AT SCHOOL

Violence at school can take many forms and can be interpersonal, institutional, and structural, as well as physical. These various expressions of violence may lead to insecurity, or to feelings of insecurity, among students. In the example above, systemic violence was experienced by a whole class; the problem was more than one of a degrading physical punishment being inflicted on two apparently recalcitrant students with a persistent record of lateness. Although the term "violence in schools" is now commonly used internationally, there was, until the late 1990s, a preference among scholars and practitioners for terms such as *antisocial behavior* (Debarbieux, 2001). In England, one commonly used term is *disaffection*. These terms focus attention on the individual or group thought to be antisocial or disaffected. A focus on individual students as the source of the problem may disguise certain problematic institutional processes.

In a study of girls' experiences of exclusion from school (Osler, 2006; Osler, Street, Lall, & Vincent, 2002; Osler & Vincent, 2003), girls' own experiences of exclusion were investigated. In contrast to boys (who in England remain more vulnerable to exclusion from school as a disciplinary measure), girls engaged in forms of withdrawal that were less likely to draw attention to their difficulties (academic, social, or emotional); they were more likely to disguise learning problems; and less likely to access forms of support. Professionals working with young people confirmed that teachers, under pressure to improve academic attainment, focused on the potential disaffection of boys, and tended to ignore girls' challenges to behavioral codes, since these were less likely to be disruptive to others' learning. As an educational psychologist explained to the research team:

> There is someone I am working with at the moment. . . . She's very emotionally distressed, as shown by crying, worrying, refusing to do her homework and those sorts of things. Whilst the school are concerned about her, it's not as pressing as a 6-foot kid who's throwing desks about. (quoted in Osler, 2006, p. 574)

The study revealed what other studies of school violence, including studies of cyberbullying (Cassidy, Faucher, & Jackson, 2013; Cassidy, Jackson, & Brown, 2009; Jackson, Cassidy, & Brown, 2009), illustrate, namely, that indirect and psychological bullying among girls leads to a "hidden culture of aggression" (Simmons, 2002), causing a significant minority of students to live in fear. Such bullying has long-term damaging effects but is nonetheless largely invisible to adults. For those students interested primarily in the extrinsic benefits of school, such as good test results, unfavorable judgments by teachers and being placed in low tracks or sets may be experienced as a form of violence.

Our study (Osler & Vincent, 2003) concluded that in order to address the culture of school violence, policymakers and teachers need to move away from the "gender seesaw" (Collins, Kenway, & McLeod, 2000) where first boys, and then girls, and then boys again, are targeted as needing support, and recognize a more complex picture. Gender equity and justice requires a more nuanced approach and not simply an effort to even up achievement data and exclusion rates. By centering students' own perspectives, it becomes possible to view their experiences through a lens that addresses the everyday incivilities of school culture, and explore links between these incivilities and school violence and exclusion. In centering students' perspectives in keeping with international human rights standards, research can contribute to a more complex "gender jigsaw" (Collins et al., 2000), which recognizes that questions of race and ethnicity, sexuality, poverty, and so on are not necessarily interrelated in a linear causal way to each other but are interwoven in young peoples' lives.

The CRC standard, which requires adult decisionmakers to take young people's perspectives into consideration, can also be built into research design (Emerson & Lundy, 2013; Osler, 2010b; Starkey, Akar, Jerome, & Osler, 2014), as well as into everyday educational practices. In other words, students move away from being the objects of research and have opportunities to feed into the research design: namely, to collect data (thus equipping them with new skills) and to contribute to the interpretation, presentation, and dissemination of research findings. These processes bring a range of benefits to a research team and to the students concerned, not least of which is the acquisition of a set of transferable research skills.

U.N. CONVENTION ON THE RIGHTS OF THE CHILD

The CRC is the most widely recognized U.N. human rights treaty, with 193 of 194 sovereign states being parties to the Convention. The exception is the United States, which signed the treaty in 1995, indicating the nation's intention to ratify. In 2008, during a youth debate, U.S. presidential candidates were asked: "As President, would you seek the ratification of the U.N. Convention on the Rights of the Child?" Barack Obama said it was "embarrassing" that the United States was in the company of Somalia, "a lawless country," in not ratifying the convention.[4] He promised to review the CRC and "ensure that the United States resumes its global leadership in human rights" (Obama, 2008). The next stage is for the Convention to be presented to the Senate, which must reply in the affirmative before it can be ratified by the President.

The CRC has encountered notable opposition in the United States, both within the Senate and with sections of the public, due to misconceptions about its intent and provisions. A number of politically conservative organizations in the United States have opposed the CRC, including the Christian Coalition of America, Concerned Women for America, Eagle Forum, and the National Center for Home Education. These organizations portray the CRC as a threat and raise unfounded concerns relating to national sovereignty. Their various claims include that the CRC would undermine parental authority, curtail the rights of individual states, and undermine parent–child relationships, encouraging children to have abortions, and sue parents. Effectively, they suggest the United Nations would determine how America's children are raised and educated. Ratification is likely to be difficult until a more favorable political climate is realized.

These claims and perceptions stem from misconceptions and misunderstandings about how international human rights treaties are implemented in the United States. Some provisions criticized by opponents were in fact proposed by the United States in the CRC drafting process, under the administrations of Presidents Reagan and Bush, and reflect rights American children already have under the U.S. Constitution. This does not imply, however, that all are protected under the Constitution. Were the United States to ratify the CRC, these rights would be extended to cover resident children who do not hold U.S. citizenship, thereby ensuring equity for these marginalized young people.

The CRC applies to all young people under the age of 18 years. It is legally binding in international law, but the Convention has no external controlling mandates: Governments (and NGOs if they wish) report periodically —generally every 5 years—to the Committee on the Rights of the Child. They are required to report on their progress in implementing the convention according to guidelines that require, in the case of education, updated information on laws, policies, and other measures that enable children to enjoy their rights from early years through to tertiary and vocational levels, addressing, in particular, the needs of children and young people who are marginalized and vulnerable. Reporting is required under Article 44 of the CRC, and includes the right to education (Article 28); the aims and quality of education (Article 29) including human rights education and civic education; and the cultural rights of children from indigenous and minority communities (Article 30).

The committee welcomes additional reports from NGOs, who may, and often do, consult with children in the process of producing material to present to the committee. NGO reports are then set alongside the government–drafted responses to the committee, enabling a more rounded perspective of policy implementation and potential gaps in provision. The committee then conducts a hearing at which it questions government officials on progress and also calls other parties it wishes to consult. At the end of this process, the committee publishes concluding observations. Although these comments are generally rather brief and do not allow systematic comparison of progress across states with regard to human rights education—since the committee's specific focus of attention may vary considerably between countries (Gerber, 2013)—they nevertheless provide a benchmark against which civil society can judge progress and engage in children's rights advocacy.

In the United States, as in many other nations, such treaties are non-executing, which means that that they can only be implemented through domestic legislation—enacted, in the case of the United States, by Congress or by state legislatures. When nations ratify the CRC, they can reject or clarify specific provisions in the convention. Thus neither the United Nations nor the Committee on the Rights of the Child undermines the sovereignty of the nation. By ratifying the treaty, the U.S. federal government would carry a duty to fulfill specific provisions.

Broadly, the CRC is concerned with children's freedom from violence, abuse, hazardous employment, exploitation, abduction, or sale; adequate nutrition; free compulsory primary education; adequate health care; equitable treatment regardless of gender, race, or cultural background; freedom of thought; the right to express opinions in matters affecting them; and access to leisure, play, culture, and art. The children's human rights agenda is broad, encompassing children's civil and political rights, as well as their economic, social, and cultural rights. They have been elaborated extensively and codified in international law and enacted in the policies of nations worldwide, as the provisions of the CRC are incorporated into legal frameworks and domestic policies. Effectively, near-universal adoption of the CRC has supported nation-states in developing legal frameworks and implementing policies that acknowledge children's status as fellow citizens and as holders of rights, entitled to equal dignity. It marks a significant step in viewing children as rights-holders, moving away from legal frameworks and societal conceptions of childhood in which children were seen, first and foremost, as the possessions of their parents. All these ideas have been explored by scholars working in the field of the sociology of childhood (Qvortrup, Corsaro, & Honig, 2009).

As discussed in previous chapters, the civil, political, social, economic, and cultural rights enshrined in the CRC are in fact interrelated, with those lacking basic economic and social necessities ill-placed to claim their political rights, and those lacking political freedoms finding it difficult to assert their economic and social rights. Across the globe, where the CRC has been ratified, it has provided a standard against which governments can measure their progress in implementing children's human rights. It has proved to be a powerful standard-setting tool and one that can be used by NGOs representing children's interests to struggle for greater social justice.

CLOSING THE GAP BETWEEN IDEALS AND REALITIES

Following the adoption of the CRC in 1989, the World Declaration on the Survival, Protection and Development of Children (UNICEF, 1990), proclaimed at the World Summit for Children in New York, focused on the needs of the most vulnerable children, including those who, as a result of war and aggression, find themselves "as refugees and displaced children, forced to abandon their homes and their roots" (Article 4). It concludes: "There can be no task nobler than giving every child a better future" (Article 25). At the United Nations Summit, world leaders proclaimed that, within the field of education:

> We will work for programmes that reduce illiteracy and provide educational opportunities for all children, irrespective of their background and gender; that prepare children for productive employment and lifelong learning opportunities, i.e. through vocational training; and that enable children to grow to adulthood within a supportive and nurturing cultural and social context." (Article 6)

The Education for All agenda (World Conference on Education for All, 1990), taken forward by the World Education Forum in the Dakar Framework for Action (UNESCO, 2000) and subsequently the Incheon Declaration (UNESCO, 2015), stressed the commitment of the international community to the realization of high-quality and universal primary education for all children, both boys and girls, and including marginalized children, such as linguistic and ethnic minorities, migrants, indigenous peoples, those with disabilities, street children, and those who are victims of conflict.

In 1990 the international climate appeared favorable to addressing children's rights through international cooperation. Since the 1990s, economic crises, wars, and the erosion of commitments to human rights in the name of security have dulled the optimism of this period. Concern among education officials in wealthy nations commonly focuses on international competition, reflecting the concerns of governments that the nation's children should excel in international rankings of educational performance represented by PISA test scores, with scholars focusing, for example, on the impact of immigrant students on the test score outcomes of those who are native born (Brunello & Rocco, 2013). While such research has the potential to contribute to greater social justice, it might also be used to advance those who are already advantaged and reduce the chance of equitable outcomes.

Current debates on international cooperation tend to stress the threat of terrorism and the need for rights-restricting antiterror measures and not the potential of education to change lives and secure rights (Coppock, 2014). In 2015, 1,011,712 migrants were recorded as arriving across the Mediterranean to Italy, Greece, Spain, or Malta, with a further 3,770 known to have died trying to make the journey. (International Organization for Migration [IOM], 2015). This number represents nearly three-quarters of the global number of migrant deaths in 2015. Nearly 35,000 additional migrants were recorded as arriving in Europe by land in 2015. Families from Syria and Iraq make up a significant proportion of those seeking asylum in Europe and those who have perished on the journey. As of July 2015, there were 1.17 million Syrian refugees in Lebanon, 1.8 million in Turkey, more than 600,000 in Jordan, and another quarter of a million in Iraq, most of these in the autonomous region of Iraqi Kurdistan. Iraq's situation is further complicated by some 3 million internally displaced people (IDPs), many of whom have also fled to the Kurdistan Region. A further 7.6 million people are displaced within Syria.

Some 25 years after the 1990 aspiration for universal primary education, conflict in the Middle East is denying children their right to education:

> A region which—until just a few short years ago—had the goal of universal education well within reach, today faces a disastrous situation: more than 13 million children are not attending school in countries being affected—either directly or indirectly—by armed conflict. (UNICEF, 2015, p. 3)

Such children are clearly exceptionally vulnerable, yet Martha Fineman (Fineman, 2008; Fineman & Grear, 2016) draws on the concept of "universal human vulnerability"—she posits that vulnerability and dependency are inherent in the human condition—to advocate for human rights, arguing that achieving social justice in the 21st century will require a "*more active and responsive state.*" (Fineman, 2010, p. 260). Rather than rely on abstract and inevitably contested principles such as dignity and liberty to define what it means to be human, she develops critical legal studies to ensure that bodily, material, and institutional contexts are brought into the discussion.

Fineman suggests that as *embodied* beings, we are universally and individually constantly susceptible to injury, harm, and dependency over the life-course (Fineman, 2016). Since there is no position of invulnerability, there is only the possibility of resilience. Since we are not born resilient, we must gain the resources that make us resilient through social institutions and relationships. Resilience is acquired when we have sufficient resources to allow us to adapt to, ameliorate, compensate for, or contain our vulnerability.

From Fineman's perspective, human vulnerability demands that all social institutions and relationships, including those in education, require rules. Rules operate as constraints on individuals for the good of the collective, in this case, the school community. The role of the state is to ensure that socially necessary and legitimate rules are defined and enforced through law. In this way, a vulnerability analysis demands that, in fashioning and implementing those rules, the state be responsive to the needs of a legal subject who is both an embodied being and embedded in social relations. In other words, resilience is possible when the state—and its various institutions—enable conditions for resilience, enabling all to be provided for and protected, as well as to participate. This requires recognition and monitoring of the operation of social institutions and social relationships, and attention to the ways in which privilege and disadvantage are produced within them. From this perspective, it can be seen that all rights, not only economic, social, and cultural rights, but also civil and political rights, require an active and responsive state.

This analysis moves away from an argument based on human compassion to address restricted vulnerability (seen as the experience of the weak) to one where vulnerability is a characteristic of our shared humanity necessarily requiring an engaged political response. It is a matter of our common collective interest that vulnerability is transformed into resilience by state action and responsiveness. Fineman's emphasis on state responsibility does not, of course, remove the need for an active civil society, responsible for holding the state to account. There is also a compelling argument for all states to work together, taking collective responsibility in order to address issues of social justice. In other words, extending Fineman's thesis beyond the borders of the state demands a cosmopolitan understanding.

Education is an enabling right, providing access to other rights (McCowan, 2013). Yet it is still denied to around 60 million children worldwide.

Even in prosperous nations, with near-universal access to schooling, marginalized children continue to struggle to claim their right to quality education that is appropriate to their needs (Osler & Osler, 2002) and that guarantees and protects their cultural rights under the CRC (Articles 17, 29, 30, 31). The final sections of this chapter turn to the implementation of the CRC in schools and its potential to realize greater social justice in children's lives.

CHILDREN'S HUMAN RIGHTS AND EDUCATION FOR DEMOCRATIC CITIZENSHIP

The U.N. Convention on the Rights of the Child confirms the status of the child as citizen, with children and young people accorded participation rights, as well as rights relating to provision and protection. In our globalized age, a number of authors have argued it is no longer appropriate to conceive of citizenship education exclusively within the framework of the nation-state or to assume that all students in schools will be citizens or aspirant citizens (Banks et al., 2005; Osler & Starkey, 2005).

Citizenship can be understood as a *status*, a *feeling*, and a *practice* (Osler & Starkey, 2005). While not all students will necessarily have the *status* of citizen (i.e., nationality) in the country in which they are studying, with attendant rights, all have the status of holder of human rights. The status, feeling, and practice of citizenship are interrelated. While stateless persons nearly always remain highly vulnerable, the absence of formal citizenship (nationality) rights is not necessarily a bar to a *feeling* of citizenship or sense of belonging in a community. Feelings of belonging depend on an individual's sense of security and on an atmosphere of nondiscrimination. Neither is the *practice* of citizenship or engagement in the life and affairs of the community necessarily dependent on citizenship status. Working in a community food bank, for example, is an "act of citizenship" (Isin & Neilsen, 2008) that is not dependent on nationality. Nevertheless, the degree to which an individual feels empowered to engage in the community and engage in acts of citizenship (Isin & Neilsen, 2008), or the *practice* of citizenship, is likely to be influenced by the degree to which an individual has a *feeling* of citizenship and belonging.

Citizenship education that focuses on status, feeling, and practice, rather than status alone, is likely to be more inclusive of a wide range of learner identities. Educators do not need to choose between regular (national) citizenship education and what is commonly known as "global citizenship education." It is possible to examine the status, feeling, and practice of citizenship at different scales from the local to the global. This is what Osler and Starkey (2005) refer to as "education for cosmopolitan citizenship," underpinned by human rights. Learners can identify with others at all these scales. A sense of solidarity with people at all scales is a central concept within human rights.

The human rights project itself is cosmopolitan. Education for cosmopolitan citizenship requires us to reimagine the nation itself as cosmopolitan.

Similarly, an approach to multicultural education that extends beyond the nation to address power relations between nationals and nonnationals and to consider inequalities, power, and solidarity beyond national boundaries, is more likely to be appropriate in a globalized world. International migration is leading to "super-diversity" (Vertovec, 2007) in many cities. Human rights provide a framework within which students can critically examine power and develop solidarity with others at various scales from the local to the global and foster global intercultural engagement.

Article 29 of the U.N. Convention on the Rights of the Child confirms the right to education for human rights and peace. Article 29 refers to "respect for human rights and fundamental freedoms and for the principles enshrined in the Charter of the United Nations." In particular, it sets out the aims of education for all children and refers to the obligation by the nation-state to promote education for peaceful coexistence with others in the community, the nation, and the wider world. It confirms the right to a multicultural education that develops respect both for the learners' family culture and values and for the culture and values of the country in which the individual is living. As Article 29 outlines, this education should promote peace, tolerance, and understanding between "all peoples, ethnic, national and religious groups." Minimally, Article 29 implies that both teachers and young people are familiar with human rights. It also implies that all young people in multicultural nation-states have some level of engagement and integration with children and young people from backgrounds different from their own, as well as an education that builds on and respects the child's home culture and his or her own identity. Additionally, Article 30, which refers to the rights of children from ethnic, religious, or linguistic minorities or of indigenous origin to enjoy their culture, practice their religion, and their language, has direct implications for schools.

Grover (2007) argues that education for tolerance, in keeping with the provisions of Article 29, cannot be fostered where there is complete educational segregation. She concludes that it should "be acknowledged that educating for peace will require states to mandate some level of educational integration of school children from diverse ethnic, religious, cultural and language groups" (p. 60). A number of postconflict societies devise education systems that divide children on the basis of language, religion, or ethnic group. Two examples within Europe are the school system of Bosnia and Herzegovina and that of Northern Ireland.

Northern Ireland, which maintains a school system largely segregated by religious denomination, can be seen clearly to fall short of this standard, which according to Grover (2007) is essential for fulfilling the requirements of Article 29. Yet in many other parts of the United Kingdom, as well as in the United States, particularly in cities, where market forces and a focus on "parental choice" in schooling affect access to schooling, children are also divided according to social class, ethnicity, and religious affiliation. These de facto segregated school systems might equally be judged to fall short in relation to Grover's assessment of the minimum requirements for enabling education for peace and justice.

Currently, the child's right to education is frequently interpreted, legislatively and judicially, as a "parental liberty right" (to have a child educated according to parental wishes). Grover (2007) argues that this tends to work against children's rights and that "the notion of minority education is frequently erroneously translated into *completely segregated school systems* [emphasis added]" (p. 61). She suggests that "the minority and nonminority child's legal right to free association (each with the other) in the educational context is frequently disregarded both by the legislature and the courts" in nation-states across the globe (p. 61). In other words, the "parental liberty right" or right to have a child educated according to parental wishes, currently appears to trump children's right to be educated together.

Clearly, realizing social justice in education, including gender equity and the rights of minorities, means more than simply translating international instruments into national policies or implementing educational reforms. It means designing schools and curricula in which learners are provided with knowledge about their rights and equipped with the skills to claim them.

EVALUATING RIGHTS WITHIN EDUCATION

Teachers and students can be invited to evaluate the degree to which their school is compliant with the standards of the CRC. Hugh Starkey and I have identified a set of pedagogic principles that invite teachers, along with school leaders and administrators, to review the degree to which practices are in conformity with the CRC. The principles are as follows: dignity and security (various articles including 8, 11, 12, 19–20, 23–26); freedom from fear (Preamble and Articles 19, 23, 28.2, 29); participation (Articles 12, 13, 14, 15, 31); identity and inclusivity (Preamble and Articles, 2, 7, 8, 16, 23, 28, 29, 31); freedom (Article 12, 13, 14, 15); access to information (Article 17); and privacy (Article 16) (Osler & Starkey, 2010, pp. 135–137).

Another tool we have devised that can be used by both teachers and students is a questionnaire entitled: *Does Your School Environment Give Everyone a Chance to Enjoy Their Rights?* (see Appendix C). It allows an exploration of the degree to which schools are accessible, acceptable, and adaptable to all children (Tomaševski, 2001; see Figure 2.1). It encourages reflection by teachers and students on their own schools, focusing in particular on acceptability (curriculum and teaching) and adaptability (the addressing of minority needs) against internationally agreed-upon standards, namely those of the CRC. The questionnaire has been used with both teachers and students to consider the provisions of the CRC and critically examine various aspects of schooling against human rights standards in three broad categories of rights: provision, protection, and participation. The questionnaire is made up of a series of statements, each linked to one or more articles in the CRC. For example, "The student newspaper is treated like any other publication, subject to the law, but is not subject to additional censorship (Article 13)." Readers are invited to judge, from their experience, whether each standard is realized always, sometimes, or never. Using this tool, students can work individually, in pairs, or in groups to examine the processes of their own schooling.

Teachers can also complete the exercise, and then students and teachers can compare their different responses and perspectives on schooling. As well as introducing the CRC, this tool raises challenging questions about adult–child power relationships (Osler, 2010b; Osler & Starkey, 2010) and about the role of schools in teaching for democratic citizenship. Banks and his colleagues (2005) identified a further principle in educating citizens in a global age: "Students should be taught knowledge about democracy and democratic institutions *and provided opportunities to practice democracy* [emphasis added]" (p. 5). This tool opens the way to engage students in democratic decisionmaking processes within the school. The CRC Article 12 states that children and young people should have opportunities to express their opinions in relation to decisions that affect them and for these opinions to be "given due weight" in decision-making processes.

At a second stage, students can check the statements in *Does Your School Environment Give Everyone a Chance to Enjoy Their Rights?* against the CRC to establish how the authors derived each statement from the convention. In this way they are becoming familiar with the provisions of the convention and of ways in which they apply to the everyday processes of schooling.

SUMMARY

In this chapter I have sought to illustrate how children's rights have changed from the 1960s and early 1970s, when Hillary Rodham Clinton saw them as little more than a slogan (Rodham, 1973), to become a significant force across the globe. I have explored the significance and impact of the CRC on policy and practice in education.

Although a number of myths persist in the United States about the CRC, its near-universal ratification and the ways in which it brings together children's civil, cultural, economic, political, and social rights in one instrument make it a unique tool for positive change in children's lives, and one that teachers and students, as well as other members of civil society, can use to strengthen educational structures and curricula so that they effectively serve the ends of children and young people.

The effect of the CRC has been to place child rights at the center of debates about child protection and welfare, educational provision, and the role of children and young people as citizens. Today, understandings of childhood and recognition of the role of children as citizens, rather than citizens-in-waiting, has informed debates about students' participation rights at school. These understandings have particular significance for the development of social studies and civic education curricula.

Without an understanding of children's rights, and particularly their participation rights in school, the underlying utopian vision of human rights (Osler & Starkey, 2010; Starkey, 2012)—that of realizing peace and justice in the wider world—is seriously undermined. The next chapter concludes this volume by reflecting on the importance of a cosmopolitan vision for the project of education and on ways in which the gap between cosmopolitan ideals and the everyday realities of schooling might be more effectively bridged through a closer attention to the discourse and practice of human rights both in schools and in the professional education of teachers.

CHAPTER 8

Reimagining a Cosmopolitan Future

Human rights are understood, from the perspective of the international community, as a legal framework designed to protect and empower individuals. Learning about human rights structures and institutions is one means of empowering people, whether they are from privileged or marginalized communities, to claim rights for themselves and for others in a spirit of solidarity. Yet at a more fundamental level, human rights are an expression of the human urge to resist oppression. The urge to resist oppression is universal in the sense that it does not belong to one culture or tradition.

The struggle for justice is a common human struggle, even if human concepts for justice vary over time and space. While scholars may trace the modern human rights project back through one tradition to the European Enlightenment, activists across the globe may make links between local traditions and beliefs and contemporary human rights standards. It seems that the roots of the modern human rights project are less important, in this sense, than the ability of those struggling for justice to use human rights to strengthen their cause. In the same way that languages borrow words from each other, each culture draws on others in its process of development. As this book has argued, the key issue to consider is not cultural differences so much as asymmetrical power relations, both within and between communities, at all levels from the local to the global. For practical purposes, anyone anywhere can appeal to the international community's vision of human rights as a framework in a struggle for rights. This is the cosmopolitan vison and cosmopolitan promise of human rights.

People need to know they have rights in order to claim them. This is a starting point for human rights education. But rights are rarely realized without struggle. So a second stage involves empowering learners with the skills to claim rights. Neither knowledge, nor knowledge and skills combined, can be the endpoint. Knowledge about human rights involves sharing a vision of greater justice. Equipping learners with skills implies equipping them with the action skills through which they can take the next step to shape and realize a more just society. It is to this vision, and to this challenge of imagining a more just society, that I now turn. In this respect I am moving from consideration of the moral obligations of the teacher toward learners to the political responsibilities of the teacher in an unjust world. I will seek to illustrate this through the story of a small group of citizens in Italy and the political acts that followed when they encountered a refugee in Milan Central Station.

EDUCATION AND POLITICAL ACTS

In November 2015 I attended a special screening of the documentary film *On the Bride's Side* (Augugliaro, del Grande, & al Nassiry, 2014), followed by a Q&A session with one of the film's directors, journalist Gabriele del Grande. The film came about as a result of a chance meeting at the main train station in Milan, Italy, on an autumn afternoon in 2013. Three friends—Gabriele del Grande, poet Khaled Soliman al Nassiry, and translator Tareq al Jabr—were meeting for a coffee when a young Palestinian man named Abdallah heard them speaking Arabic. He approached the three friends and asked them from which platform the train for Sweden would depart. The three men invited Abdallah to join them. From his rather naive question, the idea to get him to Sweden, and make a film about it, developed.[1]

Abdallah was one of the survivors of a shipwreck off Lampedusa, an island in the Mediterranean Sea, on October 11, 2013. In the film, he movingly describes how he saw 250 of his fellow travelers drown, among them adults and children with whom he had formed close attachments.

After hearing his story the three friends contacted a film director friend, Antonio Augugliaro, and over a 2-week period hatched a plan to drive Abdallah, along with four other people fleeing the war in Syria, some 3,000 kilometers (about 1,900 miles) across Europe to Sweden, often selecting indirect routes to avoid detection. They decided to fake a wedding: "What border police officer would stop a bride and ask to see her documents?" With the help of an old friend, Palestinian Tasneem Fared (who holds a European passport), posing as the bride in traditional white gown, and several friends who agreed to act as wedding guests, together with a film crew, they set out to make an uncertain, exhausting, emotional, and in many ways risky journey to Sweden.

On November 14, 2013, the group of 23 people—Italians, Palestinians, and Syrians—all smartly dressed as if they were actually going to a wedding, gathered at the Milan station, to set out on a journey to demonstrate that people from both sides of the Mediterranean can cooperate and demonstrate solidarity. The film makes the point, reinforced by Gabriele del Grande, that no one would need to make the journey of death across the Mediterranean Sea, paying US$1,000 each as Abdallah had done, if the governments of various European nations had matched their promises of asylum for refugees fleeing Syria with safe passages to Europe. The conflict is, of course, one in which many of those same governments, along with that of the United States, are implicated, and it is not easily solved. Yet the means existed to save those who were forced to make this journey of death.

The 4-day journey to Sweden from Milan involved crossing an ancient mountain trail on foot into France and then avoiding various police motorway checkpoints as the "wedding party" made their way across France, Germany, Luxembourg, and Denmark. Along the way, they are shown in the film in Marseilles, France, and Bochum, Germany, before crossing Luxembourg and eventually arriving in Copenhagen, Denmark, from there to complete the last leg of the journey by rail to Malmö, Sweden, and on to Stockholm.

Various European citizens are shown supporting the group in their courageous act of civil disobedience. In Marseilles, supporters threw a party to express their solidarity with the refugees and filmmakers, since there were many more citizens willing to offer the travelers a bed for the night than were in fact needed. The team were able to realize their ambitions through drawing on friendships in these different countries. As Gabriele del Grande explained, they are the "Erasmus generation," students who have benefited from European-wide university mobility opportunities under the European Union–funded Erasmus scheme, who have now a European network of like-minded friends.

Through this network, they are supported, advised, and welcomed along the way, and when we see them partying in Marseilles the scene is reminiscent of an actual wedding. At the party, one of the refugees, a young boy named Manar, who has ambitions to be a rap artist, entertains the guests. Manar raps his own story, making links between his experiences as a refugee and those of a previous generation exiled from their Palestinian homeland, telling of grandparents who kept the keys of their now nonexistent former homes, holding onto the dream of return.

The film's directors explain (on their website at www.iostoconlasposa. com/en/) that *On the Bride's Side* is

> both a documentary and a political act. . . . The filming, therefore, always had to adapt to the political act, because we really had to get to Sweden, it wasn't just for the film. . . . The fact that we were sharing a great risk and a great dream inevitably united us. And this experience also changed our way of seeing things and helped us in the search for a new perception of the border, for a language, which, without falling into the trap of victimism, was able to transform the monsters of our fears into the heroes of our dreams, the ugly into the beautiful, and numbers into names.

The documentary itself, and the story it tells, are examples of cosmopolitan acts of citizenship and of human rights in action on the part of the various members of the group: the directors, those posing as wedding guests, and those who gave assistance along the journey. All who showed solidarity with the refugees were seeing their home city of Milan, Italy, Europe, and the Mediterranean region as cosmopolitan spaces, where diversity is recognized and not feared and where people's humanity comes before their nationality, religion, or other characteristics.

In working together to realize their goal, the people engaged in these acts, in making a film and in supporting a group of refugees in reaching their destination, were themselves changed; they were enabled to rethink their perceptions of Europe and its external and internal borders. The film does not tell the viewer what to think—it is not heavy-handed—but it certainly provoked many questions in my mind, questions about borders, about what it means to be European, and about what we choose to teach about the present and about the past. While these questions are not all new, and are not all yet fully resolved, I know I have gained new insights.

This is citizen action at both a local and a European level, with those engaged in these actions not only taking risks in defying the law, but documenting their efforts. The processes of documentation and distribution of the film—"turning numbers into names"—are themselves acts that serve to raise wider awareness of the plight of refugees and might therefore be recognized as educational. Del Grande suggests that one reason no government has called them to account for their defiance of the law is the fact that they have a vast range of supporters, who through crowdsourcing subsequently supported the completion and distribution of the film. It certainly shows a level of compassion and care for refugees both in Italy and across Europe. But del Grande also points out that the decision to make the film did not come from nowhere—many of those involved had previously taken refugees into their homes for some nights.

Teachers might use this film to explore parallels with past efforts to show support for those fleeing oppression, such as the Underground Railroad, the network of secret routes, safe houses, and people acting in solidarity, which enabled many fleeing slavery in the United States during the 19th century to make the journey north to safety and freedom in Canada. The *On the Bride's Side* team also chose to defy the law, because this law was seen by them to be not only unworkable, but unjust and inhumane. Teachers can consider the importance of examining historical struggles and enabling their students to make links with those of the present, examining past struggles for justice as part of a ongoing process rather than as something fully achieved. Not to do so is to present an incomplete and inaccurate vison of our world, suggesting that somehow we are morally or politically superior to those of previous generations.

Imagining and reimagining a vision of a cosmopolitan future is a challenging but essential task of education. Enabling students, at all levels of education, to contribute to this vison, or utopia, is a collective process. A more just society cannot be reached by individuals working alone, but it is one worth struggling for in a spirit of solidarity. In this sense the processes of education are a political intervention in the lives of all in the learning community, students and teachers alike.

Paulo Freire (1970), working with marginalized learners in Brazil, sought to develop a "pedagogy of the oppressed," in which learners were no longer seen as the recipients of knowledge—what he referred to as the "banking model"—but were engaged in processes of knowledge creation. Freire advocated dialogue, which is not just about learners developing their understanding, but is about a community of learners making a difference, building on their lived experience. So today, all students of human rights, whether from marginalized or privileged backgrounds, need to be involved in knowledge creation; yet for those who enjoy privilege, the next stages are likely to involve processes of unlearning and an understanding of power relations that generally go unquestioned. In Chapter 4 I explored how learners, by exploring untold stories or narratives (including their own), can work to create new knowledge, add layers of nuance and complexity to old knowledge, and even potentially overturn established ways of looking at the world.

The challenge of making a difference, particularly in enabling learners to do this through the processes of formal schooling, remains considerable. The story of *On the Bride's Side* requires educators not just to see teaching itself as an act of citizenship but to acknowledge that teaching has a political as well as a moral dimension. It is a political act. There can be no neutral position concerning social justice; not to act is to endorse and sustain inequality and injustice. As Kumashiro (2012) reminds us: "Teaching involves both intended and unintended lessons, and it is often in the unintended hidden lessons that oppression finds life and reinforcement" (p. 111). Anti-oppressive education requires teacher self-awareness, which is a step toward recognizing teaching as a political act. While some teachers may balk at the concept of teaching as a political act, fearing political indoctrination, the consciousness of teaching as a political act—or to put it another way, the teacher's self-awareness—seems to be an essential step in avoiding the processes of banking education that Freire challenged. It is in fact these banking processes of rote learning, unquestioning memorization, and absorption of textbook knowledge that leave the learner open to indoctrination.

There need to be many alternative spaces for human rights learning, not least among those accessing university and college education. Traditionally, human rights education has taken place in law schools, effectively restricting study primarily to those planning careers in the legal professions. This has meant that not only has human rights education generally been restricted to a specific professional group, but that even this group has generally not benefitted from an interdisciplinary approach to human rights, or from opportunities to explore human rights alongside those who are not would-be lawyers. Other professional groups clearly have a particular need for human rights education, notably journalists, who have a considerable influence on the ways human rights are understood or misunderstood in the wider society. There is clearly a strong case for specific professional human rights learning, tailored to professional needs. Additionally, since human rights learning is an interdisciplinary activity, and one that students need to relate to the here-and-now, human rights education should ideally bring together students across difference, addressing diverse sociocultural identities as well as specific professional ones. As Chapter 2 highlighted, human rights education is itself a human right, and thus a universal entitlement, applicable to all. In order to realize this right all possible spaces for human rights education need to be explored. As well as opening up new spaces for exploring human rights and social justice, teachers need to utilize those already in existence, transforming them to more readily meet the needs of diverse learners in an unequal world and in unequal communities.

In many regions of the world, university and college students are encouraged, and even expected, to engage in civic learning. At the same time, there has been a renewal of interest at national and international levels in education for democratic citizenship that targets children and young people in elementary and high schools across the globe (Banks, 2004; Cogan & Derricott, 2000; Council of Europe, 2002, 2011; European Commission, 1997; Osler & Starkey, 1999; Parker, 2003; Torney Purta, Lehmann, Oswald, & Schulz, 2001; Torney-Purta, Schwille, & Amadeo, 1999). Opportunities for civic learning at schools and universities are complementary: They can contribute both to the strengthening of democracy in schools and to the enhancement of democratic practices and processes in communities. This educational goal remains critical, as Osler and Starkey (2006) have noted:

> In both established democracies and newly established democratic states, such as those of Eastern and Central Europe and Latin America, there is a recognition that democracy is essentially fragile and that it depends on the active engagement of citizens, not just in voting, but in developing and participating in sustainable and cohesive communities. (p. 433)

The development of communities to which citizens contribute is essential to democracy, but it also is essential to effective learning and to teaching as an act of citizenship and as a political act.

Increasingly, programs are moving from a framework in which civic learning is designed for the national sphere (to which learners are assumed to have a natural affinity) to one that encompasses local, global, and other scales of belonging. Here I reflect on a framework for civic learning that might be applied at various levels of education to support what has been termed "education for cosmopolitan citizenship" (Osler, 2011b; Osler & Starkey, 2003, 2005).

Education for cosmopolitan citizenship aims to support learners' citizenship engagement at different scales, including the local, the national, and the international, and to understand the interconnections between these different scales. Such education must necessarily equip learners with knowledge and skills, but also with a disposition to take action to promote greater social justice, acknowledging not only their common humanity and global interconnectedness, but also learners' diverse affinities and identities. Civic educational programs that focus exclusively on the national level are no longer appropriate since, as Castles (2004) has observed, the "principle of each individual being a citizen of just one nation-state no longer corresponds with reality for millions of people who move across borders and who belong in various ways in multiple places" (p. 18).

As I have argued in previous chapters, educational programs that ignore a social justice dimension are not neutral, but are likely to compound existing disadvantages. In a deeply unequal world and in divided and deeply stratified societies, as Sensoy and DiAngelo (2012) point out, "Each of us does have a choice about whether we are going to work to interrupt these systems or support their existence by ignoring them. There is no neutral ground" (p. xxii). Therefore, teachers cannot be neutral in engaging in civic education.

Education for cosmopolitan citizenship is necessarily about enabling social justice. Yet, as researchers have argued (Sensoy & DiAngelo, 2010; Sleeter, 2005, 2015), inadequate theorizing can undermine teachers' efforts to promote social justice outcomes with unintended consequences. It is important to consider what universities currently aspire to realize within civic learning programs and to consider how these programs relate to changing conceptions of citizenship and changing concepts of citizen rights.

EDUCATION, CHANGING CITIZENSHIP, AND HUMAN RIGHTS

The Association of American Colleges and Universities (AACU) commissioned a National Task Force on Civic Learning and Democratic Engagement to review the components of effective civic education. The task force concluded that education for action was of key importance, and that the components of such learning should include, among other goals:

- Knowledge of the political systems that frame constitutional democracies and of political levers for influencing change
- Knowledge of diverse cultures and religions, in the United States and around the world
- Critical inquiry and reasoning capacities
- Deliberation and bridge-building across differences
- Open-mindedness and capacity to engage different points of view and cultures
- Civic problem-solving skills and experience
- Civility, ethical integrity, and mutual respect (National Task Force . . ., 2012, p. 4)

The task force found that 70% of U.S. college students report participating in some form of volunteering, community service, or service learning, and around one-half reports participation in credit-bearing service learning activities (National Task Force . . . , 2012). While the task force noted that research indicates that service learning is positively associated with a variety of civic learning outcomes, it also found that over time students' civic learning is neither robust nor persuasive.

A framework is needed whereby service learning extends beyond activities that encourage charity or goodwill to the less fortunate to activities in which students are encouraged to show solidarity with their fellow human-kind. A human rights framework, it is argued here, would support such a development and offer a strong, robust, and unifying foundation for such learning. Ideally, students should be able to make links between local struggles for justice and global efforts to promote human rights. In doing so, it enables students to look critically at injustice close to home, ensuring that rights are not used solely as a discourse or justification for foreign policy intervention. A human rights framework offers greater coherence to diverse civic learning initiatives and enables higher education institutions to support students in enhancing and strengthening democracy and justice at home.

European nations (all 47 member states of the Council of Europe, 28 of which are also members of the European Union) have made both a rhetorical and a legally binding commitment to human rights. The Council of Europe exists to promote and protect human rights, and all member states have ratified the 1950 European Convention on Human Rights (ECHR), a treaty designed to protect human rights, democracy, and the rule of law, which covers all people living under the jurisdiction of these states, regardless of their citizenship status. Nevertheless, as we have seen in Chapter 2, within Europe concrete national commitments to support education for democratic citizenship (EDC) and human rights education (HRE) vary somewhat.[2]

At the same time, in this second decade of the 21st century, Europe faces considerable challenges in enabling a human rights culture through education. Many of these challenges also apply in other regions. One challenge relates to the danger of far-right activists who have expressed racist and Islamophobic views, incompatible with democratic principles; these dangers have been exacerbated by senior political leaders who have engaged in populist rhetoric (Council of Europe's Group of Eminent Persons, 2011; Osler, 2015a&b).

The second challenge facing educators, and indeed all those engaged in broader social policymaking, relates to the nature of recent migration in Europe. The current era has been characterized as one of "super-diversity" (Vertovec, 2007), a term coined to acknowledge that national communities are today increasingly diverse and that newcomers are no longer necessarily linked to places with which states have longstanding colonial or other historical links. Since 2004 and the expansion of the EU, countries in western Europe have seen significant migration from the east to the west, and the continent now faces the issue of large numbers of undocumented migrants and asylum seekers arriving across the Mediterranean, as well as overland from Syria and north Africa.[3] The tardy response by western European governments to put in place adequate measures to rescue such migrants and address their needs once they arrive has called Europe's human rights standards and the efficacy of its political institutions into question.

This situation places a crucial responsibility on teachers of citizenship and human rights to enable learners, first, to understand and engage with international (EU) and national policy responses to migration and changing demographics; and second, to understand the interconnectedness of Europe with the places from which these migrants come. Students need opportunities to examine the stratified and often unequal relationships between European nations and the places migrants and refugees are fleeing, relationships that are mediated through colonial history and recent conflicts and through policies developed in response to resources and trading opportunities.

A third and significant challenge facing educators in schools and universities across Europe relates to government initiatives against radicalization. Educators are expected to address the perceived risks of radicalization and, sometimes, to inform the authorities about persons at risk. In particular, schoolteachers are being asked to safeguard children from these risks (Coppock, 2014). In Norway, for example, the Oslo municipality has engaged in a project to counter radicalization through social studies classes in the capital, with schools collaborating with the police in an education initiative that forms part of a broader government strategy against extremism. The apparent purpose of the initiative is not simply to counter radicalization but "to allow the teacher to *capture evidence of harmful radicalization* [emphasis added]" (Slettholm, 2015, my translation). It is not clear what is supposed to happen if such "evidence" is found.

In the United Kingdom, between 2000 and 2011, six major British antiterrorism acts were passed. These were tied to the government's antiterrorist strategy known as *Prevent*, which has an educational dimension. Schools and universities are supposed to act as part of the government's antiterrorist strategy. In 2011 the then Conservative education minister sought to strengthen the educational dimension of the antiterrorist strategy by setting up the Preventing Extremism Unit within England's education ministry. He instructed the chief inspector of schools to "ensure that children are safeguarded from extremists and their unacceptable messages" (Gove, 2011). In such situations where the role of the police and the role of teachers become confused and intertwined, trust between schools and students and their families is undermined. Although the ministry also provided examples of approaches to teaching resilience against extremism, such as lessons on how to deconstruct media representations and propaganda, little emphasis has been given to supporting teachers in such initiatives (Bonnell et al., 2011). There is a real risk that, without such training and support, efforts by schools to implement *Prevent* may undermine children's rights, for example, Article 13 (freedom of expression) and Article 14 (freedom of thought, conscience, and religion) under the Convention on the Rights of the Child (U.N., 1989).

Directly and indirectly, education policy discourses have begun to address the education of Muslim children and youth with reference to security, radicalization, and extremism (Coppock, 2014), rather than developing human rights education to counter extremism of all kinds so that young people develop solidarity with each other, regardless of characteristics such as religious faith (Davies 2008a, 2008b).

The media's tendency to focus on protecting young people from the dangers of radicalization often results in the playing down of concerns about achievement gaps between minority and mainstream youth and about discrimination in the wider society more generally. Teachers also are distracted from the task of closing achievement gaps and thus enabling greater social justice. Where the security services or the police are involved in antiradicalization programs, there is a real risk that educational goals may take second place to security concerns. Such initiatives may be ill-conceived, possibly undermining rather than strengthening social cohesion. In Britain, for example, governments have focused almost exclusively on threats from Islamist terrorism and have thus neglected far-right racist and xenophobic agendas (Osler, 2011a). The targeting of Muslim children by such policies may well be in contravention of the CRC Article 2 (nondiscrimination).

The components of effective civic education identified by the AACU task force can be strengthened by a human rights framework, an argument that is further elaborated upon below. At the same time, educators need to address complex questions related to citizenship and human rights within unequal, divided, and stratified societies, whether they are addressing local, national, or global contexts. Furthermore, teachers and their students in Europe may need to challenge policies designed ostensibly to support social cohesion and challenge extremism, as they may risk undermining students' human rights and the principles of the Council of Europe.

Across Europe, the civic education of diverse racial, cultural, ethnic, religious, and linguistic groups continues to pose a number of challenges, not least because of the gap between Europe's human rights rhetoric and a growing "them" and "us" political discourse. This discourse distinguishes between "our" mainstream values and "their" values, particularly in relation to minoritized Muslim-heritage communities. Schools and universities face the additional challenge of recognizing students' religious identities within apparently secular (but never neutral) school systems (Osler, 2007; Berkeley, 2008). These challenges have been compounded by public, political, and media responses to terrorist attacks. For example, in Paris it appeared that the predominant message of those who marched in defiance of the attackers on January 11, 2015, equated human rights with freedom of expression, thereby eclipsing other rights that are also currently under threat, such as freedom of religion, nondiscrimination, security, and protection for minorities.

EDUCATION FOR HUMAN RIGHTS AND ACTION

Earlier chapters have suggested that human rights education, as currently conceived, is necessary but insufficient to enable social justice through education. Although there may be growing skepticism about international human rights institutions, this does not detract from the power of human rights discourses in popular struggles for justice (Hopgood, 2013). Yet, if human rights education is to support everyday struggles against inequalities and contribute to justice and peace in the world, I have argued that it needs greater theorization and have offered some pointers to enable this. It also needs to claim a substantive space within the school curriculum.

The AACU advocates a civic education for action (National Task Force..., 2012). Along similar lines, this chapter argues that civic education at various scales—from the local to the global—needs to be founded in human rights; it needs to be adequately theorized so as to enable social justice; and it should enable students to acquire long-lasting skills and dispositions for the strengthening of democracy.

Effective civic education also implies a form of learning that engages with students' own identities and prior experiences, extending both of these in the process. As Chapter 7 highlighted, Osler and Starkey (2005) have characterized citizenship as a status, a feeling, and a practice. Looking beyond citizenship as nationality is critical. The nation remains important, but needs to be reimagined as cosmopolitan. Education for cosmopolitan citizenship needs to engage with learners as holders of human rights (status), to support them in achieving a sense of belonging (feeling), and to equip them with skills for action (practice) so that they can make a difference.

Human rights have been recognized, by the nations of the world and by the international community, as principles for living together and as principles that should underpin education. The teacher in a democratic community who recognizes education as a political as well as moral responsibility is strengthened by this context. Students' rights are respected, their identities recognized, and their understanding of our interconnections, at all scales from the local to the global, are extended through education underpinned by the cosmopolitan vision of human rights. Education, thus conceived, implies participatory, student-centered pedagogies, and an interdisciplinary endeavor founded in human rights and real struggles for justice. It is based on an understanding of our human interdependence based on a cosmopolitan vision that embraces the nation but extends beyond it. It implies knowledge of the international human rights framework to be sure, but equally it implies an education that supports and sustains the human urge to resist oppression and strive for greater justice.

Notes

Chapter 1

1. Although economic, social, and cultural rights do often require high levels of investment, civil and political rights also have costs. They do not simply require the state to refrain from interfering with individual freedoms. Civil and poltical rights also require investment if they are to be fully realized. For example, a proper infrastructure, which includes a well-functioning court system, guarantees of minimum living conditions for prisoners, free and fair elections, and so on, also require investment for their full realization. Likewise, economic and social rights require the state to refrain from interfering. For example, the right to join a trade union requires the state not to interfere in individual freedoms.

2. According to the World Health Organization, suicide rates per 100,000 young persons aged 15–19 in the Republic of Korea were 5.9 for boys and 4.9 for girls (overall 5.4, $n = 95$) in 2001. This figure is particularly high among girls compared with other countries. For example, Japan had a suicide rate of 3.8 among girls, with an overall rate of 6.4 (Wassermann, Cheng, & Jiang, 2005). It compares with an overall rate of 4.2 in the United Kingdom, 5.6 in Germany, and 10.9 in Norway. In most countries the reported rate is higher for boys, but there are exceptions, with China being among those countries with a higher reported teen suicide rate among girls.

Chapter 2

1. Banned Books Week is an annual event, coordinated by the American Library Association (ALA), celebrating the freedom to read. Banned Books Week highlights the value of free and open access to information and aims to bring together librarians, booksellers, publishers, journalists, teachers, and readers of all types in shared support of the freedom to seek and express ideas, even those some consider unorthodox or unpopular. The ALA highlights books that have been banned over the decades and also "challenged" books. Challenges do not simply involve a person expressing a point of view; rather, they are an attempt to remove material, thereby restricting others' access. Challenges are most frequently made to children's access to books, and typically seek to remove such items from a school or public library or from the curriculum. For further details, including information about books that have been challenged or banned, see the ALA website (www.ala.org/bbooks/about).

2. The U.N. Declaration was adopted by a majority of 143 states in favor, 4 votes against (Australia, Canada, New Zealand, and the United States), and 11 abstentions.

3. On June 26, 2015 the U.S. Supreme Court in Obergefell v. Hodges ruled that states cannot ban same-sex marriage, citing the 14th Amendment and the principle of "equal dignity in the eyes of the law." Supreme Court of the United States, Obergefell et al. v. Hodges et al. No.14 -556. Argued April 28, 2015. Decided June 26, 2015. http://www.supremecourt.gov/

opinions/14pdf/14-556_3204.pdf   Liptak, A. (2015) Supreme Court Ruling Makes Same-Sex Marriage a Right Nationwide. June 26. New York Times http://www.nytimes.com/2015/06/27/us/supreme-court-same-sex-marriage.html?_r=0

Chapter 3

1. For decades Germany denied citizenship to "guest-workers" on the premise that German citizenship could only be acquired through bloodlines. Britain has had piecemeal multicultural polices, for example, in education, dependent on the commitment of specific local authorities (Figueroa, 2004; Osler, 2011a; Tomlinson, 2009).

2. These comments are especially noteworthy since they are expressed in a publication by the Council of Europe, a respected international body, and are direct criticisms of leaders of Council of Europe member-states.

3. Sojourner Truth is famed for her speech "Ain't I a woman?" delivered at the Ohio Women's Rights Convention in 1851, which implicitly adopted the concept of intersectionality.

Chapter 5

1. While such identities are commonplace in North America this is not the case in early 21st-century Europe.

2. The Greek authorities have since acted in arresting Golden Dawn leaders (see www.bbc.co.uk/news/world-europe-24391656).

3. An opinion poll carried out in 2011 found that 25% of Norwegians believed there were too many Muslims in the country, but the figure dropped to 16% in Oslo, where half of all Muslims live. See Norwegian Broadcasting Corporation (NKR), 2011.

4. Examples of countries that moved to become totalitarian states following elections include Nazi Germany in the 1930s and Egypt in the second decade of the 21st century. During the 20th century democracy was threatened by military coups in many states, including Argentina, Chile, and Greece.

5. The Nordic nations, as member states of the Council of Europe, are required to conform to the standards of the European Convention on Human Rights and comply with the rulings of the European Court of Human Rights.

6. Norway is not an EU member-state, but implements many EU polices, including movement of labor, and has signed the Schengen agreement allowing free movement across Schengen member-states.

7. Some 669,000 are themselves migrants and 135,600 are the children of migrants. The largest group of migrants are from the EU/EEA, with those from Poland amounting to 100,000 persons.

8. The Sami parliament is an important channel of political influence, and its business, as determined by the Norwegian Sami Act of 1987, is "any matter that in the view of the Parliament particularly affects the Sami people" (quoted in Josefsen, 2010, p. 9). The Sami language is an official language in Norway.

9. For further discussion, see Osler and Lybæk (2014). For the full judgment of the UNHRC see: www.unhchr.ch/tbs/doc.nsf/0/6187ce3dc0091758c1256f7000526973?Opendocument

10. Article 2 Protocol 2 of the European Convention on Human Rights relates to the right to education and the state's duty to ensure it is in conformity with parents' religious and philosophical convictions.

11. From 2014 there are indications of a change, with initiatives designed to give greater curriculum emphasis to human rights in both schools and teacher education.

Chapter 6

1. The Kurdistan Region is situated in the north of Iraq and is the country's only autonomous region.

2. Two Kurdish dialects are spoken in the region: Kurmanji in Duhok and Sorani in Erbil.

3. While some Syrian refugees are accommodated in a camp near Duhok, others are spread across the region, supported by families and communities (IOM, 2012).

4. These statistics do not include those living in the community, lodging with families or other local people.

5. Women may lack access to shelters, which in any case may close for lack of support. Some claim that shelters have allowed women at risk to be returned to their families.

6. The data were collected as part of a small-scale research and development initiative funded by the British Council's DelPHE program (British Council, 2010). A paper from this project, INTERDEMOCRATE (intercultural and democratic learning in teacher education), is published as Ahmad et al. (2012). The project builds on a longstanding partnership between University College of Southeast Norway and Duhok University, Iraq. I am grateful for the support of the principal investigator, Dr. Lena Lybæk, and project members Niroj Ahmad, Adnam Ismail, and Nadia Zako for the data collection.

7. I wish to thank Chalank Yahya both for her significant contribution to this chapter and for her insights, which have informed my understandings of the region.

8. This concern that a student should not "fail" in human rights, or indeed in citizenship, is one that is echoed by educators in widely different global contexts. It suggests that educators look closely at their assessment procedures and practices.

9. Wasta is a form of nepotism or corruption commonly linked to family and tribal affiliations or obligations.

Chapter 7

1. In fact, Hillary Rodham Clinton was at the time adopting a conservative position, making an argument for minimum state intervention in children's lives in cases where children risk serious harm, over the application of the "best interests" principle (Lindsey & Sarri, 1992).

2. In reality, the enjoyment of all human rights is interlinked. Although the UDHR makes no distinction between rights, during the Cold War period Western market economies tended to emphasize civil and political rights, while Eastern bloc nations highlighted the importance of economic, social, and cultural rights. This division led to the adoption of two separate covenants in 1966—one on civil and political rights (ICCPR) and the other on economic, social, and cultural rights (ICESCR). Today it is common to refer to civil, cultural, economic, political, and social rights.

3. They claimed that it was a breach of their freedom of religion under Article 9 of the European Convention on Human Rights. The case of R (on behalf of Williamson) v Secretary of State for Education and Employment was brought to the House of Lords (Court of Appeal). The Lords ruled that there was a difference between freedom of religion and freedom to manifest that belief, and that this freedom was restricted "in a democratic society . . . for the protection of the rights and freedoms of others," in this case, children.

4. Somalia subsequently ratified the Convention on the Rights of the Child in January 2015.

Chapter 8

1. Stockholm, Sweden's capital, is a rail journey of some 30 hours, with a minimum of four different train connections in Switzerland, Germany, and Denmark.

2. In 2006 the Spanish parliament approved the Education Act 2/2006, which introduced "Education for Citizenship and Human Rights," in line with Recommendation CM/Rec(2010)7 (Council of Europe, 2010). The law incorporated social and civic competences for all within compulsory education. Subsequently, an assault on the course by the Catholic Church hierarchy, the Popular Party, and right-wing media led to a campaign for its removal. Although the Spanish Supreme Court ruled the program legal and legitimate, following the 2011 elections in which the Popular Party came into government, the HRE/EDC proposals were suppressed by an education reform law, despite a European-wide campaign (Fundación Cives, 2013). In 2000 citizenship education (CE) was introduced into schools in England with cross-party support. Following the election of a Conservative–led coalition government in 2010, CE was no longer prioritized and became effective only in schools committed to it.

3. For the year 2014, the International Organization for Migration's (IOM) Missing Migrants Project (2015) reported that 3,279 migrants died trying to reach Europe by sea.

The Universal Declaration of Human Rights

Preamble*

Whereas recognition of the inherent dignity and of the equal and inalienable rights of all members of the human family is the foundation of freedom, justice and peace in the world,

Whereas disregard and contempt for human rights have resulted in barbarous acts which have outraged the conscience of mankind, and the advent of a world in which human beings shall enjoy freedom of speech and belief and freedom from fear and want has been proclaimed as the highest aspiration of the common people,

Whereas it is essential, if man is not to be compelled to have recourse, as a last resort, to rebellion against tyranny and oppression, that human rights should be protected by the rule of law,

Whereas it is essential to promote the development of friendly relations between nations,

Whereas the peoples of the United Nations have in the Charter reaffirmed their faith in fundamental human rights, in the dignity and worth of the human person and in the equal rights of men and women and have determined to promote social progress and better standards of life in larger freedom,

Whereas Member States have pledged themselves to achieve, in co-operation with the United Nations, the promotion of universal respect for and observance of human rights and fundamental freedoms,

Whereas a common understanding of these rights and freedoms is of the greatest importance for the full realization of this pledge,

---

* The Universal Declaration of Human Rights (UDHR) is a milestone document in the history of human rights, proclaimed by the United Nations General Assembly on December 10, 1948 in Paris. The drafting committee was chaired by Eleanor Roosevelt. Canadian John Peters Humphry provided the initial draft for the Human Rights Commission responsible for its development. The Commission consisted of representatives with different legal and cultural backgrounds from all regions of the world. It was proclaimed as a common standard of achievement for all peoples and all nations, setting out for the first time, fundamental human rights to be universally protected. It has moral rather than legally binding status.

**Now, Therefore THE GENERAL ASSEMBLY proclaims THIS UNI-
VERSAL DECLARATION OF HUMAN RIGHTS** as a common stan-
dard of achievement for all peoples and all nations, to the end that every
individual and every organ of society, keeping this Declaration constantly
in mind, shall strive by teaching and education to promote respect for these
rights and freedoms and by progressive measures, national and international, to secure their universal and effective recognition and observance, both
among the peoples of Member States themselves and among the peoples of
territories under their jurisdiction.

Article 1

All human beings are born free and equal in dignity and rights. They are
endowed with reason and conscience and should act towards one another in a spirit of brotherhood.

Article 2

Everyone is entitled to all the rights and freedoms set forth in this Declaration, without distinction of any kind, such as race, colour, sex, language,
religion, political or other opinion, national or social origin, property,
birth or other status. Furthermore, no distinction shall be made on the
basis of the political, jurisdictional or international status of the country
or territory to which a person belongs, whether it be independent, trust,
non-self-governing or under any other limitation of sovereignty.

Article 3

Everyone has the right to life, liberty and security of person.

Article 4

No one shall be held in slavery or servitude; slavery and the slave trade shall
be prohibited in all their forms.

Article 5

No one shall be subjected to torture or to cruel, inhuman or degrading
treatment or punishment.

Article 6

Everyone has the right to recognition everywhere as a person before the
law.

Article 7

All are equal before the law and are entitled without any discrimination to
equal protection of the law. All are entitled to equal protection against
any discrimination in violation of this Declaration and against any incite-
ment to such discrimination.

Article 8

Everyone has the right to an effective remedy by the competent national tribunals for acts violating the fundamental rights granted him by the constitution or by law.

Article 9

No one shall be subjected to arbitrary arrest, detention or exile.

Article 10

Everyone is entitled in full equality to a fair and public hearing by an independent and impartial tribunal, in the determination of his rights and obligations and of any criminal charge against him.

Article 11

1. Everyone charged with a penal offence has the right to be presumed innocent until proved guilty according to law in a public trial at which he has had all the guarantees necessary for his defence.
2. No one shall be held guilty of any penal offence on account of any act or omission which did not constitute a penal offence, under national or international law, at the time when it was committed. Nor shall a heavier penalty be imposed than the one that was applicable at the time the penal offence was committed.

Article 12

No one shall be subjected to arbitrary interference with his privacy, family, home or correspondence, nor to attacks upon his honour and reputation. Everyone has the right to the protection of the law against such interference or attacks.

Article 13

1. Everyone has the right to freedom of movement and residence within the borders of each state.
2. Everyone has the right to leave any country, including his own, and to return to his country.

Article 14

1. Everyone has the right to seek and to enjoy in other countries asylum from persecution.
2. This right may not be invoked in the case of prosecutions genuinely arising from non-political crimes or from acts contrary to the purposes and principles of the United Nations.

Article 15

1. Everyone has the right to a nationality.

2. No one shall be arbitrarily deprived of his nationality nor denied the right to change his nationality.

Article 16

1. Men and women of full age, without any limitation due to race, nationality or religion, have the right to marry and to found a family. They are entitled to equal rights as to marriage, during marriage and at its dissolution.
2. Marriage shall be entered into only with the free and full consent of the intending spouses.
3. The family is the natural and fundamental group unit of society and is entitled to protection by society and the State.

Article 17

1. Everyone has the right to own property alone as well as in association with others.
2. No one shall be arbitrarily deprived of his property.

Article 18

Everyone has the right to freedom of thought, conscience and religion; this right includes freedom to change his religion or belief, and freedom, either alone or in community with others and in public or private, to manifest his religion or belief in teaching, practice, worship and observance.

Article 19

Everyone has the right to freedom of opinion and expression; this right includes freedom to hold opinions without interference and to seek, receive and impart information and ideas through any media and regardless of frontiers.

Article 20

1. Everyone has the right to freedom of peaceful assembly and association.
2. No one may be compelled to belong to an association.

Article 21

1. Everyone has the right to take part in the government of his country, directly or through freely chosen representatives.
2. Everyone has the right of equal access to public service in his country.
3. The will of the people shall be the basis of the authority of government; this will shall be expressed in periodic and genuine elections which shall be by universal and equal suffrage and shall be held by secret vote or by equivalent free voting procedures.

Article 22

Everyone, as a member of society, has the right to social security and is entitled to realization, through national effort and international co-operation
and in accordance with the organization and resources of each State, of
the economic, social and cultural rights indispensable for his dignity and
the free development of his personality.

Article 23

1. Everyone has the right to work, to free choice of employment, to just
   and favorable conditions of work and to protection against unemployment.
2. Everyone, without any discrimination, has the right to equal pay for
   equal work.
3. Everyone who works has the right to just and favourable remuneration
   ensuring for himself and his family an existence worthy of human dignity,
   and supplemented, if necessary, by other means of social protection.
4. Everyone has the right to form and to join trade unions for the protection of his interests.

Article 24

Everyone has the right to rest and leisure, including reasonable limitation of
working hours and periodic holidays with pay.

Article 25

1. Everyone has the right to a standard of living adequate for the health and
   well-being of himself and of his family, including food, clothing, housing
   and medical care and necessary social services, and the right to security in
   the event of unemployment, sickness, disability, widowhood, old age or
   other lack of livelihood in circumstances beyond his control.
2. Motherhood and childhood are entitled to special care and assistance. All
   children, whether born in or out of wedlock, shall enjoy the same social
   protection.

Article 26

1. Everyone has the right to education. Education shall be free, at least in
   the elementary and fundamental stages. Elementary education shall be
   compulsory. Technical and professional education shall be made generally available and higher education shall be equally accessible to all on the
   basis of merit.
2. Education shall be directed to the full development of the human personality and to the strengthening of respect for human rights and fundamental freedoms. It shall promote understanding, tolerance and friendship among all nations, racial or religious groups, and shall further the
   activities of the United Nations for the maintenance of peace.

3. Parents have a prior right to choose the kind of education that shall be given to their children.

Article 27

1. Everyone has the right freely to participate in the cultural life of the community, to enjoy the arts and to share in scientific advancement and its benefits.
2. Everyone has the right to the protection of the moral and material interests resulting from any scientific, literary or artistic production of which he is the author.

Article 28

Everyone is entitled to a social and international order in which the rights and freedoms set forth in this Declaration can be fully realized.

Article 29

1. Everyone has duties to the community in which alone the free and full development of his personality is possible.
2. In the exercise of his rights and freedoms, everyone shall be subject only to such limitations as are determined by law solely for the purpose of securing due recognition and respect for the rights and freedoms of others and of meeting the just requirements of morality, public order and the general welfare in a democratic society.
3. These rights and freedoms may in no case be exercised contrary to the purposes and principles of the United Nations.

Article 30

Nothing in this Declaration may be interpreted as implying for any State, group or person any right to engage in any activity or to perform any act aimed at the destruction of any of the rights and freedoms set forth herein.

Unofficial Summary of the U.N. Convention on the Rights of the Child

The Preamble†

- recalls the basic principles of the United Nations and specific provisions to certain relevant human rights treaties and proclamations such as the Universal Declaration of Human Rights;
- reaffirms the fact that children, because of their vulnerability, need special care and protection; and
- places special emphasis on the primary caring and protective responsibility of the family, the need for legal and other protection of the child, the importance of respect for the cultural values of the child's community, and the vital role of international co-operation in achieving the realisation of children's rights.

Article 1: Definition of a child

Children are defined as all people under 18 years of age.

Article 2: Non-discrimination

All rights in the Convention apply to all children without exception, and the State has an obligation to protect children from any and all forms of discrimination including that resulting from their parents or guardian's status.

Article 3: Best interests of the child

All actions concerning the child must be based on his or her best interests.

Article 4: Implementation of rights

The State has an obligation to translate the rights of the Convention into reality.

---

† Children's Rights Alliance, *Summary of the UN Convention on the Rights of the Child* (July 2013). Retrieved from www.childrensrights.ie/sites/default/files/information_sheets/files/SummaryUNCRC.pdf. This unofficial summary has no legal status. Scholars wishing to study the Convention on the Rights of the Child in some depth are advised to refer to the full text provided in the references (United Nations, 1989).

Article 5: Parental guidance and the child's evolving capacities as he or she grows

The State has a duty to respect the rights and responsibilities of parents and the wider family or others involved in the upbringing of the child in a manner appropriate to the child's evolving capacities.

Article 6: Survival and development

The child has an inherent right to life, and the State has an obligation to ensure to the maximum extent possible the survival and development of the child.

Article 7: Name and nationality

The child has the right to be registered, to have a name from birth and to be granted a nationality. In addition, the child has the right to know and be cared for [by] his or her parents.

Article 8: Preservation of identity

The State has an obligation to protect and, if necessary, re-establish the basic aspects of the child's identity (name, nationality and family relations).

Article 9: Separation from parents

The child has the right to live with his or her parents unless it is not deemed to be in his or her best interests; the child has the right to maintain contact with both parents if separated from one or both.

Article 10: Family reunification

The State has an obligation to foster and enable family reunification where children and parents live in separate countries; the child whose parents live in a different state has the right to maintain personal relations and direct contact with both parents.

Article 11: Illicit transfer and non-return of children from abroad

The State has an obligation to try to prevent and to remedy the illicit transfer and non-return of children abroad by a parent or third party.

Article 12: The child's opinion

The child has the right to express an opinion, and to have that opinion taken into account, in any matter or procedure affecting the child, in accordance with his or her age and maturity.

Article 13: Freedom of expression

The child has the right to obtain and make known information, and to express his or her own views, unless this would violate the rights of others.

Article 14: Freedom of thought, conscience and religion

The child has the right to freedom of thought, conscience and religion, subject to appropriate parental guidance and national law.

Article 15: Freedom of association

The child has the right to meet with others and to join or set up associations, unless doing so would violate the rights of others.

Article 16: Protection of privacy

The child has the right to protection from interference with privacy, family, home and correspondence, and from libel or slander.

Article 17: Access to appropriate information

The State has an obligation to ensure that the child has access to information and material from a diversity of media sources and to take measures to protect children from harmful materials.

Article 18: Parental responsibilities

The State has an obligation to recognise and promote the principle that both parents or legal guardians have common responsibilities for the upbringing and development of the child; the State shall support parents or legal guardians in this task through the provision of appropriate assistance.

Article 19: Protection from abuse and neglect

The State has an obligation to protect children from all forms of abuse and neglect, to provide support to those who have been abused and to investigate instances of abuse.

Article 20: Protection of children without families

The State has an obligation to provide special protection for children without families and to ensure that appropriate alternative family care or institutional placement is made available to them, taking into account the child's cultural background.

Article 21: Adoption

In countries where adoption is recognised and/or allowed, it shall only be carried out in the best interests of the child, with all necessary safeguards for the child and under the authorization of competent authorities.

Article 22: Refugee children

Special protection is to be granted to children who are refugees or seeking refugee status, and the State has an obligation to co-operate with competent organisations providing such protection and assistance.

Article 23: Children with a disability

Children with a mental or physical disability have the right to special care, education and training designed to help them to achieve the greatest possible self-reliance and to lead a full active life in society.

Article 24: Health and health services

The child has the right to the enjoyment of the highest possible standard of health and to have access to healthcare and medical services. In its provision of health services, the State shall place special emphasis on primary and pre-ventative health care and public health education.

Article 25: Periodic review of placement in care settings

The child who has been placed in a care setting by the State for reasons of care, protection or treatment has the right to have all aspects of that place-ment reviewed and evaluated regularly.

Article 26: Social security

The child has the right to benefit from social security.

Article 27: Growing up free from poverty

The child has the right to an adequate standard of living; parents have the pri-mary responsibility to provide this, and the State has a duty to assist parents, where necessary, in fulfilling this right.

Article 28: Education

The child has the right to education; the State has a duty to make primary education compulsory and free to all; to take measures to develop different forms of secondary education and to make this accessible to all children. School discipline should be administered in a manner consistent with the child's human dignity.

Article 29: Aims of education

Education should be directed at developing the child's personality and tal-ents; preparing the child for active life as an adult; fostering respect for basic human rights; developing respect for the child's own cultural and national values and those of others; and developing respect for the natural environ-ment.

Article 30: Children of minorities or indigenous peoples

Children of minority communities and indigenous peoples have the right to enjoy their own culture, to practice their own religion and to use their own language.

Article 31: Leisure, recreation and cultural activities

The child has the right to rest and to engage in leisure, play and recreational activities and to participate in cultural and artistic activities.

Article 32: Child labour

The State has an obligation to protect children from engaging in work that negatively impacts their health, education or development; to set a minimum age for employment; and to regulate conditions of employment.

Article 33: Drug abuse

The child has a right to protection from illicit use of narcotic and psychotropic drugs and from being involved in their production and distribution.

Article 34: Sexual exploitation

The child has the right to protection from all forms of sexual exploitation and sexual abuse, including prostitution and involvement in pornography.‡

Article 35: Sale, trafficking and abduction

The State has an obligation to prevent any form of abduction of children or sale of or traffic in children.

Article 36: Other forms of exploitation

The child has the right to protection from all other forms of exploitation prejudicial to their welfare.

Article 37: Torture and deprivation of liberty

The State has an obligation to ensure that no child is subject to torture, cruel, inhuman or degrading treatment or punishment, capital punishment, life imprisonment, and unlawful arrest or deprivation of liberty. A child who is deprived of liberty must be treated with humanity and respect and in a manner that is appropriate to his or her age. Children who are detained should be separated from adults, have the right to contact with family, and access to legal and other assistance.

Article 38: Armed conflicts

The State has an obligation to respect, and to ensure respect for humanitarian law as it applies to children in situations of armed conflict. States must ensure that no child under the age of fifteen can take direct part in hostilities or be recruited into the armed forces. States must take all feasible measures

---

‡   The Optional Protocol to the UN Convention on the Rights of the Child on the Sale of Children, Child Prostitution and Child Pornography was adopted by the UN General Assembly in 2000. It prohibits the sale of children, child prostitution and child pornography and requires State Parties to adopt appropriate measures to protect the rights and interests of child victims.

to ensure protection and care of children who are affected by armed conflict.§

Article 39: Rehabilitative care

The State has an obligation to take all appropriate measures to promote the physical and psychological recovery and social integration of children who have been victims of any form of neglect, exploitation or abuse, torture or degrading treatment or of armed conflict.

Article 40: Administration of juvenile justice

Children accused of, or recognised as having committed, an offence have the right to respect for their human rights and in particular to benefit from all aspects of the due process of law, including legal or other assistance in preparing and presenting their defence. States have an obligation to promote alternative procedures and measures so as to ensure that recourse to judicial proceedings and institutional placements can be avoided wherever possible and appropriate.

Article 41: Respect for existing standards

If standards set in the national law of a country which has ratified the Convention, or in other applicable international instruments, are higher than those in the Convention on the Rights of the Child, it is the higher standard that will apply.

Articles 42-45 define how compliance with the Convention is to be monitored and fostered.

Article 42

The State has an obligation to make the rights contained in the Convention widely known to adults and children alike.

Article 43 and Article 44

States which ratify the Convention must submit a report on implementation two years after ratification and every five years thereafter. This report is submitted to the UN Committee on the Rights of the Child which consists of eighteen child rights experts elected by State Parties for the purposes of examining progress made by State Parties in implementing the Convention. State Parties are required to make their reports widely available to the general public in their own country.

---

§   The Optional Protocol to the UN Convention on the Rights of the Child on the Involvement of Children in Armed Conflict was formally adopted by the UN General Assembly on 25 May 2000. This Protocol establishes eighteen years as the minimum age for participation in armed conflict, for compulsory recruitment, and for recruitment or use in armed conflict by armed groups.

Article 45

In order to "foster the effective implementation of the Convention and to encourage international cooperation," the specialised agencies of the UN (such as the ILO, WHO, UNHCR, UNESCO and UNICEF) are involved in the process of considering international reports. Non-governmental organizations (NGOs) may also submit relevant information to the UN Committee on the Rights of the Child. The Committee may invite the UN specialised agencies and NGOs to advise on the optimal implementation of the Convention.

Articles 46–54

Articles 46–54 define the conditions under which the Convention comes into force.

Does Your School Environment Give Everyone a Chance to Enjoy Their Rights?

PROVISION			
	Sometimes	Always	Never
1. Students and teachers have opportunities to learn about the UN Convention on the Rights of the Child and to consider its implications for the school (Article 29).			
2. Girls and boys have equal access to all subjects and lessons (Articles 2, 28, 29).			
3. All texts take account of cultural differences in the school population (Articles 2, 28, 29.1c, 30).			
4. In the teaching of national history, due weight is given to women and minorities and to their versions of history (Articles 2, 13, 28, 29.1c & d, 30).			
5. Resources for sport (inlcuding equipment, activities, times of use) are equally accessible to girls and boys (Articles 2, 28, 31).			
6. Extracurricular activities organized by the school are available to all regardless of ability to pay (Articles 2, 28, 31).			
7. The school is accessible to people with disabilities (Articles 2, 23, 28).			
8. The curriculum is organized so that students may opt out of religious education and this possibility is made known (Article 14).			

	Sometimes	Always	Never

9. Care is taken that students' names are recorded and pronounced appropriately (Article 7).

10. Efforts are made to ensure regular attendence (Article 28).

11. The school provides opportunities for students to express themselves through art, music, and drama (Articles 13, 14, 29, 31).

PROTECTION

12. People are careful not to cause physical harm. For example:

a. adults are not allowed to hit young people.

b. young people are not allowed to hit adults.

c. young people are not allowed to hit each other.

13. Students' lockers are considered private property (Article 16).

14. Any personal files on a student kept by the school can be inspected by the student whose file it is and the parents, if appropriate. The file can be checked and corrected if necessary (Articles 5, 16, 17, 18).

15. The contents of any files, whether personal or vocational may not be communicated to a third party without the permission of the student and her or his parents if appropriate (Articles 15, 16, 18).

16. Any person receiving information from a school file accepts that they are bound by confidentiality (Article 16).

17. No posters, images, or drawings of a racist, sexist, or discriminatory kind may be displayed anywhere on school premises (Articles 2, 17, 29.1b, c, & d).

18. People encourage each other to be tolerant, particularly of those who appear different (Article 29).

19. When there is an incident that may lead to the exclusion of a student or disciplinary action, an impartial hearing is organized. In other words, all those involved get a hearing (Articles 28.2, 40).

	Sometimes	Always	Never
20. A student accused of breaking the rules is presumed innocent until proven guilty and carries on with classes (Article 28.2, 40).			
21. Where a student has infringed someone's rights—student or adult—reparation is expected (Articles 2, 19).			
22. Adults infringing students' rights are also expected to make reparation (Articles 2, 19).			

PARTICIPATION

23. In their schoolwork, students have the freedom to express their own political, religious, or other opinions, whatever the opinions of the teachers (Articles 12, 13, 14, 17).			
24. The student newspaper is treated like any other publication, subject to the law, but is not subject to additional censorship (Article 13).			
25. Young people have created or can create an independent student union, recognized by the school authorities as representing all the students in the school (Article 15).			
26. There are formal and informal mechanisms for learners to make a complaint or suggestions for improving the life of the school (Articles 12, 13).			
27. Young people have as much right to respect as adults (Articles 12, 19, 29.1c).			
28. Students and adults (including parents, teachers, and administrative staff) are consulted about the quality of the teaching in the school (Articles 5, 12, 18).			
29. There is an elected student council (Articles 12, 13, 15, 17).			
30. Students are represented on the governing body of the school (Article 12).			

Source. "Appendix 4" in *Changing Citizenship: Democracy and Inclusion in Education*, A. Osler and H. Starkey, 2005. Maidenhead, United Kingdom: Open University Press/McGraw Hill, pp. 195–198.

List of Abbreviations

AACU	Association of American Colleges and Universities
ANC	African National Congress
CEDAW	Convention on the Elimination of Discrimination Against Women 1979
CERD	International Convention on the Elimination of All Forms of Racial Discrimination 1965
CESCR	International Covenant on Economic, Social and Cultural Rights 1966
CRC	UN Convention on the Rights of the Child 1989
DIHR	Danish Institute for Human Rights
ECHR	European Convention on Human Rights 1950
EDC	Education for democratic citizenship
EFAGMR	Education for All Global Monitoring Report
EU	European Union
HCZ	Harlem Children's Zone
HRE	Human rights education
ICCPR	International Covenant on Civil and Political Rights 1966
IOM	International Organisation for Migration
KDP	Kurdistan Democratic Party
KRG	Kurdistan Regional Government
LDS	Church of Jesus Christ of Latter Day Saints (Mormon Church)
LGBT	Lesbian, gay, bisexual, and transgender
MDG	Millennium Development Goal
PACE	Parliamentary Assembly of the Council of Europe
PUK	Patriotic Union of Kurdistan
UDHR	Universal Declaration of Human Rights 1948
UN	United Nations
UNESCO	United Nations Educational, Scientific, and Cultural Organization
UNICEF	United Nations International Children's Emergency Fund
WIDE	World Inequality Database on Education
WHO	World Health Organization

References

Ahmad, N., Lybæk, L., Mohammed, I., & Osler, A. (2012). Democracy and diversity: Teaching for human rights and citizenship in post-conflict Iraqi Kurdistan. *Race Equality Teaching, 30*(3), 28–33.

al-Ali, N., & Pratt, N. (2011). Between nationalism and women's rights: The Kurdish women's movement in Iraq. *Middle East Journal of Culture and Communication, 4,* 337–353.

Alexander, M. (2012). *The new Jim Crow: Mass incarceration in the age of color blindness.* New York, NY: The New Press.

Appiah, K. A. (2006). *Cosmopolitanism: Ethics in a world of strangers.* New York, NY: Norton.

Archer, L. (2003). *Race, masculinity, and schooling: Muslim boys and education.* Maidenhead, United Kingdom: Open University Press.

Arendt, H. (1968). *The origins of totalitarianism.* San Diego, CA: Harcourt.

Arthur, J. (2015). Extremism and neo-liberal education policy: A contextual critique of the Trojan horse affair in Birmingham schools. *British Journal of Educational Studies, 63*(3), 311–328. doi:10.1080/00071005.2015.1069258

Au, W. (2009). High-stakes testing and discursive control: The triple bind for non-standard student identities. *Multicultural Perspectives, 11*(2), 65–71.

Augugliaro, A., del Grande, G., & al Nassiry, K. S. (2014). *On the bride's side* [Film notes]. Retrieved from www.iostoconlasposa.com/en/

Avery, P. G., Levy, S. A., & Simmons, A.M.M. (2013). Deliberating controversial public issues as part of civic education. *The Social Studies, 104*(3), 105–114. doi: 10.1080/00377996.2012.691571

Baildon, M., & Sim, J. B.-Y. (2010). The dilemmas of Singapore's national education in the global society. In A. Reid, J. Gill, & A. Sears (Eds.), *Globalization, the nation-state, and the citizen: Dilemmas and directions for civics and citizenship education* (pp. 80–96). New York, NY: Routledge.

Bajaj, M. (2011). Human rights education: Ideology, location, and approaches. *Human Rights Quarterly 33*(2), 481–508.

Bangstad, S. (2015). The racism that dares not speak its name: Rethinking neonationalism and neo-racism. *Intersections: East European Journal of Society and Politics, 1*(1), 49–65.

Banks, J. A. (2002). Race, knowledge construction, and education in the USA: Lessons from history. *Race, Ethnicity and Education, 5*(1), 7–27.

Banks, J. A. (2004). Teaching for social justice, diversity, and citizenship in a global world. *The Educational Forum, 68,* 289–298.

Banks, J. A. (Ed.). (2009). *The Routledge international companion to multicultural education*. New York, NY: Routledge.

Banks, J. A. (2014). *An introduction to multicultural education* (5th ed.). Boston, MA: Pearson.

Banks, J. A., & Banks, C.A.M. (Eds.). (2004). *Handbook of research on multicultural education* (2nd ed.). San Francisco, CA: Jossey-Bass.

Banks, J. A., & Banks, C.A.M. (Eds.). (2010). *Multicultural education: Issues and perspectives* (7th ed.). Hoboken, NJ: Wiley.

Banks, J. A., Banks, C.A.M., Cortés, C. E., Hahn, C., Merryfield, M., Moodley, K., . . . Parker, W. C. (2005). *Democracy and diversity: Principles and concepts for educating citizens in a global age*. Seattle, WA: Center for Multicultural Education, College of Education, University of Washington. Retrieved from depts.washington.edu/centerme/DemDiv.pdf

Baptist, W., & Bricker-Jenkins, M. (2002). A view from the bottom: Poor people and their allies respond to welfare reform. In R. Albelda & A. Withorn (Eds.), *Lost ground* (pp. 195–210). Cambridge, MA: South End Press.

Barton, K. & Levstik, L. (2013).*Teaching history for the common good*. New York, NY: Routledge.

Baxi, U. (1996). "A work in progress?": The United Nations report to the United Nations Human Rights Committee. *Indian Journal of International Law, 38,* 34–53.

BBC News. (2010, September 13). NBA star John Amaechi in bar access row. Retrieved from www.bbc.co.uk/news/mobile/uk-england-manchester-11287865

Begikhani, N., Gill, A., & Hague, G. (with Ibraheem, K.). (2010). *Honour-based violence (HBV) and honour-based killings in Iraqi Kurdistan and in the Kurdish Diaspora in the UK* [Final report]. Bristol, United Kingdom: Centre for Gender and Violence, Bristol University. Retrieved from http://www.roehampton.ac.uk/uploadedFiles/Pages_Assets/PDFs_and_Word_Docs/Staff_Profiles/Aisha-Gill/Report_HBV_IK_UK_KurdishDiaspora_MCopy_December_webcirculationonly.pdf

Bell, J. S. (2002). Narrative inquiry: More than just telling stories. *TESOL Quarterly, 36*(2), 207–213.

Berkeley, R. (2008). *Right to divide? Faith schools and community cohesion*. London, United Kingdom: Runnymede Trust.

Bernath, T., Holland, T., & Martin, P. (2002). How can human rights education contribute to international peace-building? *Current Issues in Comparative Education, 2*(1), 14–22.

Bhabha, H. J. (2003). On writing rights. In M. Gibney (Ed.) *Globalizing rights: The Oxford amnesty lectures* (pp. 162–183). Oxford, United Kingdom: Oxford University Press.

Bhabha, H. J. (2004). *The location of culture* (2nd ed.). New York, NY: Routledge.

Bhopal, K. (1998). South Asian women in east London: religious experience and diversity. *Journal of Gender Studies, 7*(2), 143–156.

Bhopal, K. (2004). Gypsy travellers and education: Changing needs and changing perceptions. *British Journal of Educational Studies, 52*(1), 47–64.

Bicknell, J. (2004). Self-knowledge and the limitations of narrative. *Philosophy and Literature, 28*(2), 406–416.

Bjornstol, E. P. (2009). Human rights law education in China. *Web Journal of Current Legal Issues, [2009]*(1). Retrieved from www.bailii.org/uk/other/journals/WebJCLI/2009/issue1/bjornstol1.html

Bonnell, J., Copestake, P., Kerr, D., Passy, R., Reed, C., Salter, R., . . . Sheikh, S. (2011). *Teaching approaches that help to build resilience to extremism among young people* (DFE-RR119). London: Department for Education.

Bowring, B. (2012). Human rights and public education. *Cambridge Journal of Education, 42*(1), 53–65.

Brabeck, M. M., & Rogers, L. (2000). Human rights as a moral issue: Lessons for moral educators from human rights work. *Journal of Moral Education, 29*(2), 167–182.

Brah, A., & Phoenix, A. (2004). Ain't I a woman? Revisiting intersectionality. *Journal of International Women's Studies, 5*(3), 75–86.

British Broadcasting Corporation (BBC) (2013). Martin Luther King: I have a dream re-visited. *BBC News Magazine.* August 27. Retrieved from http://www.bbc.co.uk/news/magazine-23853578

British Council. (2010). DelPHE-Iraq. Retrieved from www.britishcouncil.org/delphe-iraq.htm

Bromley, P. (2009). Cosmopolitanism in civic education: Exploring cross-national trends. *Current Issues in Comparative Education, 12*(1), 33–34.

Brossard Børhaug, F. (2012). How to better combine equality and difference in French and Norwegian anti-racist education? Some reflections from a capability point of view. *Journal of Human Development and Capabilities, 13*(3), 397–413.

Brunello, G., & Rocco, L. (2013). The effect of immigration on the school performance of natives: Cross country evidence using PISA test scores. *Economics of Education Review, 32,* 234–246.

Bryan, A. (2009). The intersectionality of nationalism and multiculturalism in the Irish curriculum: Teaching against racism? *Race, Ethnicity and Education, 12,* 297–317.

Bunch, C., & Frost, S. (2000). Women's human rights: An introduction. In C. Kramarae & D. Spender (Eds.), *Routledge international encyclopedia of women: Global women's issues and knowledge.* New York, NY: Routledge

Butler, J. (2006). *Precarious life: The powers of mourning and violence.* New York, NY: Verso.

Carter, C., & Osler, A. (2000). Human rights, identities, and conflict management: A study of school culture as experienced through classroom relationships. *Cambridge Journal of Education, 30*(3), 335–356.

Cassidy, W., Faucher, C., & Jackson, M. (2013). Cyberbullying among youth: A comprehensive review of current international research and its implications and application to policy and practice. *School Psychology International, 34*(6), 575–612.

Cassidy, W., Jackson, M., & Brown, K. (2009). Sticks and stones can break my bones, but how can pixels hurt me? Students' experiences with cyber-bullying. *School Psychology International, 30,* 382–482.

Castles, S. (2004). Migration, citizenship, and education. In J. A. Banks (Ed.), *Diversity and citizenship education: Global perspectives* (pp. 17–48). San Francisco, CA: Jossey-Bass.

Cha, Y., Wong, S., & Meyer, J. W. (1992). Values education in the curriculum: Some comparative empirical data. In J. W. Meyer, D. H. Kamens, & A. Benavot (Eds.), *School knowledge for the masses* (pp. 139–151). Washington, DC: Falmer Press.

Chan, A.W.H., & Cheung, H. Y. (2007). How culture affects female inequality across countries: An empirical study. *Journal of Studies in International Education 11*(2), 157–179.

Chilcott, L. (Producer), & Guggenheim, D. (Director). (2011). *Waiting for "Superman"* [Motion picture]. Los Angeles, CA: Walden Media & Participant Media.

Claire, H. (2005). "You did the best you can": History, citizenship and moral dilemmas. In A. Osler (Ed.), *Teachers, human rights and diversity: Educating citizens in multicultural societies.* Stoke-on-Trent, United Kingdom: Trentham.

Cogan, J. J., & Derricott, R. (2000). *Citizenship for the 21st century: An international perspective on education.* London, United Kingdom: Kogan Page.

Collins, C., Kenway, J., & McLeod, J. (2000). Gender debates we still have to have. *Australian Educational Researcher, 27*(3), 37–48.

Connelly, F. M., & Clandinin, D. J. (1990). Stories of experience and narrative inquiry. *Educational Researcher, 19*(5), 2–14.

Coppock, V. (2014). "Can you spot a terrorist in your classroom?" Problematising the recruitment of schools to the "war on terror" in the United Kingdom. *Global Studies of Childhood, 4*(2), 115–125.

Council of Europe. (1950). *Convention for the protection of human rights and fundamental freedoms* (European Convention on Human Rights). Strasbourg, France: Council of Europe. Retrieved from http://www.echr.coe.int/Documents/Convention_ENG.pdf

Council of Europe, Committee of Ministers. (1985). *Recommendation No. R (85) 7, of the committee of ministers to member states on teaching and learning about human rights in schools.* Retrieved from www.coe.int/t/dg4/education/historyteaching/Source/Results/AdoptedTexts/Rec(85)7_en.pdf

Council of Europe. Committee of Ministers. (2002). Recommendation of the committee of ministers to member states on education for democratic citizenship. Strasbourg, France: Council of Europe. Retrieved from https://wcd.coe.int/ViewDoc.jsp?id=313139&Site=CM

Council of Europe, Committee of Ministers. (2010). *Recommendation CM/Rec (2010)7 of the committee of ministers to member states on the council of Europe charter on rducation for democratic citizenship and human rights education* (adopted by the Committee of Ministers on 14 May 1985 at the 385th Meeting of Minsters' Deputies). Strasbourg, France: Council of Europe. Retrieved from wcd.coe.int/ViewDoc.jsp?id=1621697

Council of Europe, Group of Eminent Persons. (2011). *Living together: Combining diversity and freedom in 21st-century Europe* (Report of the Group of Eminent Persons of the Council of Europe). Strasbourg, France: Council of Europe.

Cox, L., & Thomas, D. Q. (2004). *Close to home: Case studies of human rights work in the United States.* New York, NY: Ford Foundation.

Crenshaw, K. W. (1989). Demarginalizing the intersection of race and sex: A Black feminist critique of antidiscrimination doctrine, feminist theory, and antiracist politics. *University of Chicago Legal Forum, 140,* 139–167.

Davies, L. (2008a). *Educating against extremism.* Stoke-on-Trent, United Kingdom: Trentham.

Davies, L. (2008b). Gender, extremism, and security. *Compare, 38*(5), 611–623.

Debarbieux, E. (2001). Scientists, politicians, and violence: On the road to a European scientific community to tackle violence in schools. In E. Debarbieux & C. Blaya (Eds.), *Violence in schools: Ten approaches in Europe* (pp. 11–25). Issy-les-Moulineaux, France: ESF.

Decara, C. (2013). Mapping of human rights education in Danish schools (summary report in English). Copenhagen: Danish Institute for Human Rights. http://www.humanrights.dk/files/media/dokumenter/udgivelser/mapping_of_hre_in_danish_schools.pdf [The full study is available in Danish at http://www.menneskeret.dk/udgivelser/udredninger]

Delanty, G. (2003). Citizenship as a learning process: Disciplinary citizenship versus cultural citizenship. *International Journal of Lifelong Education, 22*(5), 597–605.

Denning, S. (2001). The springboard: How storytelling ignites action in knowledge-era organizations. *Journal of Organizational Change Management, 14*(6), 609–614.

Dewey, J. (2002). Democracy and education: An introduction to the philosophy of education. In S. J.Maxcy (Ed.), *John Dewey and American education* (vol. 3). Bristol, UK: Thoemmes. (Original work published 1916)

DiAngelo, R., & Sensoy, O. (2010). "OK, I get it! Now tell me how to do it!" Why we can't just tell you how to do critical multicultural education. *Multicultural Perspectives, 12*(2), 97–102.

Donnelly, J. (2013). *Universal human rights in theory and practice.* Ithaca, NY: Cornell University Press.

Education Act. (1998). Act of 17 July no. 61 relating to primary and secondary education and training (the Education Act). Reformulated with amendments as of 19 December 2008. Norway. Retrieved from http://www.ub.uio.no/ujur/ulovdata/lov-19980717-061-eng.pdf

Education for All Global Monitoring Report (EFAGMR). (n.d.). World Inequality Database on Education (WIDE). Paris: UNESCO. Retrieved from www.education-inequalities.org/

Eidsvoll 1814 (n.d.) Retrieved from http://www.eidsvoll1814.no/?aid=9060947

Emerson, L., & Lundy, L. (2013). Education rights in a society emerging from conflict: Curriculum and student participation as a pathway to the realization of rights. In B. B. Swadener, L. Lundy, J. Habashi, & N. Blanchet-Cohen (Eds.), *Children's rights and education: International perspectives* (pp. 19–38). New York, NY: Peter Lang.

Eriksen, T. H. (2012). Xenophobic exclusion and the new right in Norway. *Journal of Community and Applied Social Psychology, 22*(3), 206–209.

Eriksen, T. H. (2013) *Immigration and national identity in Norway.* Washington, DC: Migration Policy Institute.

European Commission. (1997). *Education and active citizenship in the European Union.* Brussels, Belgium: Commission of the European Communities.

Feteke, L. (2012). The Muslim conspiracy theory and the Oslo massacre. *Race and Class, 53*(3), 30–47.

Figueroa, P. (2004). Multicultural education in the United Kingdom: Historical development and current status. In J. A Banks & C.A.M. Banks (Eds.), *Handbook of research on multicultural education* (2nd ed., pp. 997–1026). San Francisco, CA: Jossey Bass.

Fineman, M. A. (2008). The vulnerable subject: Anchoring equality in the human condition. *Yale Journal of Law and Feminism, 20*(1), 1–24.

Fineman, M. A. (2010). The vulnerable subject and the responsive state. *Emory Law Journal, 60,* 251–275.

Fineman, M. A. (2016). Equality, autonomy and the vulnerable subject in law and politics. In M. A. Fineman & A. Grear (Eds.), *Vulnerability: Reflections on a new ethical foundation for law and politics* (pp. 13–28). Abingdon, United Kingdom & New York, NY: Taylor and Francis.

Fineman, M. A., & Grear, A. (2016). Vulnerability as heuristic: An invitation to future exploration. In M. A. Fineman & A. Grear (Eds.), *Vulnerability: Reflections on a new ethical foundation for law and politics* (pp. 1–12). Abingdon, United Kingdom: Taylor and Francis.

Flanagan, O. J. (1992). *Consciousness reconsidered.* Cambridge, MA: MIT Press.

Flowers, N. (2004). How to define human rights education? A complex answer to a simple question. In V. Georgi & M. Seberich (Eds.) *International Perspectives in Human Rights Education*. Gütersloh, Germany: Bertelsmann Foundation Publishers.

Foster, S. J. (2006). Whose history? Portrayal of immigrant groups in U.S. history textbooks: 1800-present. In S.J. Foster & K.A. Crawford (Eds.), *What shall we tell the children? International perspectives on school history textbooks* (pp. 155–178). Greenwich, CT: Information Age Publishing.

Foucault, M. (1995). *Discipline and punishment: The birth of the prison*. New York, NY: Vintage Books.

Frankenberg, E., & Lee, C. (2003). Charter schools and race: A lost opportunity for integrated education. *Education Policy Analysis Archives, 11*(32). Retrieved from epaa.asu.edu/ojs/article/view/260

Freire, P. (1970). *Pedagogy of the oppressed*. London, United Kingdom: Penguin Books.

Fundación Cives. (2013, January). *Memorandum to the Council of Europe regarding the Spanish government's project to remove democratic citizenship and human rights education in school curriculum*. Madrid, Spain: Author. Retrieved from www.fundacioncives.org/images/noticias/mas_informacion/files/44.pdf

Gay, G. (2010). *Culturally responsive teaching: Theory, research, and practice* (3rd ed.). New York, NY: Teachers College Press.

Gerber, P. (2013). *Understanding human rights: Educational challenges for the future*. Cheltenham, United Kingdom: Edward Elgar.

Gillborn, D., & Mirza, H. (2000) *Educational Inequality: mapping race class and gender*. London, United Kingdom: Ofsted.

Gobbo, F. (2011). Intercultural education and intercultural learning in Europe. In J. A. Banks (Ed.), *Encyclopedia of diversity in education* (Vol. 2, pp. 1217–1220). Los Angeles, CA: Sage.

Golding, V. (2014). Museums and truths: The elephant in the room. In A. B. Fromm, V. Golding, & P. B. Rekdal (Eds.), *Museums and truth* (pp. 3–28). Newcastle upon Tyne, United Kingdom: Cambridge Scholars.

González, N., Moll, L. C., & Amanti, C. (Eds.). (2005). *Funds of knowledge: Theorizing practices in households, communities, and classrooms*. New York, NY: Routledge.

Gostin, L. O., & Friedman, E. A. (2015). A retrospective and prospective analysis of the west African Ebola virus disease epidemic: Robust national health systems at the foundation and an empowered WHO at the apex. *The Lancet, 38*(9980), 1902–1909. doi:10.1016/S0140-6736(15)60644-4

Gove, M. (2011). *Preventing extremism in schools and protecting children from extremist views*. Letter from Secretary of State for Education to Her Majesty's Chief Inspector of Schools.

Government of Norway (2013). Centenary of women's right to vote in Norway 1913-2013. Norwegian Embassy, Canada. 11 January. Retrieved from http://www.emb-norway.ca/News_and_events/News/Centenary-of-Womens-Right-to-Vote-in-Norway-1913-2013/#.UlStub5wYic

Grant, C., & Sleeter, C. E. (1986). Race, class, and gender in education research: An argument for integrative analysis. *Review of Educational Research, 56*, 195–211.

Grant, C., & Sleeter, C. E. (1988). Race, class, and gender and abandoned dreams. *Teachers College Record, 90*(1), 19–40.

Grant, C. A., & Zwier, E. (2011). Intersectionality and student outcomes: sharpening the struggle against racism, sexism, classism, ableism, heterosexism, nationalism, and linguistic, religious, and geographical discrimination in teaching and learning.

Multicultural Perspectives, 13(4), 181–188.

Griffiths, M. (2010). *Girls education in Iraq.* Retrieved from irak.alterinter.org/IMG/pdf/UNICEF_Girls_Education_in_Iraq_2010.pdf

Grover, S. (2007). Children's right to be educated for tolerance: Minority rights and the law. *Education and Law, 19*(1), 51–70. doi:10.1080/09539960701231272

Gullestad, M. (2002). Invisible fences: Egalitarianism, nationalism and racism. *Journal of the Royal Anthropological Institute, 8*(1), 45–63.

Gullestad, M. (2004). Blind slaves of our prejudices: Debating "culture" and "race" in Norway. *Ethnos: Journal of Anthropology, 69*(2), 177–203.

Hall, S. (2002). Political belonging in a world of multiple identities. In S. Vertovec & R. Cohen (Eds.), *Conceiving Cosmopolitanism.* Oxford, United Kingdom: Oxford University Press.

Harber, C. R. (2004). *Schooling as violence.* Abingdon, United Kingdom: Routledge.

Harikar. (2011). Enhance Women Rights Education, Heritage and Life in Dohuk and Nineveh Governorates. Retrieved February 27, 2012, from www.harikar.org/index.php?page=view&id=68

Harlem Children's Zone (HCZ). (n.d.). *The HCZ Project: 100 blocks, one bright future.* Retrieved from www.hcz.org/about-us/the-hcz-project

Heater, D. (2002). *World citizenship: Cosmopolitan thinking and its opponents.* London, United Kingdom: Continuum.

Held, D. (1997). Globalization and cosmopolitan democracy. *Peace Review, 9*(3), 309–314. doi:10.1080/10402659708426070

Henry, A. (2010). Race and gender in classrooms: Implications for teachers. In J. A. Banks & C.A.M. Banks (Eds.), *Multicultural education: Issues and perspectives* (7th ed., pp. 183–207). Hoboken, NJ: Wiley.

Hill Collins, P. (1990). *Black feminist thought: Knowledge, consciousness and the politics of empowerment.* New York, NY: Routledge.

hooks, b. (1981). *Ain't I a woman: Black women and feminism.* Boston, MA: South End Press.

Hopgood, S. (2013). *The endtimes of human rights.* Ithaca, NY: Cornell University Press.

Inter-American Commission on Human Rights, Rapporteurship on the Rights of the Child. (2009). *Report on corporal punishment and human rights of children and adolescents.* Retrieved from www.cidh.org/Ninez/CastigoCorporal2009/CastigoCorporal.1eng.htm

International Organization for Migration (IOM). (2010a, January–March). Victiems of trafficking are safely brought home. IOM Mission in Iraq. *IOM Iraq Newsletter,[2010],* 2. p5. Retrieved from www.iom.int/jahia/webdav/shared/shared/mainsite/activities/countries/docs/iom_iraq_vol210_newsletter.pdf

International Organization for Migration (IOM). (2010b, June 12). *Northern Iraq seeks more aid for Syrian refugees* [Press release]. Retrieved August 12/ 2012, from www.iom.int/jahia/Jahia/media/press-briefingnotes/pbnAF/cache/offonce/lang/en?entryId=31884

International Organization for Migration (IOM). (2012, June 11). Northern Iraq seeks more aid for Syrian refugees. [Press release] Retrieved from www.iom.int/news/northern-iraq-seeks-more-aid-syrian-refugees

International Organization for Migration (IOM). (2015). *Missing migrants project.* http://doe.iom.int/docs/Flows%20Compilation%202015%20Overview.pdf

Isin, E. F., & Neilsen, G. M. (2008). *Acts of citizenship.* New York, NY: Palgrave Macmillan.

Jackson, M., Cassidy, W., & Brown, K. (2009). "you were born ugly and youl die ugly too": Cyber-bullying as relational aggression. *In Education, 15*(2), 68–82.

Josefsen, E. (2010). *The Saami and the national parliaments: Channels for political influence.* Geneva, Switzerland and New York, NY: Inter-Parliamentary Union (IPU) & United Nations Development Programme (UNDP). http://www.ipu.org/splz-e/chiapas10/saami.pdf

Josselson, R. (Ed.). (1996). *Ethics and process in the narrative study of lives.* Newbury Park, CA: Sage.

Keet, A. (2006). *Human rights education or human rights in education: A conceptual analysis* (Unpublished doctoral dissertation). University of Pretoria, Pretoria, South Africa.

Keet, A. (2012). *Human rights education: A conceptual analysis.* Saarbrücken, Germany: Lambert.

Kumashiro, K. K. (2012). Anti-oppressive education. In J. A. Banks (Ed.), *Encyclopedia of diversity in education* (Vol.1., pp. 111–113). Thousand Oaks, CA: Sage.

Kurdistan Regional Government (KRG). (2009) *Basic Education School System. Secondary Education School System.* Kurdistan Region-Iraq, Council of Ministers, Ministry of Education. School System. (Official translation in English).

Kymlicka, W. (1996). *Multicultural citizenship: A liberal theory of minority rights.* Oxford, United Kingdom: Oxford University Press.

Kymlicka, W. (2003). Multicultural states and intercultural citizens. *Theory and Research in Education, 1*(2), 147–169.

Ladson-Billings, G. (1995). But that's just good teaching! The case for culturally relevant pedagogy. *Theory into Practice, 34*(3), 159–165.

Laqueur, W., & Rubin, B. (1979). *The human rights reader.* New York, NY: Meridian.

Larrabee, M.J. (1993). Gender and moral development: a challenge for feminist theory. In M.J. Larrabee (Ed.), *An ethic of care: Feminist and interdisciplinary perspectives.* New York, NY: Routledge.

Lelic, S. (2001). Fuel your imagination: KM and the art of storytelling. *Inside Knowledge, 5*(4). Retrieved from www.ikmagazine.com/xq/asp/sid.0/articleid.07FC4A03-F54E-491F-ACE7-7D44DE201C33/eTitle.Fuel_your_imagination_KM_and_the_art_of_storytelling/qx/display.htm

Levstick, L. (2000). Articulating the silences: teachers' and adolescents' conceptions of historical significance. In P. Stears, P. Seixas, & S. Weinberg (Eds.), *Knowing, teaching, and learning history* (pp. 284–305). New York, NY: New York University Press with American Historical Association.

Lile, H. K.(2011). FNs barnekonvensjon artikkel 29(1) om formålet med opplæring: En rettssosiologisk studie om hva barn lærer om det samiske folk. [UN Convention on the Rights of the Child Article 29(1) the purpose of education: A sociological study of what children learn about the Sami people]. PhD thesis, University of Oslo. Retrieved from http://www.jus.uio.no/smr/forskning/arrangementer/disputaser/hadi_lile.html

Lindsey, D., & Sarri, R. (1992). What Hillary Rodham Clinton really said about children's rights and child policy. *Children and Youth Services Review, 14,* 473–483.

Lister, R. (1997). *Citizenship: Feminist perspectives.* Basingstoke, United Kingdom: Macmillan.

Lister, R. (2013). "Power not pity": Poverty and human rights. *Ethics and Social Welfare, 7*(2), 109–123.

Loa, L.-S. (2010, September 13). Teachers create human rights lessons for contest. *Taipei Times,* p. 3. Retrieved from www.taipeitimes.com/News/taiwan/

archives/2010/09/13/2003482761/1

Lundy, L. (2007) "Voice" is not enough: conceptualizing Article 12 of the United Nations Convention on the Rights of the Child. *British Education Research Journal* 33(6), 927–942.

Mandela, N.R. (1994). *Long walk to freedom*. London, United Kingdom: Little, Brown and Company.

Mann, M. (2004). "Torchbearers upon the path of progress": Britain's ideology of a "moral and material" progress in India. An introductory essay. In H. Fischer-Tiné & M. Mann (Eds.), *Colonialism as civilizing mission. Cultural ideology in British India* (pp.1–28). London, United Kingdom: Wimbledon Publishing.

Martin, R. J. (2004). Charter school accessibility for historically disadvantaged students: The experience in New Jersey. *St. John's Law Review, 78*(2), 327–384.

Martin, S., & Feng, A. (2006). The construction of citizenship and nation building: The Singapore case. In G. Alred, M. Byram, & M. Fleming (Eds.), *Education for intercultural citizenship: Concepts and comparisons* (pp. 47–66). Clevedon, United Kingdom: Multilingual Matters.

Matsuura, K. (2004). Why education and public awareness are indispensable for a sustainable future. In UNESCO, *Educating for a sustainable future: Commitments and partnerships*. Proceedings of the high-level conference on education for sustainable development at the World Summit on Sustainable Development. September 2–3 2002, Johannesburg, South Africa.

Mayo, C. (2010). Queer lessons: Sexual and gender minorities in multicultural education. In J. A. Banks & C.A.M. Banks (Eds.), *Multicultural education: Issues and perspectives* (7th ed.) (pp.209–227). Hoboken, NJ: Wiley.

McCowan, T. (2012). Human rights within education: Assessing the justifications. *Cambridge Journal of Education, 42*(1), 67–81. doi:10.1080/0305764X.2011.651204

McCowan, T. (2013). *Education as a human right: Principles for a universal entitlement to learning*. London, United Kingdom: Bloomsbury.

McDowall, D. (2003). *A modern history of the Kurds*. London, United Kingdom: I. B. Tauris.

Mertus, J., & Flowers, N. (2008). *Local action, global change: A handbook on women's human rights*. Boulder, CO: Paradigm.

Mikkelsen, R., Fjeldstad, D. T., & Lauglo, J. (2011). *Morgendagens amfunnsborgere Norske ungdomsskoleelevers prestasjoner og svar på spørsmål i den internasjonale demokrati-undersøkelsen ICCS* [Tomorrow's citizens. Norwegian high school students' performance and responses in the international democracy ICCS study] (International Civic and Citizenship Education Study 2009, Acta Didactica Oslo 2/2011). Oslo, Norway: Department of Education and School Research, University of Oslo.

Minow, M. (1999). Reforming school reform. *Fordham Law Review, 68*(2), 257–298.

Mohanty, C. T. (1984). Under western eyes: Feminist scholarship and colonial discourses. *Boundary, 12/13, 3*(1), 333–358.

Muižnieks, N. (2013). Report of Council of Europe Commissioner for Human Rights, following his visit to Greece, from 28 January to 1 February 2013. CommDH (2013) 6. 16 April. Council of Europe, France: Strasbourg. Retrieved from https://wcd.coe.int/ViewDoc.jsp?id=2053611

Muñoz Ramírez, A. (2014, June 25). *Education for citizenship and human rights and the impact of neoconservative-Catholic influences in Spain*. Paper presented at Buskerud and Vestfold University College, Norway.

Murphy-Shigematsu, S. (2012) *When half is whole: Multiethnic Asian American identities.* Stanford, CA: Stanford University Press.

Murray, N. (1986). Anti-racists and other demons: the press and ideology in Thatcher's Britain. *Race and Class, 27*(3), 1–19.

Mutua, M. W. (2001). Savages, victims, and saviors: The metaphor of human rights. *Harvard International Law Journal, 42*(1), 201–243.

National Task Force on Civic Learning and Democratic Engagement. (2012). *A crucible moment: College learning and democracy's future.* Washington, DC: Association of American Colleges and Universities (AACU).

Noddings, N. (1986). *Caring: A feminine approach to ethics and moral education.* Berkeley, CA: University of California Press.

Nordic Council of Ministers (Norden). (2010). Strategy for children and young adults in the Nordic region. Copenhagen, Denmark: Nordic Council of Minsters Secretariat. Retreived from norden.diva-portal.org/smash/get/diva2:701574/FULLTEXT01.pdf

Norwegian Broadcasting Corporation (NKR). (2011, October 26). *En av fire nordmenn ser på islam som en trussel* [One in four Norwegians see Islam as a threat]. Retrieved from www.nrk.no/nyheter/norge/1.7847186

Norwegian Directorate for Education and Training. (2006). *Læreplanverket for kunnskapsløftet i grunnskolen. (Kunnskapsløftet)* (Quality framework) (Oslo: Norwegian Directorate for Education and training). Retrieved from www.udir.no/Upload/larerplaner/Fastsatte_lareplaner_for_Kunnskapsloeftet/5/prinsipper_lk06_Eng.pdf?epslanguage=no

Nussbaum, M. C. (2006). Education and democratic citizenship: Capabilities and quality education. *Journal of Human Development, 7*, 385–395. doi:10.1080/14649880600815974

Obama, B. (2008, October). Walden University Presidential Youth Debate. Author.

O'Cuanachain, C. (2010). Foreword. In A. Osler & H. Starkey (Eds.), *Teachers and human rights education* (pp. xi–xiii). Stoke-on-Trent, United Kingdom: Trentham.

Okafor, C. O., & Agbakwa, S. C. (2001). Re-imagining international human rights education in our time: Beyond three constitutive orthodoxies. *Leiden Journal of International Law, 14*, 563–590.

Orange, R. (2012, April 15). "Answer hatred with love": How Norway tried to cope with the horror of Anders Breivik. *The Observer.* Retrieved from http://www.theguardian.com/world/2012/apr/15/anders-breivik-norway-copes-horror

Osler, A. (1997). *The education and careers of Black teachers: Changing identities, changing lives.* Buckingham, United Kingdom: Open University Press.

Osler, A. (2005). *Teachers, human rights, and diversity: Educating citizens in a multicultural society.* Stoke-on-Trent, United Kingdom: Trentham.

Osler, A. (2006). Excluded girls: Interpersonal, institutional, and structural violence in schooling. *Gender and Education, 18*(6), 571–589. doi: 10.1080/09540250600980089.

Osler, A. (2007). *Faith schools and community cohesion: Observations on community consultations.* London, United Kingdom: Runnymede Trust.

Osler, A. (2008). Citizenship education and the Ajegbo report: Re-imagining a cosmopolitan nation. *London Review of Education, 6*(1), 11–25.

Osler, A. (2009). Patriotism, multiculturalism, and belonging: Political discourse and the teaching of history. *Educational Review, 61*(1), 85–100.

Osler, A. (2010a). École: l'égalité raciale peut-elle être inspectée? *Migrations Societé, 22*(131), 185–200.

Osler, A. (2010b). *Students' perspectives on schooling*. Maidenhead, United Kingdom: Open University Press/McGraw Hill.

Osler, A. (2011a). Education policy, social cohesion, and citizenship. In I. Newman & P. Ratcliffe (Eds.), *Promoting social cohesion: Implications for policy and frameworks for evaluation* (pp. 185–205). Bristol, United Kingdom: Policy Press.

Osler, A. (2011b). Teacher interpretations of citizenship education: National identity, cosmopolitan ideals, and political realities. *Journal of Curriculum Studies, 43*(1), 1–24.

Osler, A. (2012a). Higher education, human rights, and inclusive citizenship. In T. Basit & S. Tomlinson (Eds.), *Higher education and social inclusion*. Bristol, United Kingdom: Policy Press.

Osler, A. (2012b). Universal Declaration of Human Rights and education. In J. A. Banks (Ed.), *Encyclopedia of diversity in education*. Thousand Oaks, CA: Sage.

Osler, A. (2013a). Bringing human rights back home: Learning from "Superman" and addressing political issues at school. *The Social Studies, 104*(2), 67–76. Retrieved from dx.doi.org/10.1080/00377996.2012.687408

Osler, A. (2013b). *Human rights and democracy in action—looking ahead: The impact of the Council of Europe Charter on Education for Democratic Citizenship and Human Rights Education*. EDC/HRE Conference 2012. Retrieved from www.coe.int/t/dg4/education/standingconf/Source/Reference_textes/EDCHRE_Conference2012_report_en.pdf

Osler, A. (2014a). Human rights, scholarship and action for change. In C. Grant & E. Zwier (Eds.), *Intersectionality and urban education: Identities, policies, spaces, and power* (pp. 249–265). Charlotte, NC: Information Age.

Osler, A. (2014b). Identitet, demokrati og mangfold i skoler: Nasjonale og internasjonale perspektive [Identity, democracy and diversity in schools: National and international perspectives]. In J. Madsen & H. Biseth (Eds.), *Må vi snakke om demokrati? Om demokratisk praksis i skolen* (pp. 46–62). Oslo, Norway: Universitetsforlaget.

Osler, A. (2015a). The stories we tell: exploring narrative in education for justice and equality in multicultural contexts. *Multicultural Education Review, 7*(1–2), 12–25.

Osler, A. (2015b). Human rights education, postcolonial scholarship, and action for social justice. *Theory & Research in Social Education, 43*(2), 244–274.

Osler, A. (2016). National narratives, conflict and consensus: Challenges for human rights educators in established democracies. In C. Lenz, S. Brattland, & L. Kvande (Eds.), *Crossing borders: Combining human rights education and historical learning*. Berlin, Germany: Lit Verlag.

Osler, A. (in press). Diversity and citizenship education in Europe: Policy and practice in two jurisdictions—England and Norway. In J. A. Banks (Ed.), *Global migration, structural inclusion, and citizenship education across nations*. Washington, DC: American Educational Research Association.

Osler, A. & Lybæk, L. (2014). Educating "the new Norwegian we": An examination of national and cosmopolitan education policy discourses in the context of extremism and Islamophobia. *Oxford Review of Education, 40*(5), 543–566.

Osler, A., & Osler, C. (2002). Inclusion, exclusion and children's rights: A case study of a student with Asperger Syndrome. *Journal of Emotional and Behavioural Difficulties, 7*(1), 35–54.

Osler, A., & Starkey, H. (1996). *Teacher education and human rights*. London, United Kingdom: David Fulton.

Osler, A., & Starkey, H. (1999). Rights, identities, and inclusion: European action programmes as political education. *Oxford Review of Education, 25*(1/2), 199–216.

Osler, A., & Starkey, H. (2003). Learning for cosmopolitan citizenship: Theoretical debates and young people's experiences. *Educational Review, 55*(3), 243–254.

Osler, A., & Starkey, H. (2005). *Changing citizenship: Democracy and inclusion in education*. Maidenhead, United Kingdom: Open University Press/McGraw Hill.

Osler, A., & Starkey, H. (2006). Education for democratic citizenship: A review of research, policy, and practice, 1995–2005. *Research Papers in Education, 21*(4), 433–466.

Osler, A., & Starkey, H. (2009). Citizenship education in France and England: Contrasting approaches to national identities and diversity. In J. A. Banks (Ed.), *The Routledge international companion to multicultural education* (pp. 334–347). New York, NY: Routledge.

Osler, A., & Starkey, H. (2010). *Teachers and human rights education*. Stoke-on-Trent, United Kingdom: Trentham.

Osler, A., Street, C., Lall, M., & Vincent, K. (2002). *Not a problem? Girls and school exclusion*. London, United Kingdom: National Children's Bureau.

Osler, A., & Vincent, K. (2002). *Citizenship and the challenge of global education*. Stoke-on-Trent, United Kingdom: Trentham.

Osler, A., & Vincent K. (2003). *Girls and exclusion: Rethinking the agenda*. London, United Kingdom: RoutledgeFalmer.

Osler, A., & Yahya, C. (2013). Challenges and complexity in human rights education: Teachers' understandings of democratic participation and gender equity in post-conflict Kurdistan–Iraq. *Education Inquiry, 4*(1), 189–210. Available at www.education-inquiry.net/index.php/edui/article/view/22068

Osler, A., & Zhu, J. (2011). Narratives in teaching and research for justice and human rights. *Education, Citizenship, and Social Justice, 6*(3), 223–235. Retrieved from esj.sagepub.com/content/6/3/223

Parekh, B. (2000). *Rethinking multiculturalism: Cultural diversity and political theory*. London, United Kingdom: Macmillan.

Parker, W. C. (2003). *Teaching democracy: Unity and diversity in public life*. New York, NY: Teachers College Press.

Parliamentary Assembly of the Council of Europe (PACE). (2000). Recommendation 1438. Threat posed to democracy by extremist parties and movements in Europe. Adopted 25 January. Retrieved from http://www.assembly.coe.int/ASP/XRef/X2H-DW-XSL.asp?fileid=16765&lang=EN

Parliamentary Assembly of the Council of Europe (PACE). (2003). Resolution 1344. Threat posed to democracy by extremist parties and movements in Europe. Adopted 29 September. Retrieved from http://www.assembly.coe.int/ASP/XRef/X2H-DW-XSL.asp?fileid=17142&lang=EN

Parliamentary Assembly of the Council of Europe (PACE). (2004). *Europe-wide ban on corporal punishment of children* (Recommendation 1666). Retrieved from assembly.coe.int/nw/xml/XRef/Xref-XML2HTML-en.asp?fileid=17235&lang=EN

Pavlenko, A. (2002). Narrative study: Whose story is it, anyway? *TESOL Quarterly, 36*(2), 213–218.

Perugini, N., & Gordon, N. (2015) *The human right to dominate*. New York, NY: Oxford University Press.

Peshkin, A. (1988). In search of subjectivity—one's own. *Educational Researcher, 17*(7), 17–22.

Popkewitz, T. S. (2007). *Cosmopolitanism and the age of school reform: Science, education and making society by making the child*. New York, NY: Routledge.

Qvortrup, J., Cosaro, W. A., & Honig, M.-S. (Eds.). (2009). *The Palgrave handbook of childhood studies*. Basingstoke, United Kingdom: Palgrave Macmillan.

Rauof, A. (2007). *Manual of instruction for human rights education*. Erbil, Iraqi Kurdistan: Ministry of Human Rights.

Rawls, J. (2005). *A theory of justice*. Cambridge, MA: Harvard University Press. (Original work published 1971)

Reid, A., Gill, J., & Sears, A. (Eds.). (2009). *Globalization, the nation-state and the citizen: Dilemmas and directions for civics and citizenship education*. New York, NY: Routledge.

Reimers, F. M., & Chung, C. K. (2010). Education for human rights in times of peace and conflict. *Development, 53*(4), 504–510.

Riessman, C. (1991). When gender is not enough: Women interviewing women. In J. Lorber & S. Farrell (Eds.), *The social construction of gender* (pp. 217–236). Newbury Park, CA: Sage.

Rodham, H. (1973). Children under the law. *Harvard Educational Review, 43*, 487–514.

Roosevelt, E. (1958). Excerpt from a speech made at the presentation of "In Your hands: a guide for community action for the tenth anniversary of the Universal Declaration of Human Rights." March 27, 1958. United Nations, New York. Retrieved from www.udhr.org/history/biographies/bioer.htm

Ryan, P. (2006). Interculturality, identity, and citizenship education in Mexico. In G. Alred, M. Byram, & M. Fleming (Eds.), *Education for intercultural citizenship: Concepts and comparisons* (pp. 11–22). Clevedon, United Kingdom: Multilingual Matters.

Saint, A. (1987). *Towards a social architecture: The role of school building in post-war England*. New Haven, CT: Yale University Press.

Savin-Baden, M., & Van Niekerk, L. (2007). Narrative inquiry: theory and practice. *Journal of Geography in Higher Education, 31*(3), 459–472.

Schaffer, K., & Smith, S. (2004). *Human rights and narrated lives: The ethics of recognition*. New York, NY: Palgrave.

Schwaller, N., & Døving, C.A. (Eds.) (2010). *Minority narratives and national memory*. Oslo, Norway: Unipub.

Sen, A. (1992). *Inequality re-examined*. Oxford, United Kingdom: Oxford University Press.

Sen, A. (2010). *The idea of justice*. London, United Kingdom: Penguin.

Sensoy, Ö., & DiAngelo, R. (2012). *Is everyone really equal? An introduction to key concepts in social justice education*. New York, NY: Teachers College Press.

Simmons, R. (2002). *Odd girl out: The hidden culture of aggression in girls*. Orlando, FL: Harcourt.

Sleeter, C. (2005). *Un-standardizing curriculum: Multicultural teaching in the standards-based classroom*. New York, NY: Teachers College Press.

Sleeter, C. (2013). Foreword. In J. Hall (Ed.), *Children's human rights and public schooling in the United States* (pp. vii–ix). Rotterdam, Netherlands: Sense Publishers.

Sleeter, C. (2015). Multicultural curriculum and critical family history. *Multicultural Education Review, 7*(1–2), 1–11.

Slettholm, A. (2015, February. 23). *Oslo Kommune: Trusselen fra radikal islam er i stor grad medieskapt*. Aftenposten Osloby. Retrieved from http://www.osloby.no/nyheter/Oslo-kommune-Trusselen-fra-radikal-islam-er-i-stor-grad-medieskapt-7912041.html

Smith, C. (1995). The development of Sami rights since 1980. In T. Brantenberg, J. Hansen, & H. Minde (Eds.), *Becoming visible: Indigenous politics and self-government*. Tromsø, Norway: University of Tromsø, Sámi dutkamiid guovddáš - Centre for Sámi Studies. Retrieved from http://www.sami.uit.no/girji/n02/en/105smith.html

Smith, D. J. (2010). *Young Mandela*. London, United Kingdom: Phoenix.

Snowden, D. (2002). Narrative patterns: Uses of story in the third age of knowledge management. *Journal of Information and Knowledge Management, 1*(1), 1–6.

Spivak, G. C. (1999). *A Critique of postcolonial reasons: Towards a history of the vanishing present.* Cambridge, MA: Harvard University Press.

Stanley, S., & Wise, L. (1993). *Breaking out again: Feminist ontology and epistemology* (2nd ed.). London, United Kingdom: Routledge.

Stansfield, G.R.V. (2003). *Iraqi Kurdistan, political development and emergent democracy.* London, United Kingdom: Routledge Curzon.

Starkey, H. (1991). *The challenge of human rights education.* London, United Kingdom: Cassell.

Starkey, H. (2007). Language education, identities, and citizenship: Developing cosmopolitan perspectives. *Language and Intercultural Communication, 7*(1), 56–71.

Starkey, H. (2012). Human rights, cosmopolitanism, and utopias: Implications for citizenship education. *Cambridge Journal of Education, 42*(1), 21–35. doi: 10.1080/0305764X.2011.651205

Starkey, H., Akar, B., Jerome, L., & Osler, A. (2014). Power, pedagogy and participation: Ethics and pragmatics in research with young people. *Research in International and Comparative Education, 9*(4), 426–440.

Starratt, R. J. (2003). *Centering educational administration: Cultivating meaning, community, responsibility.* Mahwah, NJ: Erlbaum.

Statistics Norway (Statistick sentralbyrå). (2015). Immigrants and Norwegian-born to immigrant parents, 1 January 2015. Published March 4. https://www.ssb.no/en/befolkning/statistikker/innvbef

Stromquist, N. P. (2006). Gender, education, and the possibility of transformative knowledge. *Compare, 36*(2), 145–161.

Subrahmanian, R. (2005). Gender equality in education: Definitions and measurements. *International Journal of Educational Development, 25*(4), 395–407.

Svendsen, S.H.B.(2013). Learning racism in the absence of "race." *European Journal of Women's Studies, 21*(1), 9–24.

Swalwell, K., & Apple, M. (2011). Reviewing policy: Starting the wrong conversations: The public school crisis and "Waiting for Superman." *Educational Policy, 25*(2), 368–382.

Tai, E. (2010). Local and global efforts for human rights education: A case from the Osaka Human Rights Museum. *The International Journal of Human Rights, 14*(5), 771–788.

Tan, T. W. (1994). Moral education in Singapore: A critical appraisal. *Journal of Moral Education, 23*(1), 61–73.

Tarrow, N. (1993). Human rights education: Alternative conceptions. In J. Lynch, C. Modgil, & S. Modgil (Eds.), *Cultural diversity and the schools: Vol 4. Human rights, education and global responsibilities.* LondonUnited Kingdom: Falmer Press.

Tibbitts, F. (2008). Human rights education. In M. Bajaj (Ed.), *Encyclopedia of peace education.* Charlotte, NC: Information.

Todd, S. (2007). Promoting a just education: Dilemmas of rights, freedom and justice. *Educational Philosophy and Theory, 39*(6), 592–603.

Todd, S. (2009). Living in a dissonant world: Towards an agonistic cosmopolitics for education. *Studies in Philosophy and Education, 29,* 213–228.

Tomaševski, K. (2001). *Human rights obligations: Making education available, accessible, acceptable and adaptable.* Right to Education Primers, no. 3. Lund,